I0753699

THE

AMERICAN ENGINEER,

DRAFTSMAN, AND MACHINIST'S ASSISTANT.

THE

AMERICAN ENGINEER,

DRAFTSMAN, AND MACHINIST'S ASSISTANT;

DESIGNED FOR

PRACTICAL WORKINGMEN, APPRENTICES,

AND THOSE INTENDED FOR

THE ENGINEERING PROFESSION.

ILLUSTRATED WITH

TWO HUNDRED ENGRAVINGS ON WOOD AND FOURTEEN LARGE ENGRAVED LITHOGRAPHIC PLATES

OF RECENTLY CONSTRUCTED

AMERICAN MACHINERY AND ENGINE-WORK.

BY

OLIVER BYRNE,

MATHEMATICIAN; CIVIL, MILITARY, AND MECHANICAL ENGINEER;

AUTHOR OF

"THE HANDBOOK FOR THE ARTISAN, MECHANIC, AND ENGINEER;"

"The Practical Model Calculator;" Compiler and Editor of the "Dictionary of Machines, Mechanics, Engine-work, and Engineering;" "The Pocket Companion for Machinists, Mechanics, and Engineers;" "The Practical Cotton Spinner;" "The Practical Metal-worker's Assistant;" Author and Inventor of the "Calculus of Form," a New Science, a substitute for the Differential and Integral Calculus; "The Doctrine of Proportion;" "The Elements of Euclid, by Colors;" "A Practical Treatise on Spherical Trigonometry;" "The New and Improved System of Logarithms;" "The Practical, Complete, and Correct Gauger;" "Lessons on Military Art and Science;" "Practical Short and Direct Method of Calculating Logarithms;" etc. etc. etc.;

SURVEYOR-GENERAL OF THE ENGLISH SETTLEMENTS IN THE FALKLAND ISLANDS; PROFESSOR OF MATHEMATICS IN THE COLLEGE FOR CIVIL ENGINEERS, LONDON; CONSULTING ACTUARY TO THE PHILANTHROPIC LIFE ASSURANCE SOCIETY, ETC. ETC. ETC.;

INVENTOR OF

The Patent Calculating Instruments; A New Mathematical Instrument termed the Byrnegraph; A Mathematical Science termed the Calculus of Form; The Method of Teaching Geometry and other Linear Arts and Sciences by Colors; A New Theory of the Earth, which accounts for many Astronomical, Geographical, and Geological Phenomena, hitherto unaccounted for; etc. etc. etc.

PHILADELPHIA:

C. A. BROWN AND COMPANY,

N. W. CORNER OF FOURTH AND ARCH STREETS.

1853.

PHILADELPHIA:
T. K. AND P. G. COLLINS, PRINTERS.

This Work

I INSCRIBE TO

THE MEMORY OF MY BROTHER,

THE LATE

JOHN O'BYRNE, C.E.,

TO

WHOSE TALENTS AND ENTERPRISE

THE ENGINEERING PROFESSION IS LARGELY INDEBTED.

HE WAS

BORN IN WICKLOW, IRELAND, ON THE 27TH OF MAY, 1812,

AND

DIED IN NEW YORK ON THE 6TH OF APRIL, 1851.

THOSE WHO RESPECT HIS MEMORY MOST

WERE

BEST ACQUAINTED WITH HIS PRIVATE CHARACTER.

THE AUTHOR.

PREFACE.

To fill the vacant *niche* in the library of the Apprentice, Engineer, and Mechanic, for which this work is designed, has been considered a great requirement by practical men. This vacancy became apparent to every one who made the inquiry—where can I get a plain practical elementary work to guide and instruct an American mechanical engineering apprentice or student?—one who wishes to acquire the art and mystery of making practical working drawings and practical working machines? The assurances already received, and a long professional experience, furnish sufficient reasons to entertain the strongest hopes that this work is the one so often sought for and so much required. The details introduced, and the working drawings, are taken from American machinery and engine-work recently constructed, that have peculiar functions, and are well adapted to their respective employments; so that the student and amatorial machinist may save time by studying the machinery now in operation, and not that which is foreign, or which has been laid aside or fallen into disuse. The examples will be found striking and familiar, the developments scientific and practical, and the arrangement systematic and clear. The attention of the well-tutored apprentice, the educated amateur, and the accomplished draftsman, is directed to a class of geometrical problems operated upon by compasses only, without the use of a straight edge, or any other instrument; the method of coloring machinery, exhibited in Plate I.; and the erroneous principles of mechanics taught in colleges and schools, and laid down by Newton, Hutton, Gregory, Barlow, Tredgold, and other English writers and engineers. The experienced engineer and expert machinist may here, also, find many things of importance and interest, some of them entirely new, and now for the first time made public. I shall only mention the Coal-burning Locomotive of F. P. Dimpfel, C. E., of Philadelphia, for burning anthracite coal; Wright's Rotary Engine; Dunn's Electric Steam Gage; the Steam Indicator; the true cause of the explosion of boilers; the improvements introduced into steam machinery by J. T. Sutton & Co., of the Franklin Iron Works, Kensington, Philadelphia; Ericsson's Caloric Engine; and a direct method to find the true path of the piston-rod when a parallel motion is employed to guide it. No apology is offered for the mathematical proofs that set aside erroneous doctrines, or establish new facts, however illustrious the propounder or proposer of the former may be, or however strange the latter may seem; for the writer or inventor who by mathematical demonstration can substantiate his claims, no matter how uncommon they may appear, places beyond all doubt their certainty; but with respect to advanced opinions, of a practical nature, how far such may happen to be right, is left to the decision of uninterested and experienced Engineers. And in offering opinions contrary to those already received, it is particularly to be understood, that, in doing so, the Author is not actuated by any feelings of envy or dislike towards any individual or establishment whatever, but merely because he would be acting unjustly in a public capacity were the expression of the opinions withheld, to which allusion is made.

OLIVER BYRNE.

CONTENTS.

MATHEMATICAL AND DRAWING INSTRUMENTS DESCRIBED AND APPLIED.

	PAGE
Frontispiece	1
Title-page	3
Dedication	5
Preface	7
Contents	9
List of Plates	12
Compasses	13
Parallel Ruler. Fig. 1	13
Plane Scale	13
Diagonal Scale. Fig. 2	13
Line of Chords. Fig. 3	14
To measure any given angle	14
To lay down an angle	14
The Protractor. Fig. 4	14
The Sector. Fig. 5	15
The Line of Lines. Fig. 6	15
The Sectoral Line of Chords. Fig. 7	16
Lines of Sines and Tangents. Fig. 8	17
The Tangent	17
The Lines of Polygons. Fig. 9	18
The Byrnegraph	18
A Pocket-Case of Mathematical Instruments. Fig. 10	18
Hair Compasses. Fig. 11	19
The T Square. Figs. 12 and 13	19
The T Square and Protractor. Fig. 14	19
The Draftman's Squares. Figs. 15, 16, and 17	19
The Engineer's Curves and Shapes. Figs. 18 to 35	20
The Draftsman's Drawing-Board; manner of mounting Drawing-Paper, Lead-Pencils, &c.	20
The first requisite for the Mechanical Draftsman	20

GEOMETRICAL PROBLEMS AND FIGURES.

	PAGE
Problem 1. To erect a perpendicular on a given right line from a given point in that line near the centre. Fig. 36	21
Second Method. Fig. 37	21
Problem 2. To erect a perpendicular to a given right line from a given point in that line near either extremity. Fig. 38	21
Problem 3. To let fall a perpendicular upon a given right line from a given point nearly above the centre of that line. Fig. 39	21
Problem 4. To let fall a perpendicular upon a right line from a given point nearly above the extremity of that line. Fig. 40	21
Problem 5. To draw a line perpendicular to a given line from a point at some distance from that line. Fig. 41	22
Second Method. Fig. 42	22
Problem 6. To bisect a given line. Fig. 43	22
Problem 7. To draw a line at any required angle to a given straight line. Fig. 44	22
Problem 8. To measure any given angle	23
Problem 9. To draw a line parallel to a given line. Fig. 45	23
Problem 10. To divide a given right line into any number of equal parts. Fig. 46	23
Problem 11. To bisect a given angle. Fig. 47	23
Problem 12. To find the centre of a given circle. Fig. 48	23
Problem 13. To describe a circle of which any given arc or segment is a portion. Fig. 49	23
Problem 14. To describe a circle through three given points. Fig. 50	23
Problem 15. To cut off any portion of a circle whose diameter is given. Fig. 51	24

PROBLEMS ON CIRCLES OF LARGE RADII.

	PAGE
Problem 16. Given the length of the chord and versed sine of a curve to draw the curve without having recourse to the centre. Fig. 52	24
Method Second. Fig. 53	24
Problem 17. Given the arc line of a segment to extend it to any length by finding points at any given distance from each other without having recourse to any centre. Fig. 54	24
Problem 18. Given the length of the chord and height of an arc composed of three segments with the centre of the middle segment to find centres in the line for describing the segment at the two ends. Fig. 55	25
Problem 19. To describe an equilateral triangle on a given right line	25
Problem 20. To describe a circle within a given equilateral triangle. Fig. 56	25
Problem 21. To describe a circle about a given equilateral triangle	25
Problem 22. To construct a triangle equal to three given straight lines, any two of those lines being greater than the third. Fig. 57	25
Problem 23. To construct a right-angled triangle on a given straight line, the lesser angles being unequal, and one of them being given in quantity. Fig. 58	26
Problem 24. To construct a triangle the interior angles of which shall contain any given quantity or number of degrees. Fig. 59	26
Problem 25. To reduce any given right-lined figure to a triangle of equal area. Fig. 60	26

PAGE
Method Second. Fig. 61 26
Method Third. Fig. 62 26
Problem 26. To construct a square on a given right line. Fig. 63 27
Problem 27. To inscribe or describe a square within or without a given circle, and a circle within or without a given square. Fig. 64 27
Table of Polygons 27
Problem 28. To construct a regular pentagon on a given right line. Fig. 65 28
Problem 29. To inscribe or describe a regular pentagon within or without a given circle. Fig. 66 . . 28
Problem 30. To construct a regular hexagon upon a given right line. Fig. 67 28
Problem 31. To inscribe or describe a regular hexagon within or without a given circle. Fig. 68 . . 29
Problem 32. To cut off the corners of a given square, so as to form an octagon. Fig. 69 . . . 29
Problem 33. To describe an ellipse, having two diameters given. Fig. 70 29
Problem 34. To construct an ellipse, having the major and minor axes given. Fig. 71 . . . 29
Problem 35. To draw an oval of the first kind, having the length given. Fig. 72 30
Problem 36. Second Method. Fig. 73 . . 30
Problem 37. To draw an oval by means of the divisions of two circles, having the length and breadth of the oval given. Fig. 74 30

PROBLEMS ON THE SPIRAL.

Problem 38. Given the height and centre of the proportional spiral, to find any number of points in the curve through which to trace the spiral. Figs. 75 and 76 . 30
Method Second. Fig. 77 31

PROBLEMS ON THE PARABOLA.

Problem 39. Given any diameter and double ordinate, to describe a parabola by finding any number of points in the curve. Fig. 78 31
Method Second. Fig. 79 31
Method Third. Fig. 80 31
Method Fourth. Fig. 81 32
Method Fifth. Fig. 82 32
Problem 40. To describe a parabola whose parameter shall be equal to a given line. Figs. 83 and 84 . 32
Problem 41. To describe an hyperbola, the vertex and assymptotes being given. Fig. 85 33
Problem 42. To describe a cycloid, the axes being given. Fig. 86 33
Problem 43. To describe a catenarian curve, having the chord and depth of the curve given. Fig. 87 . 34

ON THE COVERING OF SOLIDS.

Problem 44. To find the envelop for a given cone. Fig. 88 34
Problem 45. To find the envelop of a given frustum of a cone. Fig. 89 34
Problem 46. To find the envelop of a given cylinder . 34
Problem 47. To find the envelop of a given cylinder, having a portion cut off so that one of the ends shall be a given angle to its sides. Figs. 90 and 91 . . 35

COVERING OF CIRCULAR ROOFS.

Problem 48. To cover a dome by bending the boards horizontally, and considering the surface as the surfaces of as many conic frustums as there are boards; the axial section of the dome being given. Fig. 92 . . 35
Problem 49. To find the form of the boards at the bottom of a dome, considering the surface to be covered in the same manner as former problem. Fig. 93 . . 36
Problem 50. To cover a dome on the second principle. Figs. 94 and 95 36
Problem 51. To find the form of the envelop, having the breadth of the board given, and without the use of the axial section. Figs. 96 to 101 . . 36
Application to Boiler-making. Figs. 102 to 107* . 37

GEOMETRICAL PROBLEMS BY THE COMPASSES ONLY, AND WITHOUT THE USE OF A RULER OR ANY OTHER INSTRUMENT.

To find the centre of a given circle. Fig. 108 . 41
To divide the circumference of a circle into four equal parts without the use of a ruler or straight edge. Fig. 109 41
To divide a given distance into two equal parts. Fig. 110 41
To construct a square on one of its diagonals, with compasses only. Fig. 111 41
To divide an arc equally, by compasses only. Figs. 112 and 113 41
To divide the circumference of a circle into five equal parts. Fig. 114 42
To describe a five-sided regular polygon, on a given line. Fig. 115 42
To describe an eight-sided regular polygon, on a given straight line. Fig. 116 42
To describe a ten-sided polygon on the line. Fig. 117 43
To describe a five-point or star. Fig. 118 . . 43

BRACKETS AND PILLOW-BLOCKS.

Elevation, End View, and Plan of Pillow-Blocks, Pedestals, Brackets, &c. Figs. 119 to 135 . . 43
Spur Mortise-Wheel 47
Proportional Scale for Geering. Fig. 136 . . 47
Undershot Water-Wheel 48
Detailed Drawings of a Meter-Wheel 48
Bevel-Wheel and Pinion 49
Bement's Lubricator. Figs. 137 and 138 . . 50
Details of Locomotives 51
Boiler for Generating Steam by burning of Anthracite, invented by F. P. Dimpfel. Plate X., and Figs. 139, 140, and 141 52
Dimensions of the Engine 52
Cost of Running 52
Boilers at the Merrimack Print Works, Lowell . . 55
Safety-Valves. Observations by Henry Howson, C. E. Figs. 142 to 150 56

	PAGE
Electric Steam-Gage. Invented by Arthur Dunn	61
House's Printing Telegraph, the Magnet of	62
Table of the Elastic Force of Steam	62
Wright's Rotary Engine	63
Wright's Hollow Cylinder Cut-off Valves	64
Locomotives. M. W. Baldwin's	65
High-Pressure Steam-Engines. J. T. Sutton & Co's	66
Horse-Power	69
The Unit of Work	69
Boiler and Foundations, arranged for a High-Pressure Engine, with 16 inch cylinder, and 48 inch stroke. Plate XIII	70
Engines of the Steamship Benj. Franklin. Plates XI. and XII	71
Boilers of Steamship Benj. Franklin. Figs. 151 and 152	75
Indicator Diagrams of Steamship Benj. Franklin. Figs. 153 to 157	75
Horse-power of the Engine as found from the Indicator Diagram	76
M. V. Regnault's Formula for the Volume of Steam	77
Steam-Pumping Engine, arranged for supplying railway tanks with water. Plate VIII	78
Strength of Materials, Metal, Wood, &c.	79
The Indicator. Figs. 158 to 166	82
Action of the Indicator. Fig. 161 and 162	83
Allowance made in finding the available horse-power of an Engine	84
Morin's Indicator	85
Nominal Horse-Power	87
Discovery of Dr. Black	87
Boyle, Gay-Lussac, and Regnault	88
Pumping-Engine, U. S. Dry Dock, Brooklyn, N. Y. Plate XIV	89
Parallel Motions. Figs. 167 to 182	91
The true course of the piston-rod here determined directly for the first time	96
Mechanical Principles, Rules, Laws, and Data	98
Parallelograms of Forces. Figs. 183 to 185	98
Parallelograms of Velocities. Fig. 186	101
Parallelograms of Accelerations. Fig. 187	101
Parallelograms of Velocities and Accelerations Fig. 188	102
Central Forces. Figs. 189 to 191	102
Principle of D'Alembert	106
True Principles upon which Practical Mechanics are based, and Machines operate	107
The Screw Propeller, and the Principles concerned in the Operation of Screw Vessels	112
Fluid Resistance	112
Newton's Third Law of Motion incorrect	113
M. Beaufoy's Results	114
Don G. Juan's Theory of the Resistance of Fluids	115
The Horse-Power necessary to accomplish any particular speed in cases of ordinary vessels and ordinary velocities	116
Beaufoy's Experiments on the friction of water	118
Laws of Fluid Resistance	118
High Speeds of Vessels	119

CONFIGURATIONS AND PROPORTIONS OF THE SCREW PROPELLER.

Thrust of the Shaft	120
Diameter of Screws	120
The Pitch of Screws	120
The number of Blades or Threads	120

POSITIVE AND NEGATIVE SLIP OF THE SCREW.

Remarkable Phenomena connected with the action of the Screw	121
Positive Slip	121
Negative Slip	122

CENTRIFUGAL ACTION OF THE SCREW.

Screw with helical Blades	122
Advantages of a deep Screw	123
Wasteful amount of Slip	123

THE CALORIC ENGINE OF ERICSSON.

Description and Horizontal Section. Figs. 192 and 193	124
The Regenerators	125
Action of the Engine when at work	125
Fallacies of the Invention	126

COMPARATIVE ADVANTAGES OF PADDLE AND SCREW VESSELS.

Screw Vessels when set to encounter Head Winds	126
Nature of Slip	127
Thrust of Screw	127
Principle of Virtual Velocities	127

NEW THEORY OF THE STRENGTH OF MATERIALS.

Nature of the forces exerted by the filaments at different points of the Cross Section, where fracture would ensue. Figs. 194 and 195	128
The fallacy of supposing a Beam to contain a neutral axis. Fig. 196	128
The End	128

LIST OF PLATES.

PLATE I.

STEAM-ENGINE WITH NINE-INCH CYLINDER AND EIGHTEEN-INCH STROKE, BY J. T. SUTTON & CO., FRANKLIN IRON WORKS, KENSINGTON, PHILADELPHIA. BUILT FOR U. S. ARSENAL, FRANKFORD, PA. SEE FRONTISPIECE PAGE 1.

PLATE II.

WATER-WHEEL AND SPUR-WHEEL. THE FIGS. OF THIS PLATE GIVE TWO VIEWS OF A MORTISE SPUR-WHEEL, AND TWO VIEWS OF AN UNDERSHOT WATER-WHEEL, CONTAINING 32 FLOATS. SEE PAGES 47 AND 48.

PLATE III.

BEVEL-WHEEL AND SECTIONS. FIG. 1 OF THIS PLATE IS A SECTION, FIG. 2 A FACE VIEW, AND FIG. 3 A SIDE VIEW OF A METER-WHEEL. PAGES 48 AND 49.

PLATE IV.

BEVEL-WHEELS GEERED. THE PAIRS OF WHEELS SHOWN IN THIS PLATE ARE OF UNEQUAL SIZE. SEE PAGES 49 AND 50.

PLATE V.

DETAILS OF LOCOMOTIVES. LEVERS FOR MOVING CUT-OFF SLIDE. SPRING AND PEDESTAL BOXES. PISTON, PACKING, CONNECTING-RODS. DETAILS OF CYLINDER. AXLES OF WHEELS. PAGE 51.

PLATE VI.

HIGH-PRESSURE STEAM-ENGINE, WITH SIXTEEN-INCH CYLINDER AND FOUR FEET STROKE. FIG. 1 IS A SIDE ELEVATION. FIG. 2 AN END VIEW LOOKING TOWARDS THE CYLINDER. FIGS. 3 AND 4 SECTIONAL VIEWS. FIGS. 5, 6, 7, 8, 9, DETAILS. SEE PAGES 66 AND 67.

PLATE VII.

WRIGHT'S REVOLVING PISTON-ENGINE. FIGS. 1 AND 2 ARE END VIEWS. FIG. 4 A MIDDLE SECTION. FIG. 3 A SIDE VIEW. FIG. 5 FIXTURES TO REGULATE THE VELOCITY OF THE PISTON. PAGES 63 AND 64.

PLATE VIII.

STEAM PUMPING-ENGINE, BY W. A. INGLIS, OF THE PEOPLE'S WORKS, PHILADELPHIA. FIG. 1 IS A SIDE ELEVATION. FIG. 2 A SECTIONAL ELEVATION. FIG. 3 A PLAN. FIG. 4 A FACE VIEW OF THE ECCENTRIC. SEE PAGES 78 AND 79.

PLATE IX.

LOCOMOTIVE, BY M. W. BALDWIN, PHILADELPHIA, CONSTRUCTED WITH EIGHT DRIVING-WHEELS, AND ITS IMPROVEMENT CONSISTS IN HAVING A FLEXIBLE TRUCK ARRANGEMENT. SEE PAGE 65.

PLATE X.

DIMPFEL'S ANTHRACITE COAL-BURNING LOCOMOTIVE, DUNN'S ELECTRIC STEAM-GAGE, AND THE BOILERS AT THE MERRIMACK PRINT WORKS, LOWELL. FOR DESCRIPTIONS SEE PAGES 51, 52, 53, 54, AND 55.

PLATE XI.

ENGINES OF THE STEAMSHIP BENJAMIN FRANKLIN, CONSTRUCTED BY I. P. MORRIS & CO. FIG. 1, PLATE XI., IS A SECTIONAL ELEVATION ON THE LINE *AB*, PLATE XII., OF THE ENGINE NEAREST THE PROPELLER. SEE PAGES 71, 72, 73, 74, 75, AND 76.

PLATE XII.

DETAILS AND SECTIONS OF THE STEAMSHIP BEN. FRANKLIN. FIG. 3, PLATE XII., IS A PLAN OF THE TWO ENGINES, ONE BEING A SECTION ON THE LINE *CD*, THE OTHER ON THE LINE *DE*, PLATE XI.

PLATE XIII.

STEAM-BOILER CONSTRUCTED BY J. T. SUTTON & CO. THIS BOILER IS OF THE REQUISITE SIZE FOR THE BEAM-ENGINE SHOWN IN PLATE VI. FIGS. 1, 2, 3, AND 4 ARE PLANS AND SECTIONS. SEE PAGES 66, 67, AND 70.

PLATE XIV.

PUMPING-ENGINE OF THE UNITED STATES DRY DOCK, BROOKLYN, ARRANGED BY W. J. M'ALPINE, C. E., AND CONSTRUCTED BY MESSRS. KEMBLE, AT THE WEST POINT FOUNDRY. SEE PAGES 89 AND 90.

MATHEMATICAL AND DRAWING INSTRUMENTS

DESCRIBED AND APPLIED.

MATHEMATICAL and drawing instruments are mechanical contrivances, enabling us to construct with ease and certainty all kinds of geometrical figures. They are usually combined in a case, popularly named a Case of Drawing Instruments. The most useful instruments are the *compasses* of various kinds, the *parallel ruler*, the *plane scales*, the *protractor*, and the *sector*. Of each of these we shall speak in order.

A pair of *compasses* is an instrument that scarcely requires general description; it consists of two pointed legs, joined at the upper end, and opening freely to any extent. The simplest and most obvious use of the compasses is that of measuring dimensions, and laying down distances. There are, however, various modifications of this instrument adapting it to more extensive usefulness. In addition to the compasses for taking dimensions, there are others with movable pen and pencil-joints, by which circular figures may be described temporarily, or permanently, according as they form necessary parts of the figure to be constructed, or are only preliminary steps in the process. For describing arcs and circles of very short radius, bow compasses are employed; these were formerly *bowed*, to bring their points more accurately together, whence their name; but they do not now differ materially from other compasses, except in being smaller, and more delicately formed.

The *parallel ruler* (Fig. 1) consists of two plane rulers moving upon joints in such a manner that they always preserve their parallelism to each other.

Fig. 1.

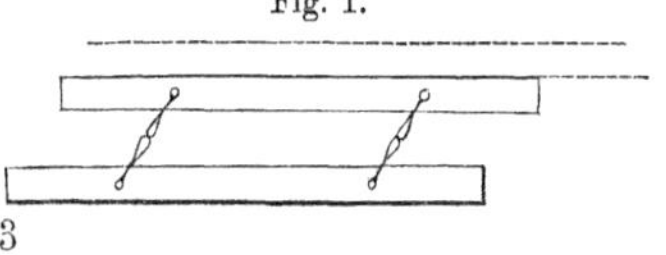

Their principal use is to facilitate the drawing of parallel lines. The mathematical principle on which this instrument depends is contained in the 27th, and two following propositions of the 1st Book of Euclid; it needs, however, no severe reasoning to prove that the scales, at every extent of opening, must be parallel; for, their outer and inner edges being all parallel to each other, and their connecting-joints being *fixed* parallel the one to the other, it is sufficiently obvious that the parallelism of the scales cannot be disturbed by any motion of the centres. In using the parallel ruler, care must be taken to keep one scale firmly pressed down whilst the other is being moved.

The *plane scale* is usually of box or ivory, and six to twelve inches in length, on which the inch is variously divided. One of the larger divisions on each scale is subdivided into tenths and twelfths; if, therefore, the large divisions be taken for units or feet, the tenths and twelfths will be decimals or inches. These scales being accurately divided, they are of instant use for laying down plans and drawings that require all their parts to have strict proportion to each other. By making ten of the larger divisions an unit, and twelve one foot, we can take from the scales, in the one instance, units and two places of decimals, and in the other, feet, inches, and firsts. To take a dimension from the plane scale, one foot of the compasses is placed against the larger division, and the other is extended into the subdivisions. Thus, to take off 8 feet 10 inches, place one foot at 8 on the selected scale, and extend the other to the tenth of the duodecimal subdivisions.

On one side of the plane scale there is given a *diagonal scale*, which has this superiority over those we have described, that from it any dimension extending to three places of figures, or to three denominations, may be taken off with the greatest readiness. The construction of this scale is very simple: eleven parallel lines inclose ten divisions of equal width; these are divided, by lines at right angles, into eleven larger divisions, the eleventh being again divided into ten equal parts, to give a second denomination, and these are subdivided by diagonal lines, so that at each intersection with the parallels of the scale, the diagonals indicate a third denomination, or the tenths of the preceding divisions.

The annexed diagram (Fig. 2) will explain the

Fig. 2.

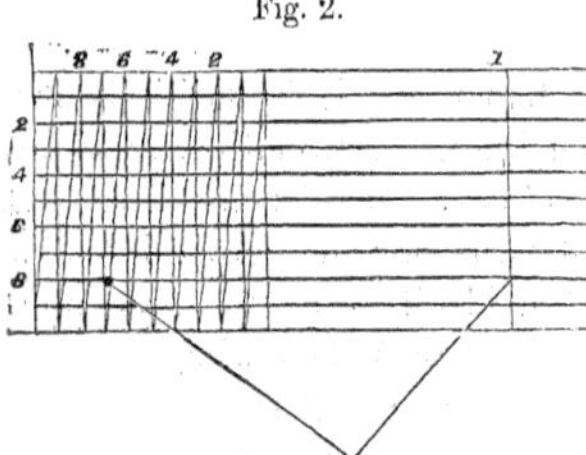

construction more clearly. The large divisions on this scale are frequently halved, and at the opposite end one of these half divisions is diagonally divided in like manner; by this means two scales are united in one. To take a dimension, say 168, place one foot of the compasses on the line 1, and extend the other to 6 of the smaller divisions, then bring the compasses down to the parallel of 8, and by opening them till the points fall exactly the one on the larger division 1, and the other on the diagonal which measures the tenths between the smaller divisions 6 and 7, you obtain the dimension required.

Above the diagonal scale there is usually laid a double scale of units and decimals. These may be taken as separate scales, or they may be used together. In the first instance, the dimension is obtained in the same manner as from the scales first described: but in the second case, the large divisions of the lower line answer for feet, and the subdivisions of the upper line for inches—one large division of the lower line coinciding with twelve subdivisions in the upper line.

Besides the scales we have described, there is sometimes on one side of the plane scale a *line of chords*, giving the chords of all angles at a fixed radius. (Fig. 3.) Constructing a quadrant of any radius, at pleasure, first draw the chord of the quadrant, or 90°; then divide the quadrant into 9 equal parts, 10, 20, 30, &c. place one foot of the compasses at A, and taking successively the distances 10, 20, 30, &c., on the quadrant, transfer them by

Fig. 3.

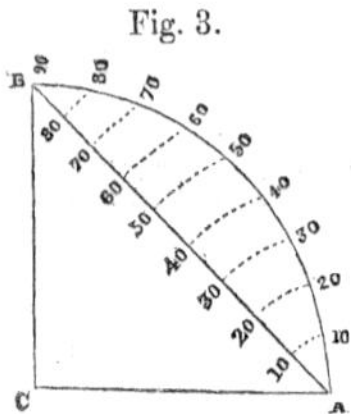

arcs from the centre A, to the line AB; the divisions on this line will then give the chords of angles from 10° to 90°, in accordance with the radius of the circle of which the described quadrant is a part. The line of chords is applied to the laying down and measuring of angles, which is done in the following manner. To *measure* any given angle, take with the compasses the chord of 60°, which is equal to radius, and placing one foot on the angular point, describe an arc across the angle. Then take the chord of this arc in the compasses and apply it to the lines of chord, which will at once show the number of degrees contained in the given angle. Suppose the given angle to be ACB; with the chord of 60° describe the arc BA, and the chord line AB applied to the line of chords will give the measure of the angle 90°. To *lay down an angle* containing a given number of degrees, draw a right line, say CA, and from C as a centre, and with the chord of 60° as a radius, describe an arc of sufficient extent; take the chord of the required angle from the line of chords, and extend it from A towards B; then drawing a right line from the angular point C, through the point of intersection in the arc, you have the required angle.

The *protractor* is an instrument by which angles are laid down or measured with greater facility than by the line of chords. It is a semicircle, or half circle of brass, having its circumference divided into 180°, every fifth and tenth degree being distinguished by lines drawn the one half-way, and the other entirely across the face of the protractor. The degrees are numbered 10, 20, 30, &c., to 180°, both ways, as indicated in the annexed diagram. (Fig. 4.)

Fig. 4.

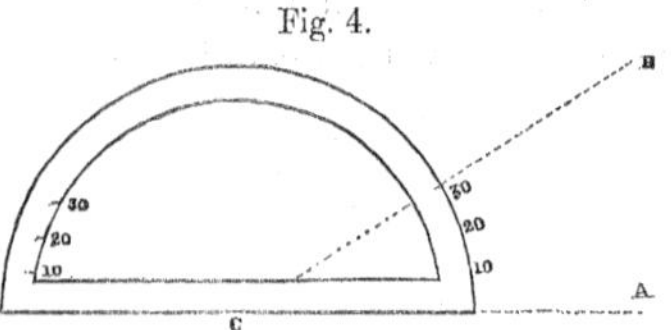

To measure a given angle by the protractor, let the centre of the instrument and the angular point C coincide, and the straight edge of the protractor lie evenly on the line CA; then will the other line CB indicate on the graduated edge of the instrument the number of degrees contained in the angle. To lay down an angle, draw a line, say CA; fix the protractor as in the former case, and with the protracting pin (which screws into the drawing pen), or with a finely-pointed pencil, mark off above the line CA and along the graduated edge, the number of degrees required for the angle; then remove the instrument and draw the line, say CB, from the angular point C through the point of measure, and the operation is completed. The angle ACB will be the angle required.

The *sector* is the most complicated instrument contained in the mathematical case, but it is at the same time the most generally useful. It consists of two scales jointed at the centre, and opening freely to their full extent. The principle of its construction results from the demonstration that similar triangles are proportional to each other in all their parts. Thus, in the triangles ACI, BCH, DCG, ECF, (Fig. 5,) the sides and bases have one common

Fig. 5.

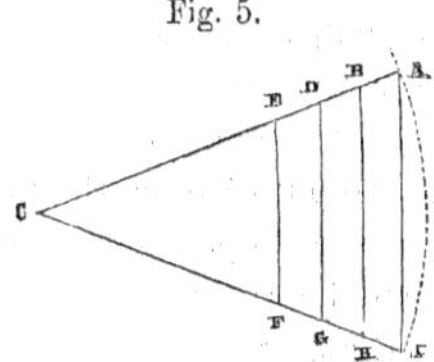

ratio; and supposing the lines AC, CI, to be the two legs of a sector, movable on the centre C, at every extent of opening the similar triangles will be proportional in all their parts. Hence the usefulness of the sector, for mechanical solutions of various problems in trigonometry. We shall, however, only refer to those parts of the sector which offer facilities for the construction of geometrical figures, and which are of service to the mechanical draftsman in laying down plans and drawings that require their details to be proportioned with mathematical precision.

On reference to the instrument it will be noticed, that there are on each side of it a number of lines radiating from the central joint, and extending over the face of the scales. Thus, on one side, we have the line of lines (L), the line of secants (S), the line of chords (C), and the line of polygons (Pol.); on the other side, we find the line of sines (S), and the two lines of tangents, the one extending to 45°, and the other to 75°. In addition to the true *sectoral* lines, we observe others disposed over the face and edges of the scales; some of these are of the same nature as the plane scales, and amongst the others are found the lines of logarithmic tangents, sines, and numbers. It will answer all the purposes we have in view, to explain and apply three of the sectoral lines, viz., the line of lines, the line of chords, and the line of polygons. The first two are laid down upon both scales in such a manner that at every opening of the sector they form equal angles; and in working these lines, the compasses must always be applied to the innermost division, as that alone runs up truly into the centre of the instrument. Distances measured on the sector are called *lateral* when taken from the centre C towards A or I, and *transverse* when taken from scale to scale, as from A to I.

The *line of lines* is merely a scale of equal parts, and the advantages it possesses over an ordinary plane scale result from the geometrical principles of the sector, to which we have already alluded. By this line, we divide a given line into any number of equal parts; find a third, or fourth, or mean proportional to any given line; construct a scale of equal parts of any given dimension; determine, from any two sides of a right-angled triangle, the length of the third side; or, divide a given line in any assigned proportion.

To divide a given line into any number of equal parts (say 10), take the length of the line in the compasses, and placing one foot on the point B of the sector, (Fig. 6,) open the instrument till the other

Fig. 6.

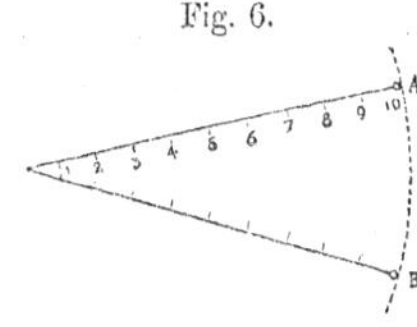

foot falls exactly on the point A; keep the sector in this position, and closing the compasses, take the transverse distance, 1.1, which will be the tenth part of the given line; and this, carried ten times over the line, will divide it as required. Had it been desired to divide the line into 8 or 9 equal parts, the length of the line would have been made a transverse distance 8.8 or 9.9 accordingly. If the given line be too long to admit of its being made a transverse distance, it must be bisected, and, if still too long, the half must be bisected. Thus, suppose it be required to divide into 40 parts, a line of which a fourth part only can be made a transverse distance; in this case, making the fourth part a transverse from 10 to 10, that is, from A to B, the transverse of 1.1 (the tenth part of the quarter line) will be the fortieth part of the given line, which is to be set off as before.

To divide a given line in any assigned proportion, say of 4 to 5, take the length of the given line in the compasses, and make this a transverse distance to 9 and 9 (9 being the sum of the proposed parts); keeping the sector in this position, take the transverse distances 4.4 and 5.5, which will divide the given line in the proportions required. If the line be too long to fall within the transverse distance, divide it as in the former case.

To construct a scale, say of 50 feet, four inches in length, take four inches in the compasses, and make this extent a transverse distance from 5 to 5 on the sector; you have then the required scale, in which every division of the line of lines, taken transversely, will be one foot. When the divisions on the sector are correctly laid down, this instrument is highly useful to the mechanical draftsman, not only in constructing any required scale, but also in reducing and enlarging other scales in any desired proportion. In selecting a sector, the purchaser should give a good price, and likewise test the accuracy of the lines in various ways; for though the instrument is *theoretically* perfect, it is *practically* useless unless it be divided with extreme delicacy and exactness.

To find a third proportional to two given lines, say lines of 4 and 5 inches in length. If it be an ascending proportion, take the lateral distance 5, and make it a transverse distance to 4.4; keeping the sector at this opening, take the transverse distance of 5.5, and this measured laterally will give the third proportional, viz. $6\frac{1}{4}$ inches: for 4 : 5 : : 5 : $6\frac{1}{4}$. Or, if it be a descending proportion, take the lateral distance 4, and make it a transverse distance to 5.5; then the transverse distance 4.4 measured laterally, gives a third proportional, viz. 3.2, or $3\frac{1}{5}$; for 5 : 4 : : 4 : $3\frac{1}{5}$. A fourth proportional to three given lines, say lines of 4, 6, and 12 inches, is found in the following manner. Take the lateral distance of the second term (6), and make it a transverse distance to the first term (4), then will the transverse of the third term (12), measured laterally, give 18, the fourth proportional required. As we cannot obtain the transverse of 12.12 from the sector, we take that of 6.6, and double the lateral measure 9 for the fourth proportional. Therefore, 4 : 6 : : 12 : 18. From the foregoing operation, we deduce a method of diminishing or increasing a line in any assigned proportion. Suppose it be required to diminish a line of 4 inches, in the proportion of 8 to 7: make the lateral distance of the second term (7), a transverse to the first term (8), then the transverse distance of the third term (4), measured laterally, will give $3\frac{1}{2}$, the proportion required. For 8 : 7 : : 4 : $3\frac{1}{2}$.

To open the sector in such a manner that the line of lines on one scale shall be at right angles to the corresponding line on the other scale. Take the lateral distance 5, and make it a transverse from 3 on one scale to 4 on the other, and the angle is formed; for 3, 4, and 5, or any of their multiples, constitute a right angle. Having thus fixed the sector, we are able, from any two given lines of a right-angled triangle, to discover the third line. Suppose the base of a right-angled triangle to be 6, and the perpendicular 5, what is the hypothenuse? We take the transverse distance of 5.6, and this measured laterally, gives $7\frac{4}{5}$, the length of the hypothenuse. Or, suppose the hypothenuse 9, and the base 6, be given to find the perpendicular: take the lateral distance 9, and placing one foot of the compasses on 6, extend the other transversely to the opposite scale, and the point where it falls exactly upon the line of lines will indicate the lateral measure of the perpendicular, viz. $6\frac{4}{5}$ *nearly*. These operations, and indeed all operations, depend, for their close approximation to truth, upon a correct subdivision of the sectoral lines.

A mean proportional to two given lines may be found when the sector is rectified for a right angle. Thus, let it be required to find a mean proportional to two lines whose respective lengths are 40 and 90. Find half the sum (65), and half the difference (25), of the given lines; take the lateral distance 65 in the compasses, and placing one foot on 25, extend the other transversely, when it will reach to 60, the mean proportional required.

It is scarcely necessary to remark, that in using the line of lines, the divisions, 1, 2, 3, &c., may be considered as units, tens, hundreds, or thousands; and the subdivisions will be decimals, units, tens, or hundreds, accordingly.

The sectoral *line of chords* has the same advantage over the scale of chords on the plane scale, that the sectoral line of lines has over the ordinary plane scales. The chords on the plane scale are confined to one radius, but those on the sector are adapted to all the radii that fall within the compass of its openings.

(Fig. 7.) To protract an angle of not more than

Fig. 7.

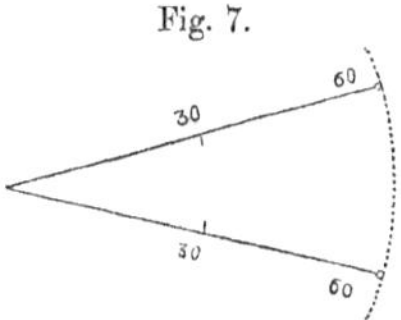

60°, say an angle of 30°: Open the sector at pleasure, and taking the transverse distance 60.60 in the compasses as a radius, describe an arc of a circle; take the transverse distance of 30°, and set it upon the arc; then from the centre draw right lines to the points of measure in the arc, and the required angle is formed. To measure an angle of not more than 60°, take in the compasses the transverse distance of 60.60 at any opening of the sector, and with this radius describe from the angular point an arc across the given angle; take the measure of the arc, included in the given angle, in the compasses, and apply this transversely to the line of chords on the sector, and the similar divisions on which the points of the compasses fall, express the true measure of the angle.

To protract an angle of more than 60°, the transverse distance of 60.60, at any opening of the sector, is taken as radius, and an arc described as in the former case; then take the transverse distance of one-half or one-third of the given number of degrees, and set off twice or three times on the arc, as the case may be; afterwards, form the required angle by right lines from the centre of the arc to the two outermost points of measure on the arc. Thus, if the angle is required to contain 100°, having described the arc, set off 50° twice, and thus obtain the required measure. Any angle of more than 60° is measured in portions, in like manner.

If it be required to protract an angle of less than 10°, it is more convenient to lay down an angle of 60°, and to set off from the arc of that angle the complement to 60°. Thus, if an angle of 7° be required, protract an angle of 60°, and set off from the arc of 60°, the complement 53°; and the remainder of the arc will then evidently contain 7°, the required measure. The reason for operating in this way for small angles, is that the divisions of the sectoral lines of chords are not readily distinguished when we approach *within* 10° towards the centre of the instrument. To measure any small angle, protract an angle of 60° that shall include it, then take the complement to 60° in the compasses, and this applied transversely to the sector will show the measure of the supplement which is to be deducted from 60°, when the remainder will express the measure of the given angle.

As the sectoral *lines of sines and tangents* afford ready means of describing eccentric curves, we offer a few words of explanation regarding them. A *sine* is a line drawn from one extremity of an arc perpendicular to a diameter passing through the other extremity. A *tangent* is a line touching a circle in one extremity of the arc, and continued, perpendicular to the diameter passing through that extremity, till it meets a line (named a *secant*) drawn from the centre of the circle through the other extremity of the arc. Thus CA (Fig. 8) is

Fig. 8.

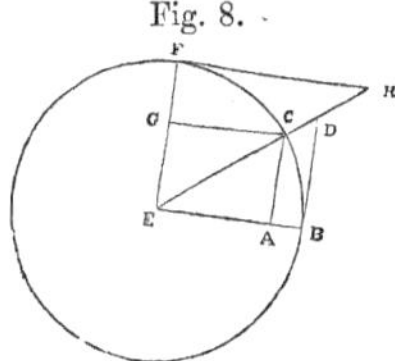

the sine, and DB is the tangent of the arc CB, or of the angle CEA; and GC is the cosine, and FH the cotangent of the same arc or angle, these last being the sine and tangent of the complementary angle to 90°. The line of sines upon the sector gives the sine of any angle to 90°, at any radius that will make a transverse distance from 90° to 90° on these lines. The line of tangents is laid upon the sector twice, on account of their length; the lower tangents extend to 45°, and the upper ones from 45° to 75°; the tangents of angles exceeding 75° are too long to fall within the compass of the sector.

To find the sine of an angle we apply the radius as a transverse distance to 90° and 90° on the line of sines, and the transverse of so many degrees as are the measure of the given angle, is the sine required. The tangent, up to 45°, is found by applying the radius transversely to 45° and 45° on the *lower* tangents, and then taking the transverse of the degrees contained in the given angle. Between 45° and 75°, the tangent is obtained by making the radius a transverse to 45° and 45° on the *upper* tangents, and taking the necessary transverse of degrees as before. And any tangent exceeding 75°, may be taken from the sector, if we can make the radius a transverse distance to the complementary degrees on the lower tangents; for in that case the transverse of 45° and 45° is the tangent required.

The *lines of polygons* (Fig. 9) are placed on the

Fig. 9.

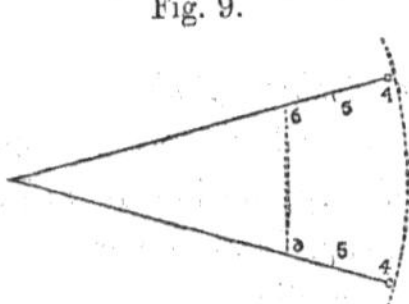

inner edges of the sector, on the under side of the line of chords (C) on one scale, and on the upper side of the line of lines (L) on the other scale. The chords of the central angles of polygons, having from 4 to 12 sides, are laid down according to a line of chords, whereof the chord of 90° is exactly equal to the chord of 60° on the sectoral lines. Hence the transverse distance of 6.6 on the lines of polygons is radius. The name of these lines sufficiently defines their use: viz., to construct regular sided figures on a given line, or *within* or *without* the circumference of a given circle.

To inscribe, say, a regular octagon (or figure of eight equal sides) in any given circle, make the radius of the circle a transverse distance to 6 and 6 on the lines of polygons, and the transverse of 8 and 8 will give the side of the octagon, which is to be set off 8 times on the circumference of the circle; chord lines drawn from point to point round the circle will complete the figure.

A polygon (say a pentagon) is constructed on any given line thus: make the given line a transverse to 5.5 on the line of polygons (5, being the number of equal sides in the required figure); with this opening of the sector, take the transverse of 6.6 for a radius, and from each termination of the given line describe an arc in such direction that the two arcs shall intersect; from the point of intersection as a centre, with the same radius, describe a circle, which will pass exactly through the terminations of the given line; the given line is then one side of the required pentagon, and requires only to be set off round the circumference of the circle to complete the figure.

To describe a regular polygon about any circle (that is, *without* the circumference), first form the *inscribed* figure; then draw lines touching the circumference, parallel to the inscribed lines, and the intersections of these outer lines will form the polygon required.

We have not touched upon all the uses to which the sectoral lines may be applied; but when those to which we have adverted are familiarly understood, the others will suggest themselves. In our next division, which explains the construction of geometric figures, the application of the several instruments we have been describing will be farther illustrated.

Mr. Oliver Byrne, the author of this work, has invented a new mathematical instrument, termed "The Byrnegraph." It is much more accurate, and supersedes the use of the *proportional compasses* and of the *sector*; it is described in his *Dictionary of Machines, Mechanics, Engine-work, and Engineering*, and may be found in Vol. I. p. 200, if the publisher, Appleton, has not changed the title of it; as he calls Byrne's Dictionary, Appleton's.

(Fig. 10.) A Pocket Case of Mathematical Instruments usually contains the following:—

1. Pair of 5-inch plain compasses.

Fig. 10.

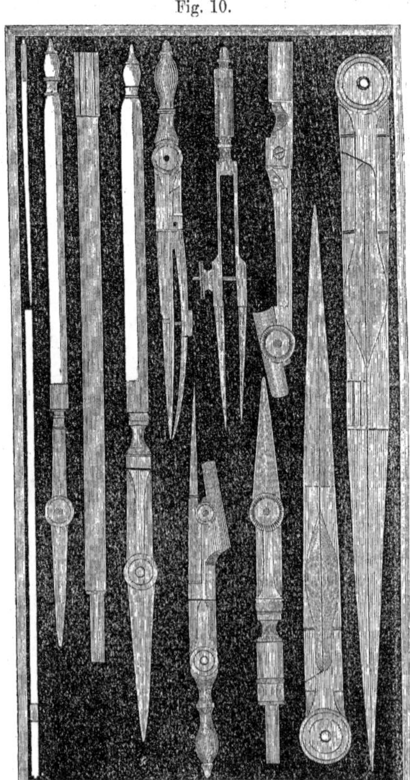

2. Pair of 6-inch drawing compasses, with one leg or point movable.
3. Pencil point.
4. Ink point.
5. One for dotting.
6. Drawing pen, with a protracting pin in the handle.
7. Protractor in the form of a semicircle.
8. Plain scale.
9. Parallel rule.
10. Sometimes a sector.
11. Also sometimes a bow pen.
12. Pencil.

Hair Compasses.—(Fig. 11.)—They are so named on account of a contrivance in the shank to set them with greater accuracy than can be effected by the motion of the joint alone. One of the steel points is fastened near the top of the compasses, and may be moved very gradually by turning the screw either backwards or forwards. To use these compasses, 1st, place the leg to which the screw is annexed, outermost; 2d, set the fixed leg on that point from whence the extent is to be taken; 3d, open the compasses as nearly as possible to the required distance, and then make the points accurately coincide therewith, by turning the screw.

Fig. 11.

The T Square.—(Figs. 12, 13.)—This is a very useful article in drawing. A ruler, about two to three feet in length, made of hard wood, or steel, is fixed, as a square, to the middle of a piece of hard wood, about one foot long and two inches wide, and on one side a loose piece is fastened by a thumb-screw, which passes through both pieces, allowing both to be clamped together at any angle, thus forming a bevel.

The head of the square, applied close to the edge of a true drawing-board, will admit of true lines being drawn as well as oblique ones, with more ease and expedition than by the common parallel rule.

The T Square and Protractor.—(Figs. 12, 13, 14.)—This instrument is formed of a divided arc of brass, usually about ten inches in diameter, whose graduation commences at the middle, and is continued each way to 90°; at the centre of the arc is attached a movable arm, about 30 inches

Fig. 12. Fig. 13. Fig. 14.

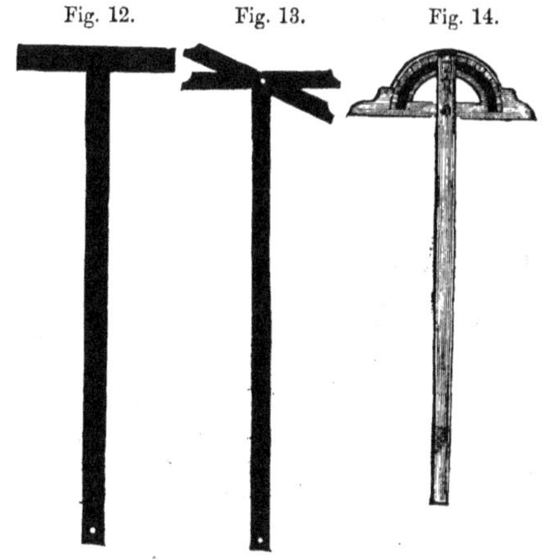

long; at the shorter end is a vernier, running on the graduated arc, and subdividing the degrees of the arc into minutes, and having a spring bent over to the under side of the arc, with a screw to clamp it fast in any position. Used on a true drawing-board, this instrument is simple and convenient, answering all the purposes of plotting and protracting of a square and bevel, and for drawing parallel lines in different directions.

Draftsman's Squares.—(Figs. 15, 16, 17).—These squares are best made of hard wood, and are

Fig. 16. Fig. 15. Fig. 17.

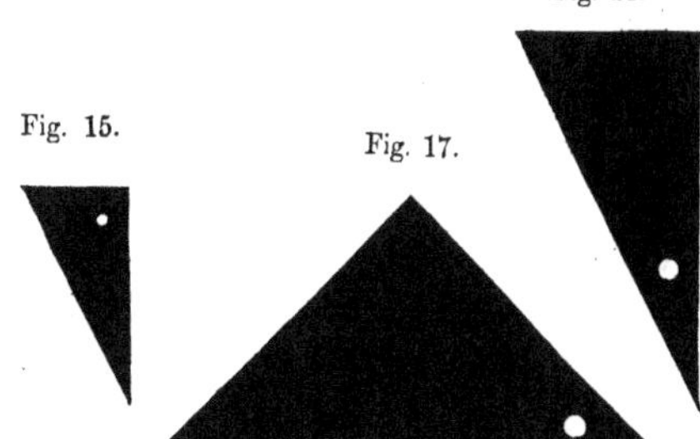

used in pairs with a common flat ruler, one of the edges of the square being placed against the rule, and, by holding the rule fast, and moving the square, parallel lines may be drawn with ease and accuracy. The squares represented are solid, having a hole for the finger to move it by. Of all the instruments used in mechanical drawing, except the compasses, these squares can be made the most useful; they are seldom out of the hands of the expert draftsman.

Curves.—(Figs. 18 to 35.)—These are various in shape and size, and from 6 to 24 inches long.

Fig. 18. Fig. 19. Fig. 20. Fig. 21.

Fig. 22. Fig. 23. Fig. 24. Fig. 25. Fig. 26.

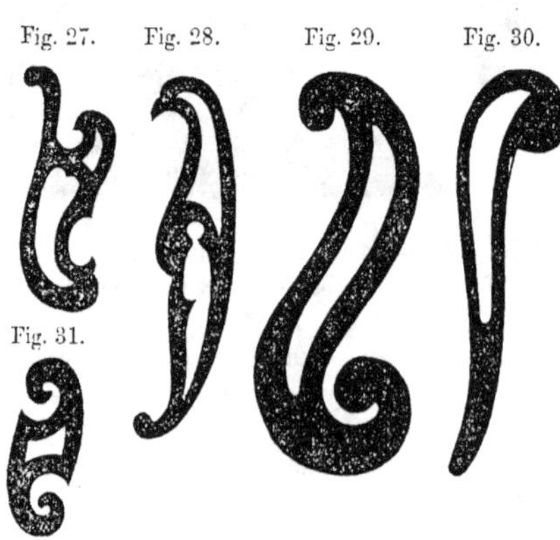

Fig. 27. Fig. 28. Fig. 29. Fig. 30. Fig. 31.

Their use is to present a variety of forms for drawing curves, and they are extensively used in naval architecture and other drawings. By the use of these curves, which are made of wood or metal, curved lines can be very steadily drawn through any number of points.

Fig 32. Fig. 33. Fig. 34. Fig. 35.

The first requisite for the mechanical draftsman is a drawing-board of suitable dimensions, whereon to mount his paper. This should be made in the following manner: A substantial frame, resembling an ordinary picture-frame, is to be prepared, grooved on the inside to admit a panel, in the same way that a picture-frame admits the back; and both the frame and panel must be made of well-seasoned wood, not liable to warp or shrink, as the usefulness of the drawing-board depends mainly on a true surface and the accurate fitting of the frame and panel, which are kept securely fixed together by two crossbars at the back. The manner of mounting the drawing-paper on a board of this description is very simple: the paper should be a little larger than the panel, and is to be damped on the back till it will lie without curling; it is then laid with the damped side downwards upon the face of the panel, and, having covered it with a sheet of clean thin paper, the hand is rubbed freely over it in all parts to make it lie smoothly and evenly; this done, the frame is to be pressed down upon the panel, forcing the latter within the grooved side, where, if the board be properly made, it is firmly held in all points; when dry, the paper will be tightly strained, and present a most agreeable surface to receive the drawing. The sides of the drawing-board should be at right angles to each other, in order that the T square may work truly.

Lead pencils of considerable hardness are a material in constant use, being the medium with which every part of the draft is at first constructed. Those marked HH, and HHH, are best suited for mechanical drawing.

GEOMETRICAL PROBLEMS AND FIGURES.

1. *To erect a perpendicular on a given right line, from a given point in that line, near the centre.*

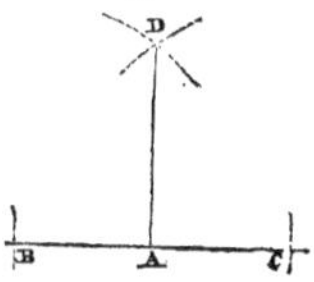

First method. (Fig. 36.) Let BC be the given line, and A the given point. From A, as a centre, with any convenient radius, cross the line BC with the arcs B and C; from the centres B and C, with a radius of more than half the given line, describe arcs intersecting each other in D; the line DA, drawn from the intersection of the arcs D to the given point A, is the perpendicular required.

Fig. 36.

Second method. (Fig. 37.) Let BC be the given line, and A the given point. Lay the protractor across the line, and cause its centre to coincide with the point A, and the division of 90° to fall exactly upon the line BC; the line DA, drawn along the straight edge of the protractor, will be perpendicular to BC, as required.

Fig. 37.

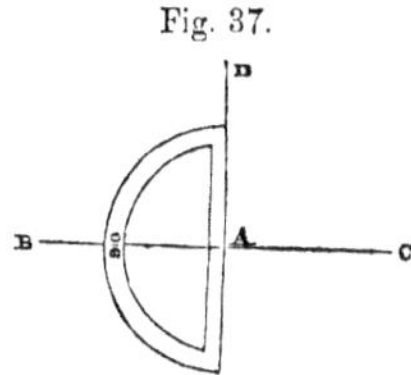

This second method is the readiest means that can be adopted for erecting a perpendicular to a right line, when the point of erection is situated anywhere *in* that line.

2. *To erect a perpendicular to a given right line, from a given point in that line, near either extremity.*

If the protractor be not at hand, the perpendicular is raised in this case, thus: (Fig. 38.) Let BC be the given line, and A the given point. Take any point F above the given line, and from that point with the radius FA, describe a portion of a circle passing through A, and cutting the given line at D; draw the line DFE by the two points D and F; and a line EA, drawn from the intersection E to the given point A, is the perpendicular sought.

Fig. 38.

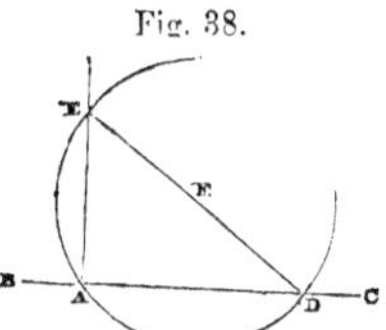

3. *To let fall a perpendicular upon a given right line, from a given point nearly above the centre of that line.*

(Fig. 39.) Let BC be the given line, and A the given point. Join CA; and from the centre C, with the radius CA, describe the arc AFD; make the arc FD equal to FA, and from the given point A, draw towards the point D; the line AE will be a perpendicular to the given line BC, falling from the point A, as required.

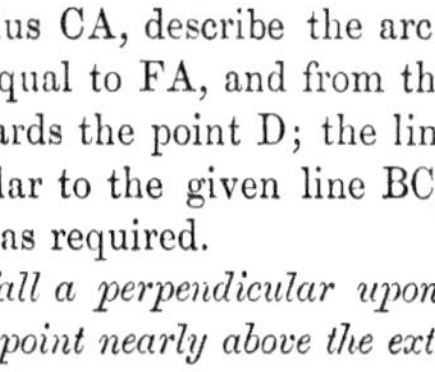

Fig. 39.

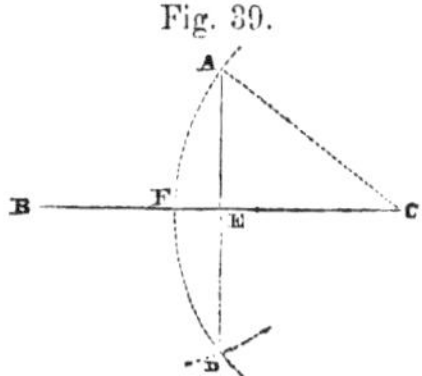

4. *To let fall a perpendicular upon a right line, from a given point nearly above the extremity of that line.*

(Fig. 40.) Let BC be the given line, and A the

Fig. 40.

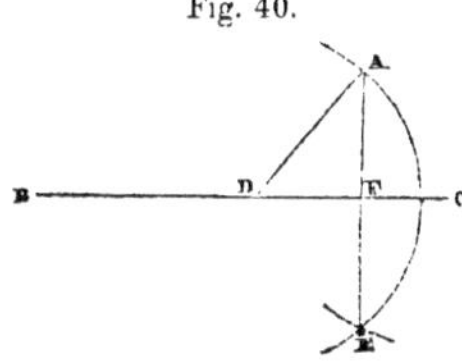

given point. Join AD; from the centre D, with the radius DA, describe the arc ACE; mark off with the compasses CE equal to CA; the line AF, part of the line AFE, is perpendicular to the line BC, and falls from the given point A.

5. *To draw a line perpendicular to a given line, from a point at some distance from that line.*

(Fig. 41.) Let BC be the given line, and A the

Fig. 41.

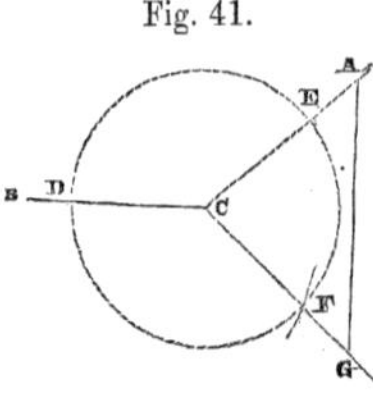

given point. Join AC; from the centre C, with any radius, describe the circle DEF; place one foot of the compasses on D, and taking the distance DE, set off DF equal thereto; draw CG indefinitely through the points C and F; make CG equal to CA; the line AG, drawn from the given point A, will be perpendicular to the given line BC.

When the point is nearly coincident with the line, that is, when it forms no sensible angle with the line, the perpendicular may be obtained in the following manner:—

(Fig. 42.) Let BC be the given line, and A the

Fig. 42.

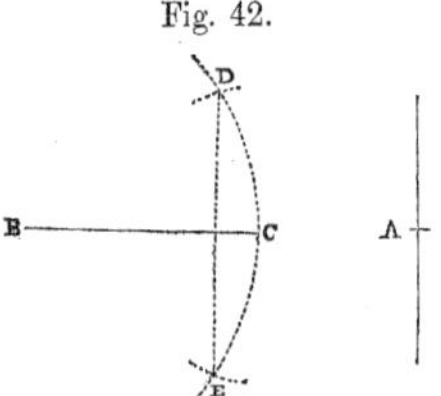

given point. From B, with the radius BC, describe the arc DCE; from C, with a shorter radius, cut the arc DCE in D and E; draw the line DE, which is perpendicular to BC; then lay one edge of the parallel ruler evenly on DE, and move the other edge till it reaches the point A, and a line drawn along the edge of the ruler through this point, will be a perpendicular to the given line BC, from the given point A, as required.

The foregoing methods of erecting and drawing perpendiculars are useful only when readier means are not at hand. Every young mechanical draftsman knows the value of the T square for drawing lines at right angles to each other; and with this beside him, he would not of course deem it necessary to erect his perpendiculars by formal constructions such as these. The T square is, however, inseparable from the drawing-board, the edges of which regulate its movements; and, as small drawings are frequently made on loose paper, in which cases the square is not available, it is necessary to acquire the methods of dispensing with its assistance. Moreover, lines may frequently require to be drawn perpendicularly to each other, that do not lie parallel to the sides of the drawing-board; and in these instances the square can be of no service. But for short lines, the draftsman's squares should always be used; for with them ten lines can be drawn, parallel or perpendicular, in any direction, before one line could be so drawn by other known methods.

6. *To bisect a given line.*

(Fig. 43.) Let AB be the given line. From A

Fig. 43.

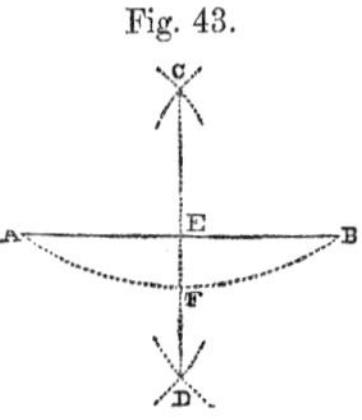

as a centre, with a radius exceeding AE, describe arcs at C and D; from B as a centre with the same radius describe arcs intersecting the former arcs in C and D; the line CD drawn through the points of intersection, bisects the given line AB. And if the given line be any portion of a circle, as the arc AFB, it is bisected in like manner; the centres A and B being taken in the extremities of the arc.

7. *To draw a line at any required angle to a given straight line.*

(Fig. 44.) Let AB be the given line. Make the centre of the protractor coincide with A, and its straight edge lie evenly upon AB; then point off the number of degrees from the circular edge with

Fig. 44.

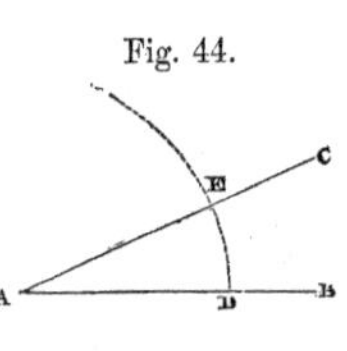

the protracting pin, and the line AC, drawn through the point E, gives the required angle. Or, let AD be the chord of 60° taken from any line of chords, and with this as radius, describe from the centre A the arc DE; take the chord of the required angle from the scale, and set it off from D to E; then draw the line AC through the point E as before. Or, with any radius, say AD, and from the centre A, describe the arc DE; apply AD transversely to 60.60 on the sectoral line of chords; take in the compasses a transverse answering to the chord of the required angle, and set it off from D to E; and draw the line AC as before.

8. *To measure any given angle.*

The measurement of any given angle either by a line of chords, by the protractor, or by the sectoral chords, is sufficiently explained in our previous descriptions of these instruments: moreover, to measure an angle is only a converse operation to the preceding proposition.

9. *To draw a line parallel to a given line.*

(Fig. 45.) Let AB be the given line. From any

Fig. 45.

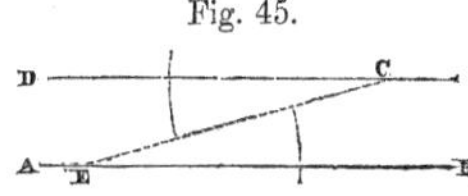

point E in the line AB, draw the line EC at any angle; make an angle DCE equal to the angle CEB; then DC, the side of the angle DCE, will be parallel to EB, the side of the angle CEB; and EB is the same line with the given line AB, therefore DC is drawn parallel to the given line AB. If a point be given through which the parallel is to be drawn, let that point be C, and draw a line from any point E to this given point C; then proceed as before.

10. *To divide a given right line into any number of equal parts.*

(Fig. 46.) Let AB be the given right line, and

Fig. 46.

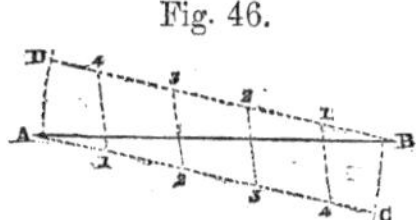

let it be required to divide it into five equal parts. Draw AC; make an angle ABD equal to the angle BAC; with any small opening of the compasses mark four divisions on the line AC, commencing at A; with the same opening mark four divisions on the line BD, commencing at B; draw the parallels 4.1; 3.2; 2.3; 1.4, and their intersections with the line AB will divide it into five equal parts as required.

11. *To bisect a given angle.*

(Fig. 47.) Let ACB be the given angle. From the centre C with any radius describe an arc AB; from A and B describe arcs intersecting each other

Fig. 47.

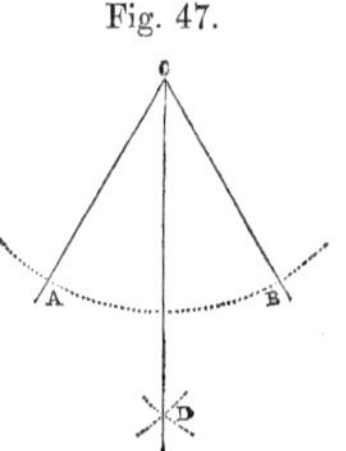

in D; draw the line CD from the angular point C through the point of intersection D, and the angle is bisected, or divided into two equal parts.

12. *To find the centre of a given circle.*

(Fig. 48.) Let the given circle be AECFBD. Draw any chord AB; bisect AB with the diameter CD; bisect CD with another diameter EF; the point of intersection G is the centre of the circle.

Fig. 48.

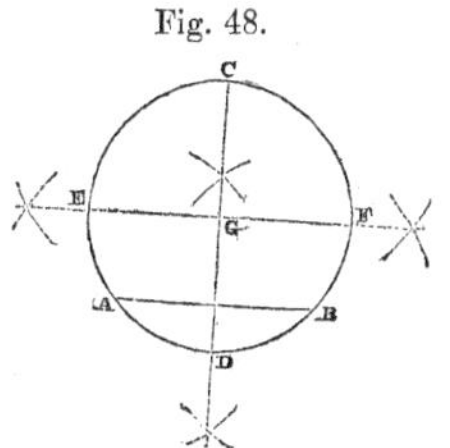

13. *To describe the circle of which any given arc or segment is a portion.*

Fig. 49.

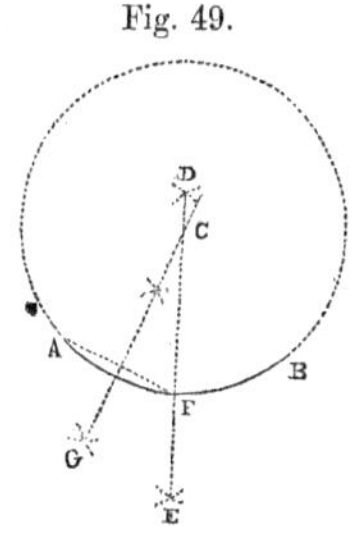

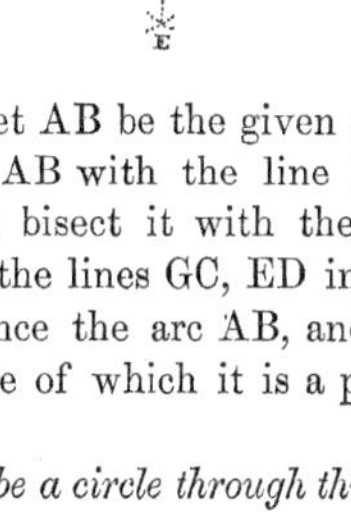

(Fig. 49.) Let AB be the given arc or segment. Bisect the arc AB with the line DE; draw the chord AF, and bisect it with the line GC; the point C, where the lines GC, ED intersect, will be the centre whence the arc AB, and consequently the entire circle of which it is a portion, may be described.

14. *To describe a circle through three given points.*

(Fig. 50.) Let A, B, and C be the three given points. Join AB and BC; bisect the lines AB and

Fig. 50.

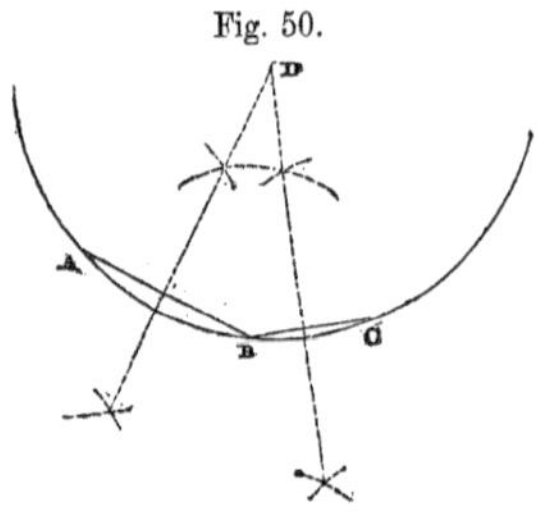

BC with lines intersecting in D; the point of intersection D will be the centre of a circle whose circumference shall pass through each of the given points A, B, and C.

15. *To cut off any portion of a circle whose diameter is given.*

(Fig. 51.) Let ABD be a part of the given circle,

Fig. 51.

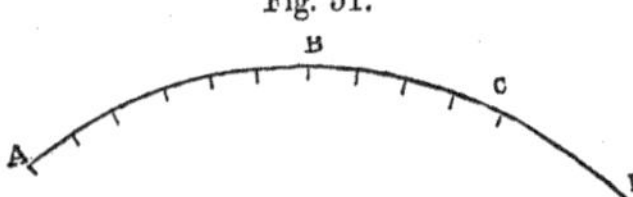

and suppose it is required to cut off a tenth part of the whole circumference. Set off the distance AB equal to half the diameter, and divide it into ten equal parts; then six of these parts as AC, will be the portion required. A very little consideration will make this evident; for since AB is measured by half the diameter, or by the radius, which is the chord of the sixth part of the circumference, it follows that each of the small spaces will be $= \frac{1}{60}$ and AC of course $= \frac{6}{60} = \frac{1}{10}$.

PROBLEMS ON CIRCLES OF LARGE RADII.

16. *Given the length of the chord and versed sine of a curve, to draw the curve without having recourse to the centre.*

(Fig. 52.) Let AB be the chord, and CD the versed sine.

Fig. 52.

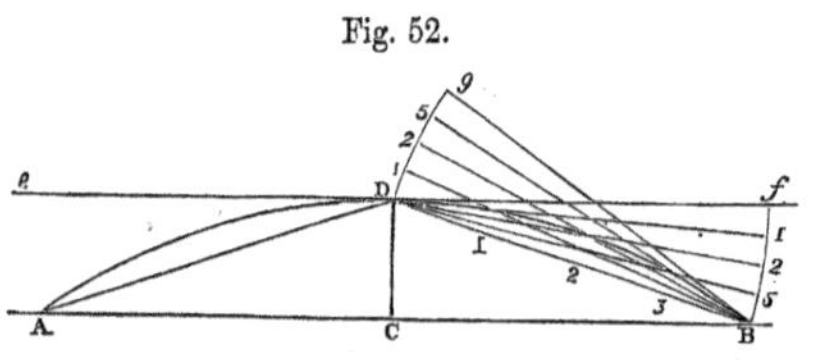

Method 1. Join AD,DB, and through D draw *ef* parallel to AB; on D with the distance DB describe an arc B*f*, cutting *ef* in *f*; on B with the same distance DB describe the arc D*g*; make D*g* equal to B*f*, and divide these arcs B*f* and D*g* each into the same number of equal parts, in the points 1,2,3, &c., numbering the one up from D to *g*, and the other down from *f* to B; from the divisions on B*f* draw lines to D, and from the points on D*g* draw lines toward B, intersecting the former lines in the points 1,2,3; these points 1,2,3 are in the arc line, through which the curve is to be traced.

(Fig. 53.) *Method* 2. Join AD, DB, and through

Fig. 53.

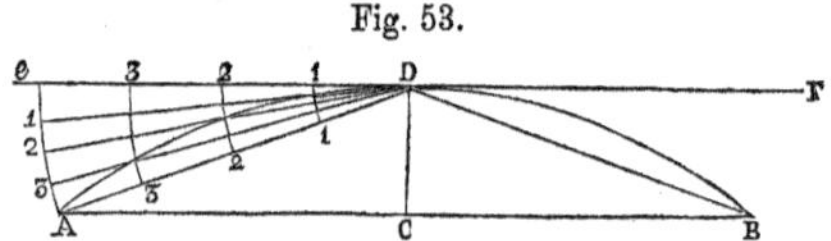

D draw *e*F parallel to AB; on D with DA describe the arc A*e*, which divide into any number of equal parts; divide either AD or D*e* into the same number of parts as A*e*, and on D as a centre describe the arcs 3,3, 2,2, 1,1; then from the points 1,2,3, on the arc A*e*, draw lines toward D, intersecting the arcs 3,3, 2,2, 1,1, in the points *h,i,k*; through these points half of the required curve is to be traced.

This last method, though not mathematically true, is sufficiently accurate for practice, when the segment DB is not greater than the quadrant of a circle; and if one quadrant be determined, the remaining three are obtained by a repetition of the operation.

17. *Given AB the arc line of a segment, to extend it to any length, by finding points in it at any given distance (as LM) from each other, without having recourse to any centre.*

(Fig. 54.) From B make BC equal to the given

Fig. 54.

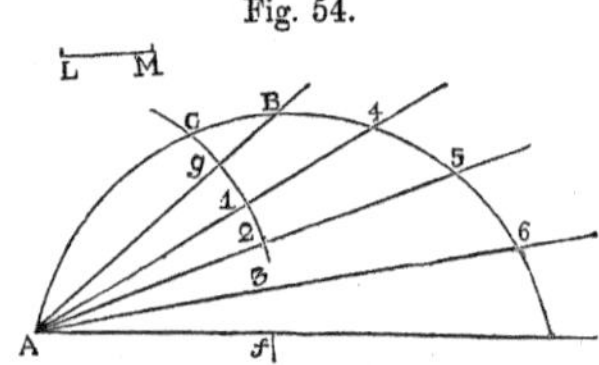

distance LM; from any other point A, in the given arc line with the distance AC describe the arc C*f* and join AB; take the distance C*g*, and from *g* turn it along towards *f*, cutting the arc C*f* in the points 1,2,3; from A through these points draw the indefinite lines A4, A5, A6; then on B with CB cut the lines A4, in 4, and on 4 with the same distance CB cut the line A5 in 5, and so on; the points 4,5,6, are in the curve of the arc line extended.

18. *Given the length AB of the chord, and height mD of an arc, composed of three segments, with the centre C of the middle segment; to find centres in the line AB for describing the segments at the two ends.*

(Fig. 55.) From the centre C of the middle seg-

Fig. 55.

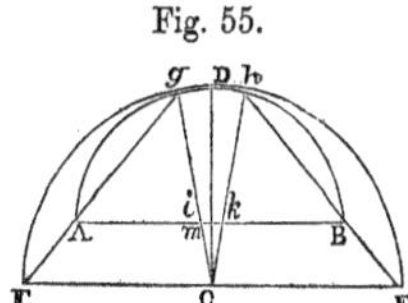

ment describe the semicircle EDF; make EF parallel to AB; through EA and FB draw lines till they intersect the arc of the middle segment in *g* and *h*, and from the points draw lines to C; then the points *i* and *k*, where these lines cut the chord AB, are the centres from which the segments A*g* and B*h* are described.

Engineers and machinists have frequent occasion to describe circular arcs whose radii are far beyond the reach of ordinary compasses; the problems 16 and 17 are, therefore, offered for their assistance in these cases; and if the draftsman has a steady hand and a good eye, the curves thus described will be sufficiently correct for all practical purposes. When, however, the mechanical artist has the requisite extent of table or flat surface to work upon, he may find the following process preferable, both in point of simplicity and truth:—

To supply the place of compasses, provide a bar of lancewood, ten feet in length, and let it be graduated into feet and inches; a brass pin in the under side, at the commencement of the graduations, will serve as a centre, and answer to the stationary foot of the compasses, and a slider that may be adjusted with a screw to any division on the bar, and provided with a pencil-holder, will answer to the revolving foot of the compasses. With this simple assistant, the draftsman can readily and correctly describe an arc of a circle of ten feet radius, or twenty feet diameter, supposing him, as before mentioned, to have extent of table or surface for his operations. If, then, he had the data in problem 16, he would bisect the semi-chords AD, DB, by perpendiculars; and these continued to their intersection would give the centre of the required curve. So, also, to continue the curve, given in problem 17, he would bisect the arc AB, draw the semi-chords, and find his centre in like manner.

19. *To describe an equilateral triangle on a given right line.*

Let the given line be AB. From the centres A and B, with the radius AB describe arcs intersecting in C; the lines CA, CB, drawn from the point C to A and B, will form an equilateral triangle.

20. *To describe a circle within a given equilateral triangle.*

(Fig. 56.) Bisect two sides, say AB, AC, the

Fig. 56.

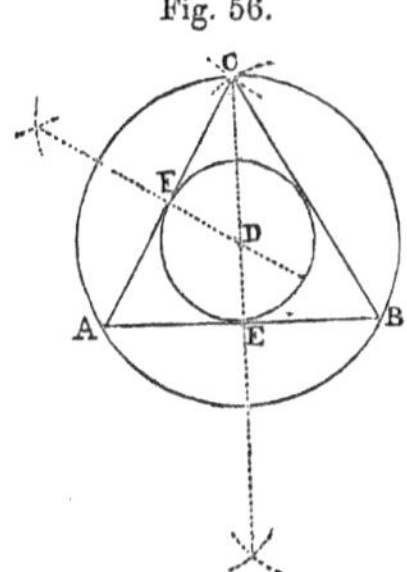

bisecting lines will intersect in D, which is the centre of the circle to be described with the radius DE or DF within the equilateral triangle ABC.

21. *To describe a circle about a given equilateral triangle.*

The operation is the same as in the preceding proposition, only that the described circle measures its radius from D to the angular points AB and C.

Circles are inscribed within, or described about all triangles in a similar manner: two sides of the triangle are bisected, to give a centre whence the circle may be inscribed or described.

22. *To construct a triangle equal to three given straight lines; any two of those lines being greater than the third.*

(Fig. 57.) Let the given lines be AD, B and C.

Fig. 57.

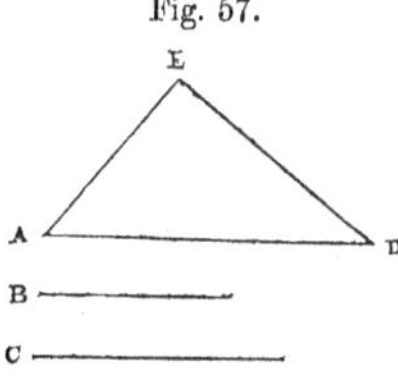

From the centre D, with a radius equal to the line C, describe an arc at E; from the centre A, with a radius equal to the line B, describe another arc at

E; the lines AE, DE, drawn to the point of intersection E, complete the triangle, which is formed of the three given lines.

23. *To construct a right-angled triangle on a given straight line; the lesser angles being unequal, and one of them being given in quantity.*

(Fig. 58.) Let AB be the given straight line, and

Fig. 58.

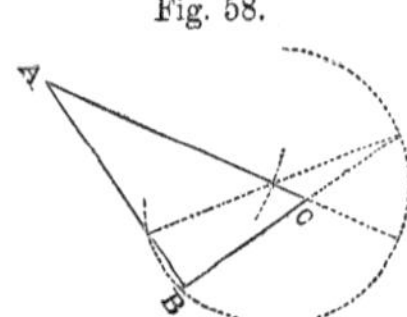

let the measure of the angle at A be 30°. From the point A draw a line AC, at an angle of 30° to the line AB; raise a perpendicular to AB on the point B; the intersection at C defines the required triangle. *Note.* The interior angles of a triangle are together equal to 180°; and in the case of a right-angled triangle, if the *base* AB and the *perpendicular* BC are equal, the angles at A and C will also be equal, and each will contain 45°. The right angle being 90°, if either angle at A or C be given, the other is known, as it must be the complement to 180°. Thus, in the diagrams, we have the right angle 90°, and the angle at A 30°; consequently the angle at C is 60°. The *hypothenuse* AC, of a right-angled triangle, is longer than the base or perpendicular.

24. *To construct a triangle, the interior angles of which shall contain any given quantity, or number of degrees, making together* 180°.

(Fig. 59.) Let it be required to construct a triangle,

Fig. 59.

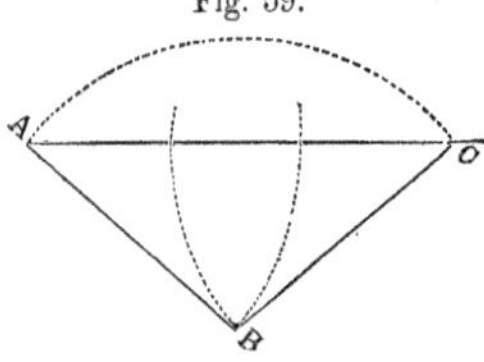

whose three interior angles shall measure respectively 40°, 100°, and 40°. Draw a line AB; draw AC at an angle of 40° to AB; draw BC at an angle of 100° to AB; the angle at C, formed by the junction of the lines AC, BC, will contain 40°, that being the complement to 180°, the sum of the interior angles. The triangle ABC has therefore been constructed in the terms of the proposition.

25. *To reduce any given right-lined figure to a triangle of equal area.*

(Fig. 60.) Let it be required to reduce the quadrilateral figure ABCD to a triangle of equal area.

Fig. 60.

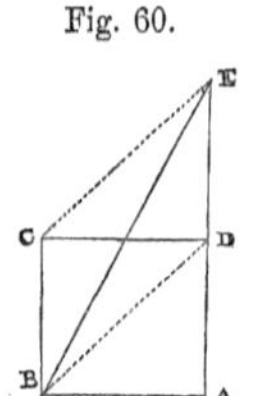

Extend AD to E; draw the diagonal BD; also CE, parallel to BD; draw another diagonal BE; then will the triangle ABE be equal in area to the quadrilateral figure ABCD. All parallelograms (four-sided figures having their opposite sides parallel) on the same base and between the same parallels are equal. Now ABCD and DECB are parallelograms on the same base BC, and between the same parallels BC, AE; therefore they are equal. And the triangle AEB, includes DAB, the half of ABCD; and EDB, which is the half of DECB, and also the half of ABCD; wherefore the triangle AEB is equal in area to the quadrilateral figure ABCD.

(Fig. 61.) Again: let it be required to reduce

Fig. 61.

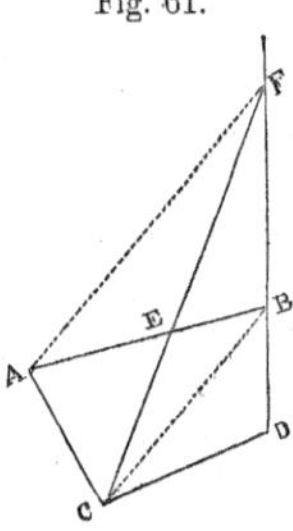

the quadrilateral figure ABCD to a triangle of equal area. Extend the side DB to F; draw CB, and, parallel thereto, draw AF; then draw the line CF, and the triangle CDF shall be equal in area to the four-sided figure ABCD. All triangles upon the same base and between the same parallels are equal in area. The triangles CAB and CFB are upon the same base CB, and between the same parallels AF and CB, therefore they are equal in area. Now CEB is common to these two triangles, consequently if it be taken from each, the remainder of the one CEA, will be equal to the remainder of the other FEB. Hence, the portion AEC of the quadrilateral ABCD, though *excluded* from the triangle CDF, is nevertheless *included* in the portion FEB of that triangle.

(Fig. 62.) Let it be required to reduce the five-sided figure ABCDE to a triangle of equal area. To do this, there must be two operations; by the first we reduce the five sides to four, and by the second we reduce the four sides to three.

1*st Operation.* Extend CD to F; draw AD, and

likewise draw EF, parallel to AD; then draw the line AF, and the four-sided figure ABCF is equal in area to the five-sided figure ABCDE.

Fig. 62.

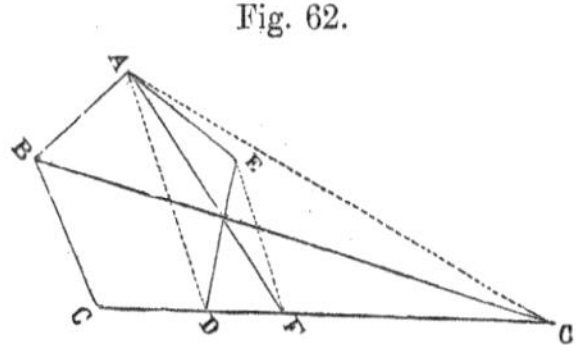

2d Operation. Extend CDF to G; draw BF, and also AG parallel to BF; join BG; then shall the triangle BCG be equal in area to the figure ABCF, and consequently equal to the given figure ABCDE.

The preceding examples are of sufficient illustration of the geometric method by which right-lined figures are reduced to the triangle. It is of no consequence how complicated the figure may be, in the number of its sides, or the irregularity of their proportions; the complexity merely involves a repetition of one and the same operation, by which the sides are progressively reduced in number till the triangular figure is at length determined. This problem is of considerable value to the mechanic and mechanical draftsman, as it renders great assistance in the calculation of areas.

26. *To construct a square on a given right line.*

(Fig. 63.) Let it be required to construct a square on the given line AB. Take AB in the compasses as radius, and describe arcs from the centres ABCDE successively. Join AF and BG; and draw HI; then will HIAB be a square constructed on the given line AB, as required. This new method of forming a square is preferable to any that has preceded it; for the points determining the whole figure are obtained very rapidly by the intersection of arcs all described with the same radius. The raising of a perpendicular upon A or B would occupy as much time as is here required for the entire operation.

Fig. 63.

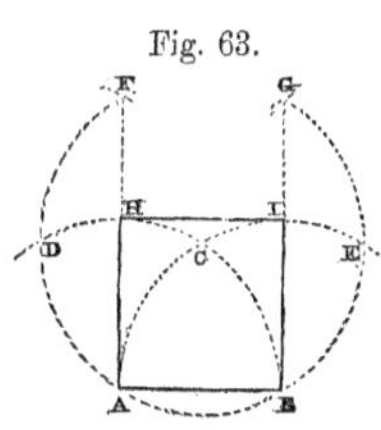

27. *To inscribe or describe a square within or without a given circle, and a circle within or without a given square.*

(Fig. 64.) To inscribe a square within the circle ABCD, draw the diameters AD, CB, at right angles, and draw the sides of the square by the points A, B, C, and D. To describe a square without the same circle, first form the inscribed square,

Fig. 64.

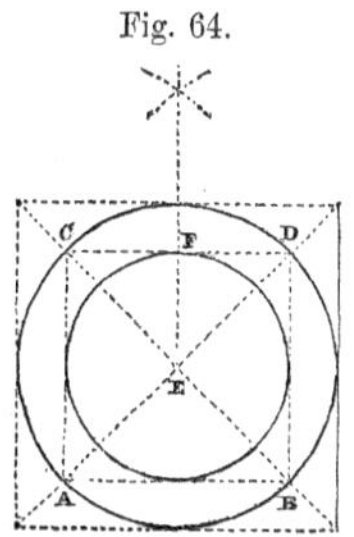

and then draw lines with the ruler, touching the circumference, parallel to the sides of the inscribed square. To inscribe a circle within a given square, draw the diagonals AD, BC, and their intersection gives the centre of the circle E; bisect one of the sides, say CD, and so obtain the radius EF; on the centre E with this radius inscribe the required circle. To describe a circle without a given square, draw the diagonals AD, BC as before; then from the centre E, with the radius EA, EB, ED, or EC describe a circle touching the square at each angle.

If a parallel ruler be not at hand, a different method must be employed to describe a square without a circle. We must first draw two diameters, say AD, BC, at right angles; then bisect one of the quadrants, say with the line EF; next obtain a tangent CD to the circle, in the point F, which tangent is a line that touches the circumference, and is at right angles to a line drawn from the centre E to the point F; lastly, on this tangental line CD a square may be constructed by the preceding proposition, and it will be described *without* the circle, of which EF is the radius.

A regular polygon is a figure contained under three or more equal lines; and is named according to the number of its angles.

TABLE OF POLYGONS.

Name.	Sides.	Angle at Cen.		Angle at Cir.	
Triangle	3	120°		60°	
Square	4	90		90	
Pentagon	5	72		108	
Hexagon	6	60		120	
Heptagon	7	51	$25'\frac{5}{7}$	128	$34'\frac{2}{7}$
Octagon	8	45		135	
Nonagon	9	40		140	
Decagon	10	36		144	
Endecagon	11	32	$43'\frac{7}{11}$	147	$16'\frac{4}{11}$
Duodecagon	12	30		150	

28. *To construct a regular pentagon on a given right line.*

(Fig. 65.) It is required to construct a regular pentagon on the line AB.

The angle at the circumference of a pentagon is 108°; therefore draw the line BC at that angle to the given line AB, and make BC equal to AB. AB and BC are two sides of the pentagon; and if we bisect these sides, the perpendiculars of bisection will intersect in the centre of a circle F, wherein the required pentagon may be inscribed; and the radius of the circle is FG or FH. Describe the circle, and taking AB in the compasses, set off the sides CD, DE, EA on its circumference; draw from point to point the lines CD, DE, EA, and the figure is completed.

Fig. 65.

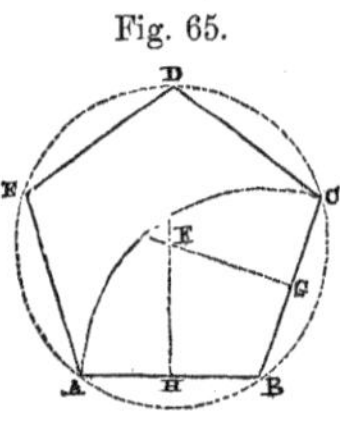

A circle is inscribed in any given pentagon by bisecting two adjacent sides with perpendiculars; then from the point of their intersection as a centre, and with the distance from the centre to the point of bisection (say FH or FG), as a radius, describe a circle touching every side of the pentagon, yet lying wholly *within* it. To describe a circle about any given pentagon, the centre is obtained as in the former case, but the radius measures from the centre to the angular points B, C, D, &c. With the radius, say FB, a circle is described touching every angle of the pentagon, yet lying wholly *without* it.

29. *To inscribe a regular pentagon within a given circle, and to describe a regular pentagon without a given circle.*

(Fig. 66.) Let it be required to inscribe a regular pentagon within the circle ABDEC. Find the centre F of the circle, and because the central angle of the polygon is 72°, lay off the angle of 72° on the circumference as, AFB; AB is then one side of the required pentagon, and if it be taken in the compasses and set off round the circle, and the lines AC, CE, ED, DB, be drawn, the figure is constructed in terms of the proposition.

Fig. 66.

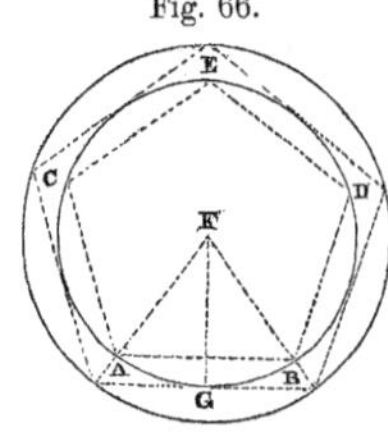

A regular pentagon may be described without a given circle by first drawing the inscribed figure, and then ruling lines, parallel to its sides, touching the outer circumference of the circle. Supposing the parallel ruler not to be at hand, proceed in this manner: obtain the angle AFB as before, and extend the sides AF, AB a little beyond the circumference of the circle; bisect AFB, and draw a tangent through the point of bisection G; the portion of this tangent falling within the extended lines FA, FB, will be a side of the required pentagon. Now, in place of drawing tangents for every side, from the centre F, with the radius FA extended, describe a circle passing through the points A and B; the tangent G then becomes the side of a pentagon to be inscribed *within* this circle.

30. *To construct a regular hexagon upon a given right line.*

(Fig. 67.) Let it be required to construct a hexagon on the line AB.

Fig. 67.

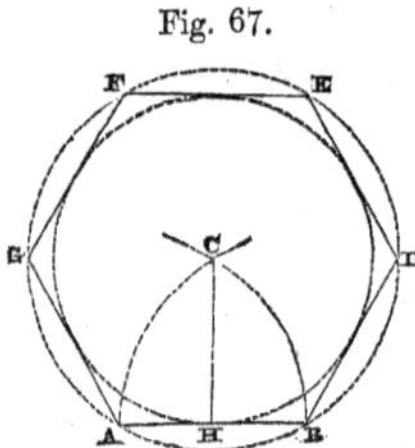

From A and B, as centres, with the radius AB, describe arcs intersecting in C; on C as the centre, with the same radius, describe a circle; and AB shall be one side of the hexagon to be inscribed within it; carry AB six times over the circumference, and through the points of measure draw the lines BD, DE, EF, FG, GA, and the hexagon is constructed as required.

To describe a circle about a given hexagon, find the centre as before; then place one foot of the compasses on this centre, and extend the other foot to any one of the angular points; describe a circle with this radius, and it will touch all the angles of the hexagon, yet lie completely *without* it. To inscribe a circle within a given hexagon, find the centre as before directed; and let the arcs which intersect at the centre C, be carried down till they intersect again on the other side of the line. Through the two intersections draw a perpendicular, bisecting the line; and CH a portion of this perpendicular, will be the radius of a circle touching the hexagon on every side, yet lying altogether *within* it.

31. *To inscribe a regular hexagon within a given circle; and to describe a regular hexagon without a given circle.*

(Fig. 68.) To inscribe a hexagon within a given

Fig. 68.

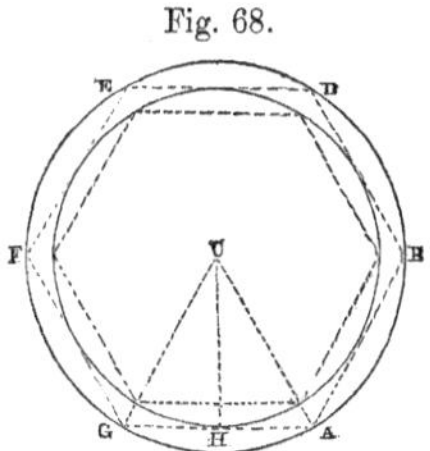

circle, first find the centre C and radius AC of that circle; the radius, carried six times over the circumference, gives the points ABDEFG, to which the sides of the required figure must be drawn. To describe a hexagon about a given circle, we may either form the inner figure, and draw outer parallel lines touching the circumference, and intersecting each other in the points ABD, &c.; or, form the central angle ACG of 60°; bisect this angle with the perpendicular CH, and draw the line CA, a tangent to the point H; GA, the portion of the tangent included within the angle ACG, will be a side of the hexagon required; and if from the centre C, with the radius CG or CA, we describe a circle passing through the points G and A, GA will then become the side of a hexagon to be *inscribed* within this circle.

It would be tedious to go through the construction of all the regular polygonal figures; since the operation is nearly the same for a figure of twelve sides as for one of five sides; and the preceding examples of the pentagon and the hexagon are sufficient to explain the general principle. It is a preferable method, when the polygon has more than five sides, to lay down in the first instance half the number of double sides on the entire circle, and afterwards to divide them. The advantage resulting from this plan is, that the error arising from doubling, or from setting off the same distance a great number of times, is thereby avoided. For instance, if in the construction of the hexagon, we first get the sides of the equilateral triangle, and then half those sides, we shall have the divisions more exact, than if we set off the hexagonal side six times on the circle; for any trifling excess or deficiency in the distance taken between the compasses, becomes a very sensible error after it has been set off four or five times.

The following problem may be added, as affording a simple and easy method of constructing an octagon.

32. *To cut off the corners of a given square, so as to form an octagon.*

(Fig. 69.) Let ABCD be the given square. Draw

Fig. 69.

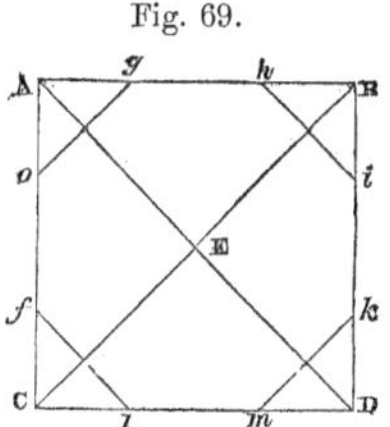

the two diagonals, bisecting each other in E; then with the distance CE, mark off from each corner of the square, Co, Cm; Dl, Di; Bk, Bg; and Ah, Af. Lastly, draw from o to g, h to i, k to m, and l to f, and the required octagon is formed.

33. *To describe an ellipse, having the two diameters given.*

(Fig. 70.) Let AB be the transverse, and CD the

Fig. 70.

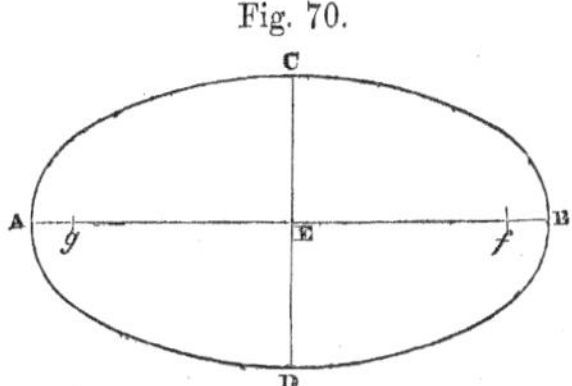

conjugate diameter. Bisect AB by a perpendicular CD, making EC, ED, each equal to half of the conjugate diameter; and from C, with a distance equal to AE, mark off the points *fg*, which are termed the foci of the ellipse; insert a pin into each of the points C*gf*, and fasten a string tightly round the pins; then withdrawing the pin from C, insert a pencil point or a tracer into the loop of the cord, and this, if carried round (taking care to keep the cord always tight), will trace out the curve of the ellipse answering to the given diameters.

34. *To construct an ellipse, having the major and minor axes given.*

(Fig. 71.) Let it be required to describe an ellipse, of which the line AB shall be the major axis, and the line DC the minor axis.

5

Draw the line AB of given length, bisect it with a perpendicular, on which lay down the minor

Fig. 71.

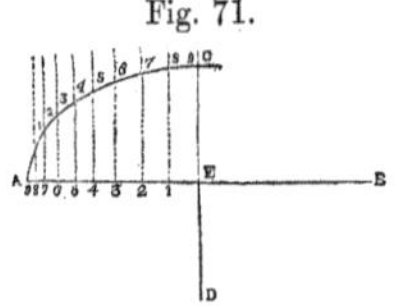

axis CD, making CE and ED equal. Take AE in the compasses, and apply it transversely to 90° and 90° on the sectoral line of sines; and then measure off successively the sines of 10°, 20°, 30°, &c., and lay them down on the line EA thus; E 1, 10°; E 2, 20°; and so on. And draw lines parallel to CE through these divisions. Again, make EC a transverse from 90° to 90° on the line of sines; and apply the transverse distances of 90°, 80°, 70°, &c., to the lines 1 8; 2 7; 3 6, &c. A series of points is thus obtained, through which one quarter of the ellipse may readily be drawn; the other quarters are determined without difficulty, by setting off in each the distances already found.

35. *To draw an oval of the first kind, having the length given.*

(Fig. 72.) Divide the given length AB into three

Fig. 72.

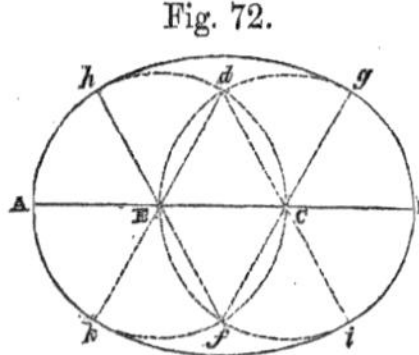

equal parts by means of the circles A*hd*C, B*gd*E, cutting each other in the points *d* and *f*; draw diameters of these circles from *d* and *f*; then from *f* as a centre with radius equal to *fg* draw the arc *hg*, and from *d* as a centre with radius *dk* draw the arc *ki*, which will complete the oval.

36. *To draw an oval of the second kind, having the length given.*

(Fig. 73.) Divide the length AB into four equal

Fig. 73.

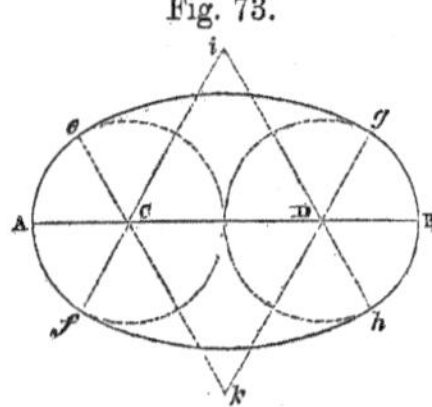

parts by means of the circles A*ef*, *g*B*h*. Set off A*e*, A*f* equal to radius AC, and B*g*, B*h* equal to radius DB; from the points *efgh* draw lines through the centres CD, cutting each other in the points *ik*; and from *k* as a centre with radius *ke* draw the arc *eg*, and from *i* as a centre with radius *i f* draw the arc *f h*, which will complete the oval.

37. *To draw an oval by means of the divisions of two circles, having the length and breadth of the oval given.*

(Fig. 74.) Let AB be the given length, and DC

Fig. 74.

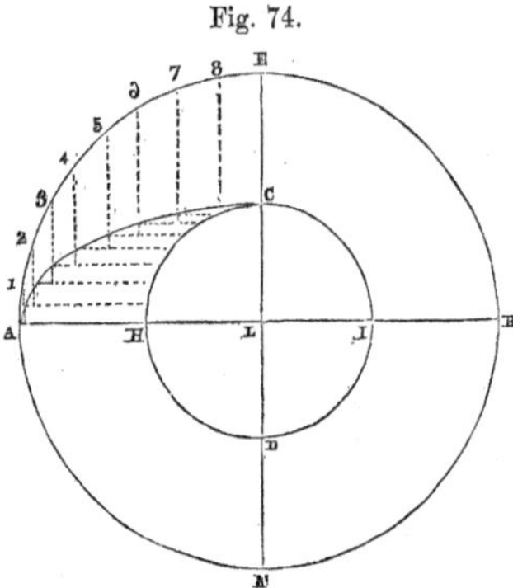

the breadth; bisect AB in L; and from L as a centre with radius AL describe the circle AEBF, and from same centre with radius equal to LC describe the circle HCID; divide each of these circles into the same number of equal parts as shown at 1, 2, 3, 4, 5, 6, 7, &c., and draw from these points in the large circle, lines parallel to EL, and from the points in the small circle, lines parallel to AL; the points where these lines intersect each other will be in the curve of the oval through which a line may be traced by the eye.

PROBLEMS ON THE SPIRAL.

38. *Given the height AB, and centre S, of the proportional spiral, to find any number of points in the curve through which to trace the spiral.*

(Figs. 75, 76.) *Method* 1. Through S draw the line 7 3 at right angles to AB; make S3 a mean proportional between AS and SB (thus on AB describe a semicircle cutting S3 in 3, then S3 is the mean proportional wanted); bisect the angles AS3 and BS3 by the lines 2 6 and 4 8, and make S2 a mean proportional between SA and S3; then from any point C without the spiral draw the lines CD and CE equal to SA and S2, join ED; and on C as a centre describe the arc E2; draw $g2$ parallel to DE, and from g describe another arc $g3$; from

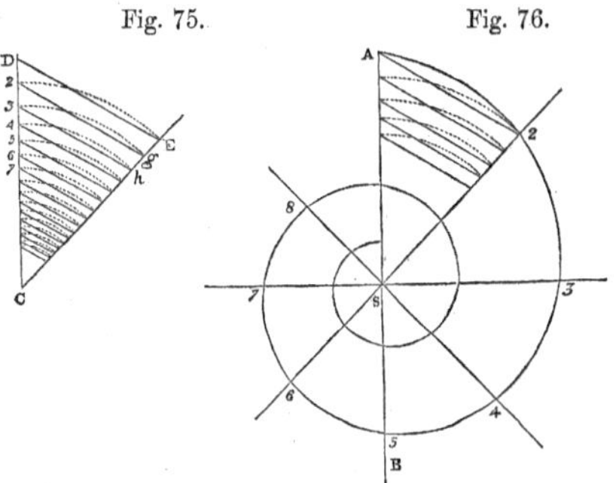

Fig. 75. Fig. 76.

3, draw $3h$ parallel to DE; thus continue the arc and parallel lines alternately, until as near to C as the spiral is wanted, near to S its centre; then transfer these distances to the spiral, making SA S2, &c., equal to CD C2, &c., and continue to follow round the centre until the whole of the lines are exhausted; the curve traced through the points A, 2, 3, 4, &c., will form the spiral.

(Fig. 77.) *Method* 2. Bisect the angles at the

Fig. 77.

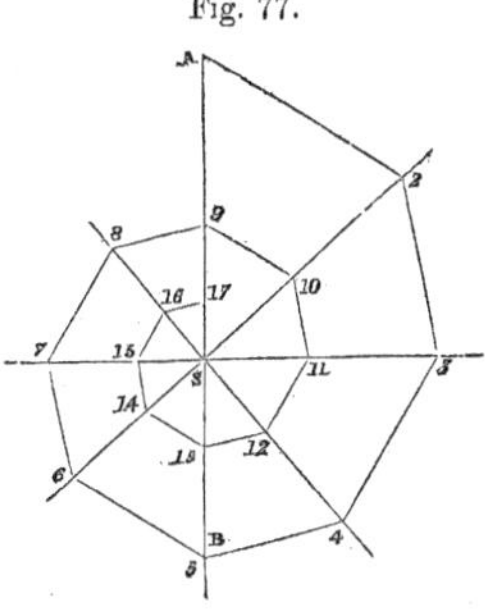

centre S by the lines 2 6, 3 7, 4 8, and find the points 2, 3, 4, 5, for the half of the first revolution by method 1. Then, beginning at 5, draw the lines 5 6, 6 7, 7 8, &c., parallel to the opposite sides A2, 2 3, 3 4, &c., and continue to follow round the centre as often as there are revolutions wanted; the points 6, 7, 8, &c., are in the curve of the spiral required.

NOTE.—The distances CD, C2, C3, in method 1, might be found more conveniently on the line SA, as is shown by the dotted lines, were it not that much confusion would be occasioned by the lines when they approached the centre S.

PROBLEMS ON THE PARABOLA.

39. *Given any diameter AB, and double ordinate CD, to describe a parabola by finding any number of points in the curve.*

(Fig. 78.) *Method* 1. Produce BA to G, and

Fig. 78.

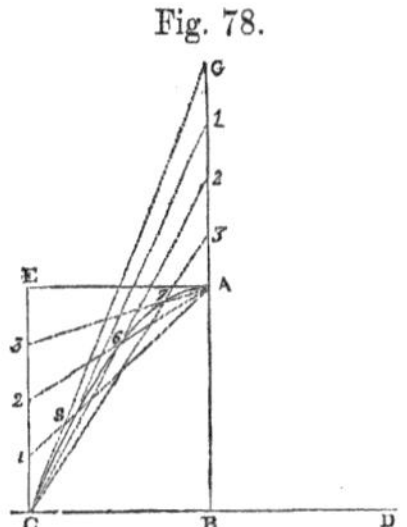

make AG=AB; draw CE equal and parallel to AB; divide EC and AG each into the same number of equal parts 1, 2, 3, reckoning the one up and the other down; draw lines from the points on EC to A, and from those on AG toward C; the points 5, 6, 7, where the corresponding numbered lines intersect are in the curve of the parabola; the points for the other half are found in the same way.

(Fig. 79.) *Method* 2. Draw DE equal and

Fig. 79.

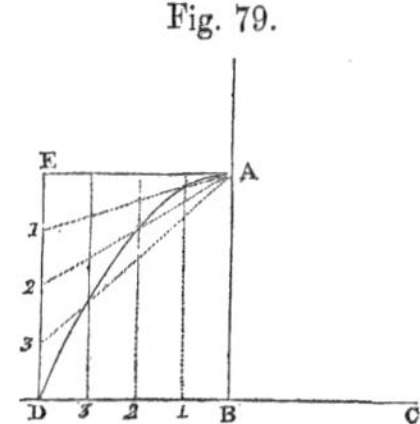

parallel to AB; divide ED and DB each into the same number of equal parts, numbering both towards D; from the points 1, 2, 3, on BD, draw lines parallel to AB; and from 1, 2, 3, on ED, draw lines toward A; the points where the corresponding numbered lines intersect are in the curve of the parabola.

(Fig. 80.) *Method* 3. Make DE equal and

Fig. 80.

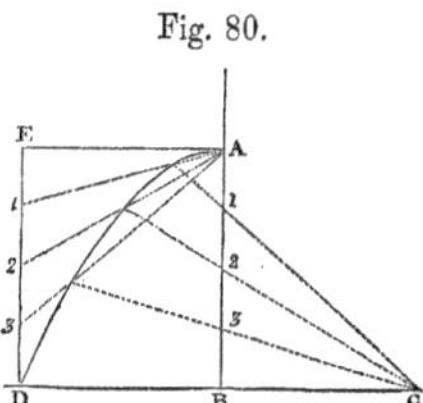

parallel to AB; divide AB and DE each into the same number of equal parts; from the points 1, 2, 3, on ED, draw lines to A, and from C draw lines through the points 1, 2, 3, on the line AB; the intersecting lines form points which are in the curve.

(Fig. 81.) *Method* 4. Divide AB and BD each

Fig. 81.

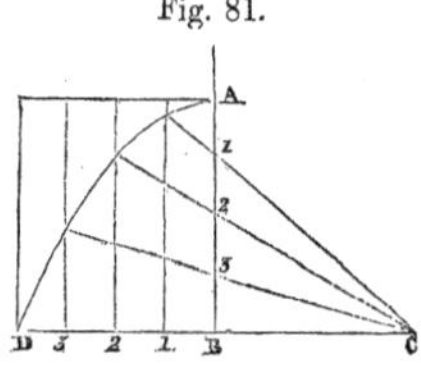

into the same number of equal parts; from 1, 2, 3, on BD, draw lines parallel to AB, and from C draw lines through 1, 2, 3, on BA; the points where the similar marked lines meet are in the curve.

(Fig. 82.) *Method* 5. Produce AB to F, and

Fig. 82.

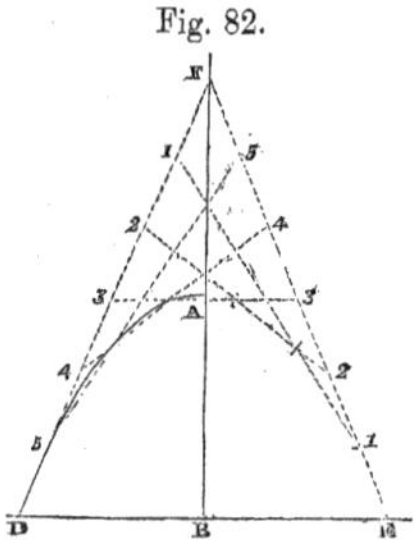

make AF equal to AB; join FD and FE; divide FD and FE each into the same number of equal parts, numbering the one from F, and the other to it; join the corresponding points 1 1, 2 2, &c., by straight lines, and they will circumscribe the parabola.

The five methods of describing a parabola, in problem 39, are adapted to cases in which the curves are of such extent that the sectoral lines cannot be applied to their construction. The parabolic curve is so frequently required by the mechanical draftsman, that we have endeavored, by variety of methods for describing it, to convey a clearer notion of its peculiarities and properties than any single operation could have given. When half the curve only is wanted, the 3d and 4th methods are perhaps the best that can be adopted; but to obtain the whole curve, method 5 is a very simple and intelligible process. It is, however, obvious that when one-half of the curve is described, the other half is readily determined. For instance, having drawn half the curve by method 4, draw lines parallel to DC, through the intersections of the dotted lines, and measure off on these parallels, from the same intersections, double distances, which will give points on the other side of AB, for the remainder of the curve. The problems which follow apply only to parabolas whose dimensions fall within the limits of the sector: these methods have no advantage over the preceding ones, but they throw additional light on the properties of the parabolic curve.

40. *To describe a parabola whose parameter shall be equal to a given line.*

(Fig. 83.) Let it be required to describe a para-

Fig. 83.

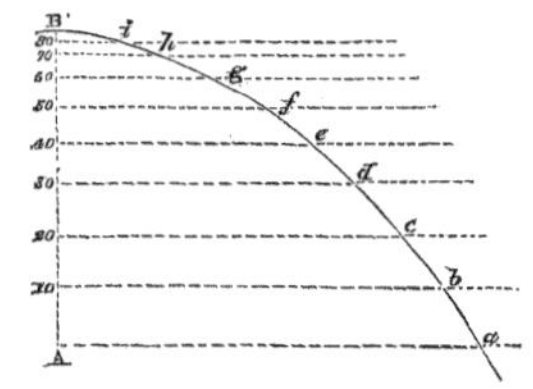

bola whose parameter is equal to the double of AB. Draw a line for the axis of the curve and set off upon it, AB equal to one-half the parameter. Take AB in the compasses, and make it a transverse to 90° and 90 on the line of *sines;* then set off on AB the transverse distances of 10°, 20°, 30°, &c., from the point A towards B; draw lines at right angles to A B through these divisions. Then set off on the lines A*a*, 10 *b*, 20 *c*, the *chords* of 90°, 80°, 70°, &c., AB being radius; but as we cannot obtain from the sectoral chords any chord exceeding 60°, we get 90°, 80°, and 70° by taking them from the scale of chords, which may be enlarged by the sector to suit AB, lesser chords may be taken from the lines of chords, having first made AB a transverse to 60.60 on these lines. Through the points *a*, *b*, *c*, *d*, &c., a curve may be drawn, which will be one-half of the required parabola; and it must be evident that, by extending the parallels A *a*, 10 *b*, &c., to the other side of AB, and by turning the compasses after marking the distances A *a*, 10 *b*, 20 *c*, on one side of AB, and setting corresponding distances on the parallels on the other side of AB, we can complete the parabola.

The nature of the parabolic curve is such, that lines drawn from the focus to all points of the curve, will be equal to lines drawn from those points perpendicular to a line placed at right angles to the axis of the curve. Hence, we obtain another method of describing the parabola.

(Fig. 84.) Let A be the focus of the parabola,

Fig. 84.

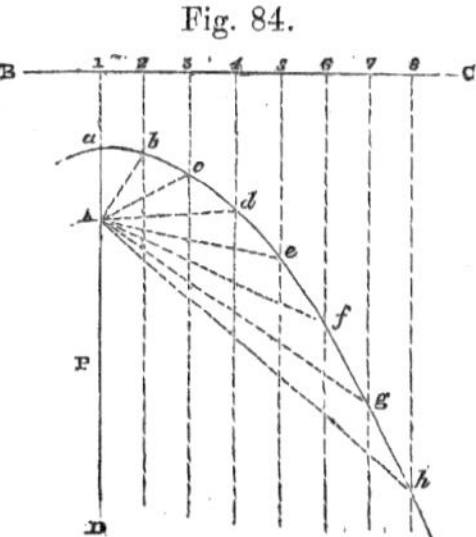

and BC be the directrix, or line drawn at right angles to the axis *a* AD. The parabola answering to these data may be constructed in this manner: Divide the space equally between A and 1, then will *a* be one point in the curve, because the lines A *a*, and *a* 1, are equal. Divide 1 C into any number of equal parts, and 1 B may be extended and similarly divided; through the points of division draw lines parallel to the axis *a* AD. Place one foot of the compasses on A, and extending the other to the parallel line 2, find by trial the point *b*, where A *b* and *b* 2 shall be equal; the point *b* so found will be a second point in the curve; keeping one foot of the compasses on A extend the other to the parallel line 3, and find by trial the point *c*, where A *c* and *c* 3 shall be equal, then will *c* be a third point in the curve; proceeding thus through all the parallels, obtain the points *d*, *e*, *f*, *g*, *h*, and if a curve be drawn from *a*, through all these points *b*, *c*, *d*, &c. to *h*, it will be one-half of the parabola answering to the data; the other half can obviously be obtained by transferring the distances to the parallels from 1 to B.

41. *To describe an hyperbola, the vertex and assymptotes being given.*

(Fig. 85.) Let it be required to describe an hyperbola, the assymptotes BH, BI, and the vertex A being given.

Draw the line BA indefinitely; and also draw AI, AC, parallel to BC and BI. Make AC a transverse to 45 and 45 on the *upper* tangents, and take successively the transverse distances of 50°, 55°, 60°, 65°, 70°, &c. from these tangents, and apply them to the line BH, from the point B; as at BD, BE, BF, BG, BH, and so on; and draw lines parallel to AC through D, E, F, G, H. Then, make AC a transverse to 45 and 45 on the *lower* tangents, and take successively the transverse distances of the complementary or cotangents, 40°, 35°, 30°, 25°, 20°, &c., and set them off on the lines D, E, F, G, H; the points *d*, *e*, *f*, *g*, *h* are thus obtained; and if through these and the point A, a smooth curved line be drawn, it will be one side of the required hyperbola. The other side can readily be found by a transfer of the distances as indicated in the diagram.

Fig. 85.

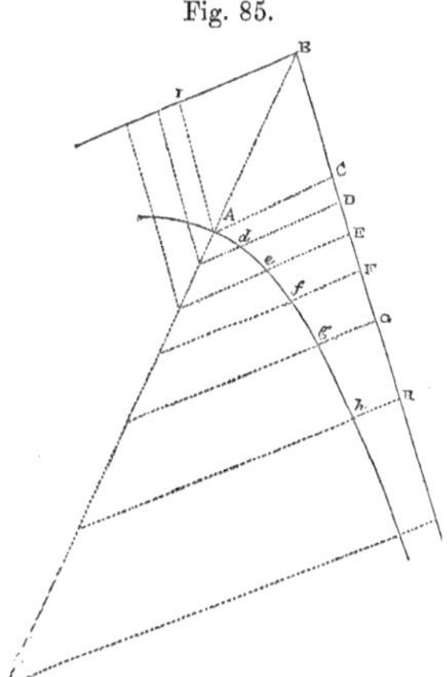

42. *To describe a cycloid, the axis being given.*

(Fig. 86.) It is required to describe a cycloid, of which the line AC shall be the axis.

Fig. 86.

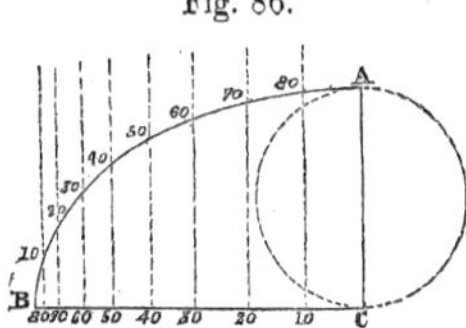

By the previous definition, the chord or base of the cycloid will be a right line equal to the circumference of the circle of which AC is a diameter. Now for practical purposes we call the ratio of the diameter of a circle to the circumference, 7 : 22. Therefore, draw the line BC indefinitely, and on the end C erect a perpendicular; make AC equal to the given axis, and dividing it into seven equal parts, let BC equal eleven of those parts; then we have AC the axis, and BC half the base of the required cycloid. Making BC a transverse to 90.90 on the line of sines, set off successively from C towards B the sines of 10, 20, 30, &c.

degrees, and draw lines parallel to AC through these divisions; then making AC a transverse to 90.90 on the sines, set off on the parallels 10, 20, 30, &c., the sines of 80, 70, 60, &c. degrees; thus we obtain a series of points through which half the cycloid may be drawn from A to B. The other half may be described in like manner.

43. *To describe a catenarian curve, having the chord and depth of the curve given.*

(Fig. 87.) Let it be required to construct a

Fig. 87.

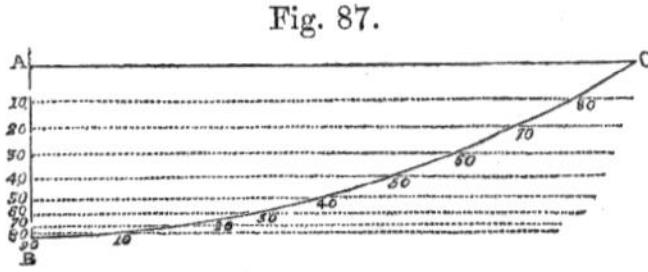

catenarian curve, AB, the depth being known, and AC half the chord of the curve being given.

Draw AB, AC at right angles to each other, and of given length. Make AB a transverse to 90.90 on the line of sines, and set off the transverse distances of 10, 20, 30, &c. degrees from A to B; draw lines parallel to AC through these divisions. Making AC the chord of 90 degrees, set off on the parallels of 10, 20, 30, &c., the chords of 80, 70, 60, &c. degrees, and thus obtain a number of points through which a curve may be drawn from C to B; this curve will be one-half of the required catenary, and the other half can be described by transfer of the points, having first extended CA in the direction of A, and continued the parallels to the other side of AB.

The mechanical construction of the eccentric curves is useful to the engineer and machinist; but it is desirable that a knowledge of their properties be obtained, and also of the mathematical formulæ applied to them.

ON THE COVERING OF SOLIDS.

Under this head, it is intended to take only a few of the most useful cases into consideration, and such as most frequently occur in practice; they may be comprehended under the sphere, cylinder, and cone; the principles upon which these are covered, will, we trust, be sufficiently plain to the practical man, from the following problems.

44. *To find the envelop for a given cone.*

(Fig. 88.) Let ABC be a cone whose diameter is AB, and slant edge BC; it is required to find the envelop.

From C, as a centre with the radius CB, describe a circle as AED; make AD equal in length to the

Fig. 88.

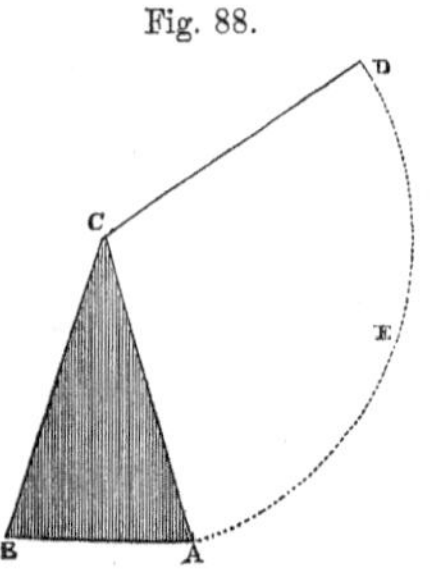

circumference of the base of the cone (which may be found by calculation), and join CD; then the figure contained under CAD will be the envelop of the cone.

45. *To find the envelop of a given frustum of a cone.*

(Fig. 89.) Let ABCD be the frustum of a cone whose base is CD, and height of slant edge BD, it is required to find the envelop.

Fig. 89.

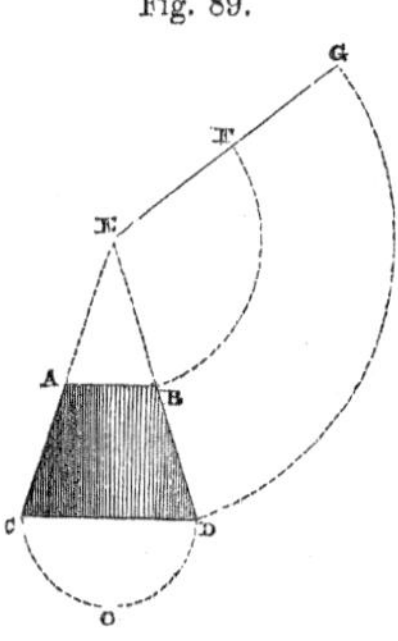

Produce AC, BD until they meet at the point E; then from E as a centre, with distance EB as a radius, describe the circle BF, and from E as a centre, with radius ED, describe the circle DG; set off DG equal to the circumference of the base of the cone, and join EG; then the figure BDFG, will be the required envelop for the frustum.

NOTE. In place of finding the length of the curve DG by calculation, as stated in last problem, the length may be found by describing a semicircle as COD, and dividing it into a number of small portions, and marking off twice the number of such divisions upon the curve DG.

46. *To find the envelop for a given cylinder.*

The envelop in this case will be easily found,

being evidently a plain square surface, or right-angled parallelogram, whose length is equal to the circumference of the base of the cylinder, and breadth equal to the height of the cylinder; when the end of the cylinder is not at right angles to the sides, the method is a little more complicated, however, and is shown as follows.

47. *To find the envelop for a given cylinder having a portion cut off, so that one of the ends shall be at a given angle to its sides.*

(Fig. 90.) Let ABCD be the given cylinder,

Fig. 90.

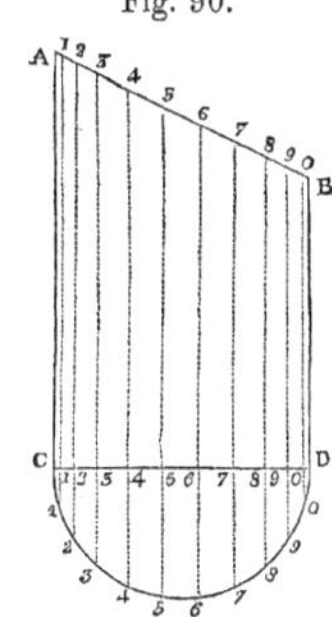

having one of its ends at an angle to the sides, as AB; it is required to find the envelop.

Upon the base CD draw a semicircle, which divide into a number of equal parts (the more the better), as 1, 2, 3, 4, 5, &c.; through these points draw the lines 1 1, 2 2, &c., parallel to the side CA of the cylinder; then set off, as in Fig. 91, the

Fig. 91.

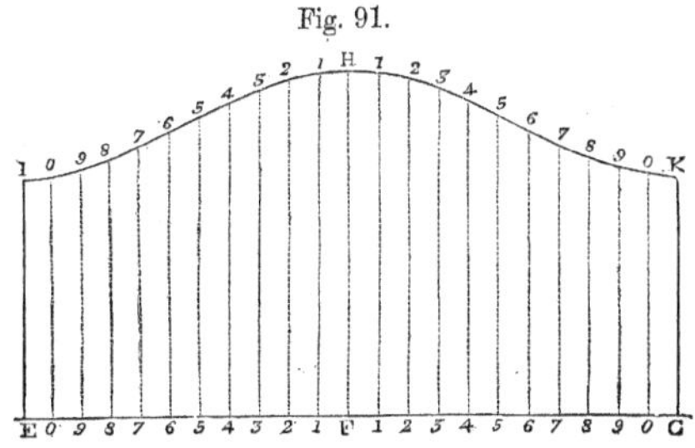

line EFG equal in length to the circumference of the base of the cylinder; or, which is the same thing, equal to twice the semicircle drawn on CD, Fig. 90; upon EFG mark off on each side of F the same number of equal distances as in semicircle CD, and draw lines as FH, 1 1, 2 2, &c. perpendicular to EFG; make FH equal in length to CA, and EI, GH, each equal to DB, also each of the perpendiculars equal to the lines in Fig. 90, bearing the same figures as, 1 1, 2 2, &c., then the line traced through these points will form a side of the envelop; the whole of which is contained in the figure EIKG.

NOTE. The above problem will be found particularly useful to copper or blacksmiths, who are in the practice of making pipes to join each other at any given angle; the shape of the plate of metal for making which will be readily found by the foregoing problem, thereby saving much time and material, when compared to the method of trial and error too commonly resorted to.

COVERING OF CIRCULAR ROOFS.

Circular roofs may be covered upon two different principles; one is by supposing the axal section to be divided into a number of small equal parts, and the roof cut by planes through the points of division parallel to the base, and then considering the portions of the solid as so many frustums of cones; and the covering of each respective portion would be found as in problem 45. The other principle is, by dividing the circumference of the base into a number of small equal parts, and supposing axal sections to be made through the points of division, and thus considering the surface of each axal portion as the surface of a cylinder; examples on both principles are given below.

48. *To cover a dome by bending the boards horizontally, and considering the surface as the surfaces of as many conic frustums as there are boards; the axal section of the dome being given.*

(Fig. 92.) Let HAF be an axal section of the

Fig. 92.

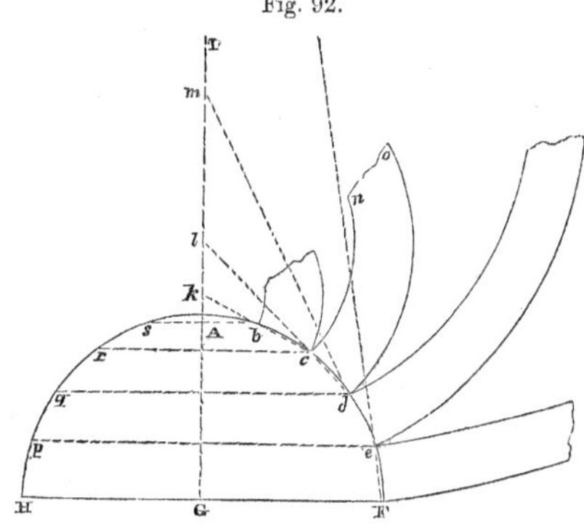

dome; draw the axis GA, and produce it to I; divide the curve of the half into equal parts, as *bc*, *cd*, *de*, *e*, F, the common measure or part being less than the breadth of the board; produce *de* to cut the axis at *l*; from 1 with the distance *lc* describe the curve *cn;* from the same centre, with the distance *ld*, describe the curve *do;* then *cdon* will be the form of the board or envelop to cover the portion *cdqr*. In the same manner, the form of the other covering for the other portions will be found; thus, by producing *bc*, *de*, *e*F, the centres *k* and *m* for covering the opposite conic frustums *bcrs*, *depq*, will be found.

It will be observed in the above figure, that the finding of the centres of the boards near the base is very inconvenient. The method of finding the forms of the boards when the centres are inaccessible, will be shown by the following.

49. *To find the form of the boards at the bottom of a dome, considering the surface to be covered in the same manner as in sec.* 48.

(Fig. 93.) Let ABC be an axal section of the

Fig. 93.

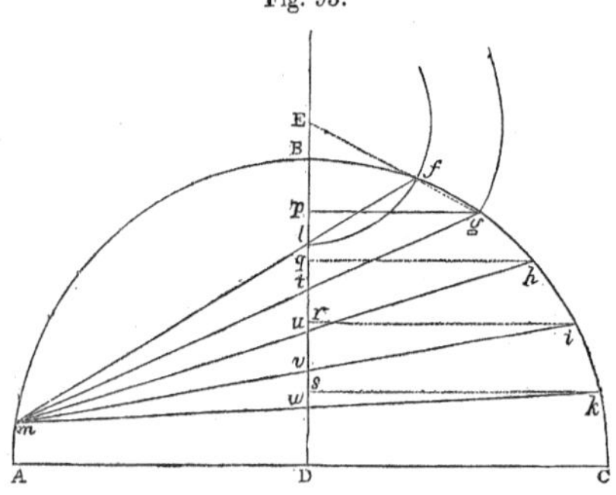

dome, and suppose *fg* to be the last board on the section; draw the representation of the axis DB, produce DB and *gf* to meet in E, from the centre E with the distance E*f* describe the arc *fl*, the concave edge of the board cutting DB at *l;* join *fl* and produce *fl* cutting the circumference AB*c*; at *m* let *gh*, *hi*, *ik*, be the places of the following boards; nearer the bottom draw *gm*, *hm*, *im*, *km*, cutting DB at *t*, *u*, *v*, *w;* draw *gp*, *hq*, *ir*, *ks*, parallel to AC, the base cutting DB again in the points *p*, *q*, *r*, *s;* then will *pg* be half the length, and *pt* the height or versed line of the first board, also *hq* half the length, and *qu* the height of the next board, *ir* half the length, and *rv* the height of the next, likewise *sk* half the length, and *sv*, the height or versed sine of the last.

NOTE. The versed sine corresponding to a stated length of each of the boards, may be easily found by calculation, the mode of doing which will be shown when we come to the application of the foregoing problems to the construction of boiler-making.

(Figs. 94, 95.) 50. *To cover a dome on the 2d principle, viz., having the joints in vertical planes. As in Fig.* 95, *supposing the axal section given, and also the breadth of the boards at the base.*

Fig. 94. Fig. 95.

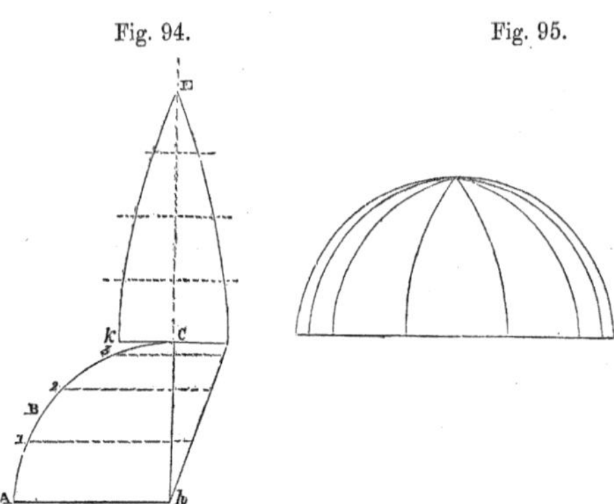

Fig. 94 shows the manner of finding the form of the envelop where the circle ABC is an axal section; the length of the board CE is made equal to the curve ABC, and *cf* half of the breadth of the board; join *fh*, and through the points of division 1, 2, 3, draw lines parallel to the base; then the lines intersected between the axis *ch* and *fh* will be the half breadth of the envelop at the corresponding division on CE, through which points a line may be drawn which will give the form of the envelop required; as E*kf*.

51. *To find the form of the envelop, having the breadth of the board given, and without the use of the axal section.*

(Fig. 96.) Let AB be the breadth of the board or envelop; bisect AB at *c*, by the perpendicular DE, make CE equal to the length of the arc from the bottom of the dome to the summit, which may be found by calculation; divide the arc AD into any number of equal parts, and draw the sines parallel to AB; divide CE into the same number of equal parts, and draw lines parallel to AB; make ordinates on each side of CE reverse to the order of the sines, and the curve, being drawn on both sides, will form the board or envelop.

Fig. 96.

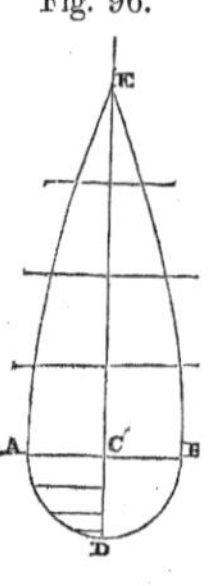

Fig. 97, A, is a segment dome, with the joints in the same manner as in problem 50.

Fig. 97.

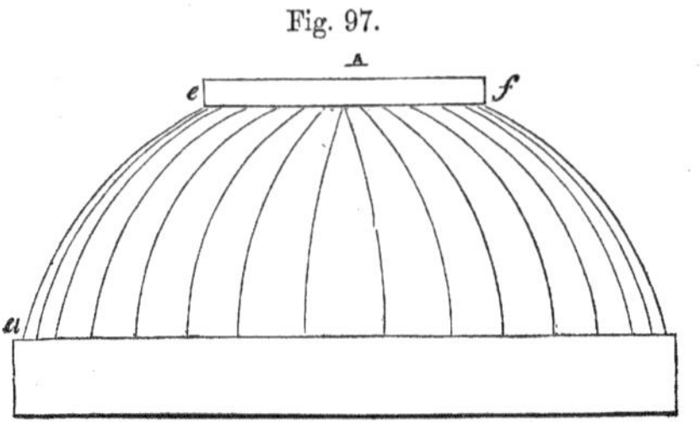

Fig. 98, B, shows the manner of finding the

Fig. 98.

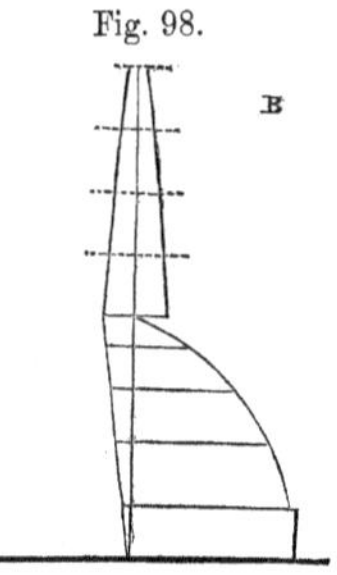

envelop for Fig. A, in the same manner as in problem 50.

Fig. 99, C, shows the method of finding the envelop for Fig. A, without the use of the axal section. In this figure, AB is the breadth of the board, AEDFB a circular zone similar in shape to the dome; the part EDF being flat, corresponding to *ef*, Fig. A, the arc AE, Fig. C, being similar to *ae*, Fig. A, and CG equal to *ae*, Fig. A. The operation is done in the same manner as in problem 51, as will be seen from the figure.

Fig. 99.

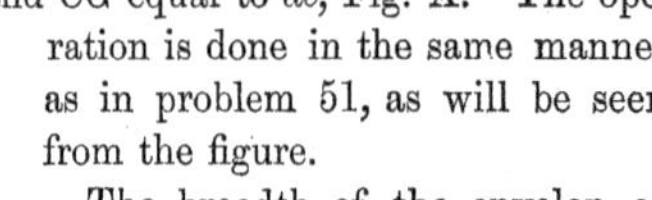

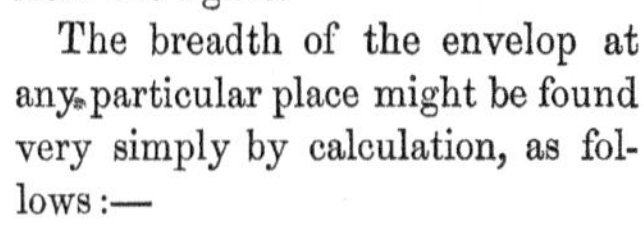

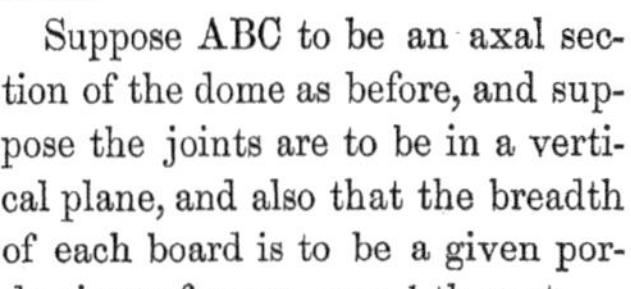

The breadth of the envelop at any particular place might be found very simply by calculation, as follows:—

Suppose ABC to be an axal section of the dome as before, and suppose the joints are to be in a vertical plane, and also that the breadth of each board is to be a given portion of the whole circumference, say $\frac{1}{24}$th part.

(Fig. 100.) Bisect AB in E, and erect a perpendicular as EC; divide the arc BC into a number of equal parts, and through the points of division 1, 2, 3, &c., draw lines parallel to AB; and since the breadth of the board is to be $\frac{1}{24}$th of the whole circumference, it is evident that the breadth at the

Fig. 100.

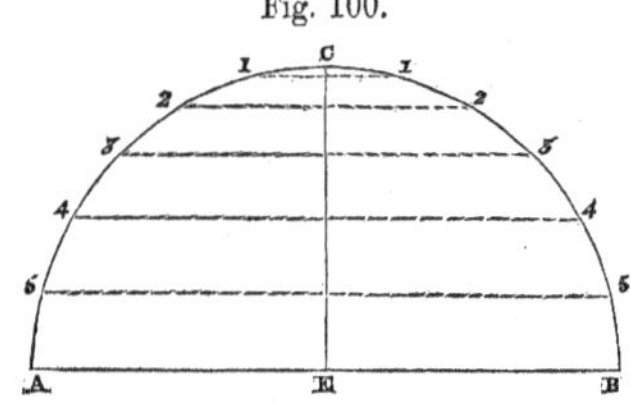

points 1, 2, 3, &c., will also be $\frac{1}{24}$th of the circumference at these points; we have only, therefore, to measure the diameters at these points, and proceed accordingly.

Thus suppose AB = 12 feet diameter.

We will find that 5 5 is	by measurement	= 11.6
and 4 4	—	= 10.4
3 3	—	= 8.5
2 2	—	= 6
and at 1 1	—	= 3.1

Then the circumference at AB will be 12 × 3.1416, or 37.6992; hence breadth of board at that point will be 37.6992 divided by 24, or = 1.57 feet.

The circumference at 5 5 will be 11.6 feet × 3.1416, or 36.44; hence breadth of board at that point will be 36.44 divided by 24, or = 1.5 feet.

Circumference at 4 4 = 10.4 × 3.1416 = 32.672; hence breadth of board = $\frac{32.672}{24}$ = 1.36 feet.

Circumference at 3 3 = 8.5 × 3.1416 = 26.703; hence breadth of board, $\frac{26.703}{24}$ = 1.11 feet.

Circumference at 2 2 = 6 × 3.1416 = 18.849; hence breadth of board = $\frac{18.849}{24}$ = 9½ inches.

Circumference at 1 1 = 3.1 × 3.1416 = 9.739; hence breadth of board, = $\frac{9.739}{24}$ = 4⅞ inches.

(Fig. 101.) If we then draw FH, and bisect it by a perpendicular IK, and set off on IK, equal distances, as 5, 4, 3, &c., same as on the dome, and make the breadths at each point same as found above by calculation, we shall, upon tracing a line through these points, have the shape of the envelop required; 24 of which will cover the whole dome.

Fig. 101.

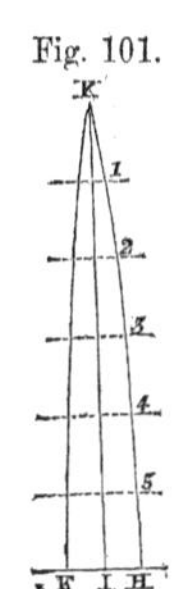

APPLICATION TO BOILER-MAKING.

The boilers of steam-engines, when made of a cylindrical form, consist of a series of conic frustums inserted into each other, and riveted together; the height of each frustum being the breadth of the plate of metal, and the diameter at the large end equal to the proposed diameter of the boiler, and of course that of the small end twice the thickness of the plates less than the larger end. This will be understood by the following figure.

Fig. 102.

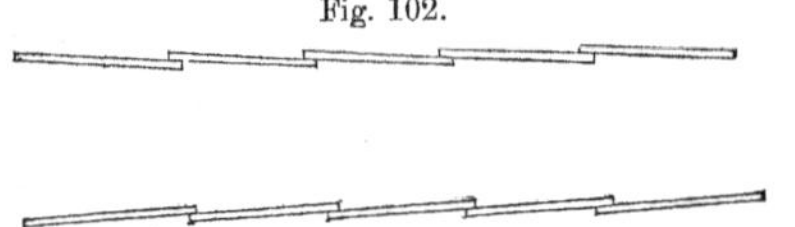

In setting about to make such a boiler, the workman generally procures a template or pattern plate, whose length is some known proportion of the circumference of the boiler, and breadth suitable to the plates of metal of which the boiler is to be made; this template is usually a thin sheet of iron, made to the proper length and shape, and pierced with holes for the rivets, so that it forms a complete pattern by which the whole of the plates can be at once drawn and punched, without resorting to the clumsy method of trial and error sometimes adopted, thereby saving much time and labor, as well as economy of material. If the template be properly made, there is not the smallest danger but that, when the plates are bent and applied to each other, the holes for the rivets will be exactly opposite: the method of making the template will be best understood by taking an example.

Suppose it was required to build a tubular boiler of 5 feet in diameter, the circumference of each portion of which was to be formed of 4 plates equal in length, and the breadth of each plate to be 22 inches, thickness $\frac{3}{8}$ths of an inch, and the distance between the holes about 2 inches.

NOTE.—In speaking of the length or breadth of a boiler-plate, in the examples to be given, we are to be understood to mean the measure as taken to the centres of the rivet-holes, as the overlap on the outside of the holes forms no part of the measurement of the boiler.

In the example given, it is clear the frustum of one of the cones composing the boiler will be thus, as, ABGH.

(Fig. 103.) The first step will be to find the vertex of the cone E, of which the frustum is a part; this will be found by the following proportion, which is derived from the 6th book of Euclid, viz., BC : BD :: BA : BE; or in words, the thickness of the boiler-plate is to the radius of the boiler, as the breadth of the plate is to the slant edge of the cone, which will, of course, be the

Fig. 103.

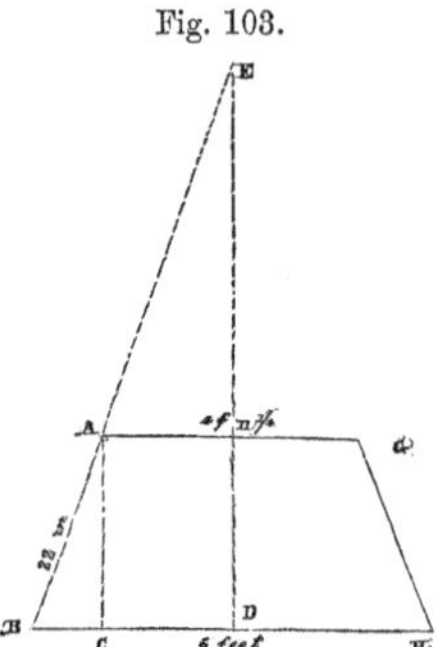

radius with which the curve of the outside of the template must be drawn—the calculation we give at length.

As $\frac{3}{8}$: 30 in. : : 22 in. : slant. edge of cone = 1760 in.

$$\begin{array}{r} 30 \\ \hline \tfrac{3}{8})660 \\ \hline 1760 \text{ inches.} \end{array}$$

The diameter of the boiler being 5 feet or 60 inches, the circumference will be $60 \times 3.1416 = 188.5$ inches; and as it is proposed to have 4 plates in the circle, the length of each plate will have to be $\frac{188.5}{4} = 47.12$ inches on the outer or larger circle. And as the diameter of the small end of the frustum is twice the thickness of the plate less than the larger, or $59\frac{1}{4}$ inches; the circumference will be $59\frac{1}{4} \times 3.1416 = 186.14$ inches; hence the length of plate on the inside will be $\frac{186.14}{4} = 46.53$ inches. The distance between the rivet-holes was to be about 2 inches, consequently the template will contain 23 divisions in the length, and 11 in the breadth of the plate. The template may now be drawn, and will stand thus: (Fig. 104.)

Fig. 104.

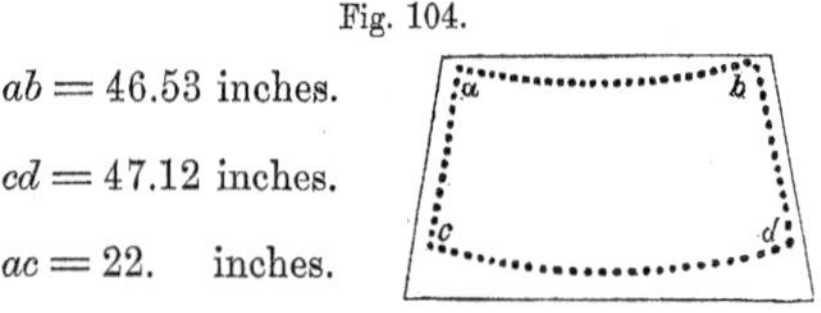

It will be perceived that, as the radius with which the outside of the template was to be drawn was 1760 inches, it would be next to impossible to attempt to draw a circle with a radius of that length by the common mode; consequently, some other method must be adopted for finding the curve; that usually taken is to calculate the versed sine corresponding to the curve of the template, and then trace the curve by means of a thin lathe bent round the three points, viz., the two extremities of the chord and the versed sine.

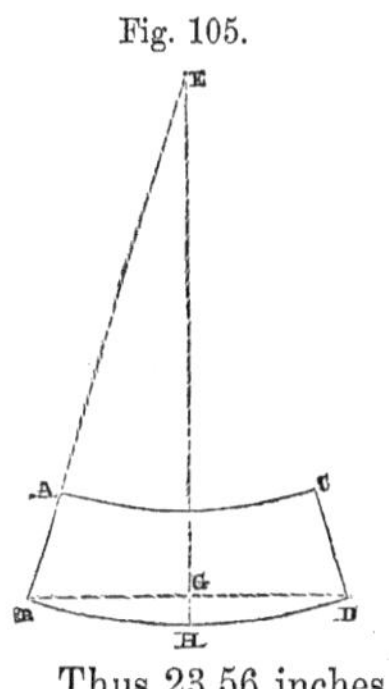

Fig. 105.

The mode of calculating the versed sine will be readily understood from the following process, which we give at length.

(Fig. 105.) In the right-angled triangle EBG, we have given EB = 1760 inches, BG $=\frac{47.12}{2}=$ 23.56 inches. Then $EB^2 - BG^2$ is $= EG^2$; hence EG can be found, and consequently GH the versed sine.

```
Thus 23.56 inches.          1760 inches.
       23.56                 1760
      ------                ------
      14136                 105600
     11780                  12320
     7068                   1760
    4712                    -------
    --------                3097600 = EB²
    555.0736 = BG²              555 = BG²
                            --------- inches.
                            3097045(1759.84 = EG.
                            1
                         27)209
                            189
                            ----
                        345)2070
                            1725
                            -----
                       3509)34545
                             31581
                             -----
                      35188)296400
                             281504
                             ------
                     351964)1489600
```

And 1760—1759.84 = .16 = GH, the versed line.

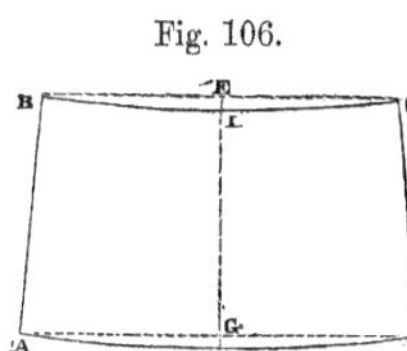

Fig. 106.

(Fig. 106.) If we then take the plate of which the template is to be made, and draw upon it a straight line, as AD = 47.12 inches, which bisect by the line EH, and set off GH = .16 the versed sine; then, by bending a thin rod around the three points AHD, the curve of the outside of the template may be drawn; the inside line may be drawn in a similar manner by marking off EB, EC, each equal, 23.26 half of the length of the inside, and AB, DC, and HI, equal to 22 inches, the breadth of the plate.

EXAMPLE 2d. Required the calculation for the template for a boiler, whose diameter is to be 36 inches, to be made of 2 plates in length; the breadth of the plate 20 inches, and thickness of plates $\frac{5}{16}$ths of an inch; the distance between the centres of the rivets to be about 2 inches.

```
         in.    in.   in.
As 5/16 : 18 : : 20 : 1152 = radius with which
          20                 the plate is to be
         ----                drawn.
   5/16)360
        ----
        1152
```

The circumference will be 36 × 3.1416 = 113 inches; hence the length of the plate $=\frac{113}{2}$ 56.5 inches for the outer edge.

The circumference of the small end of the conic frustum will be $35\frac{3}{8}$ × 3.1416 = 111 inches; hence the length of the inner edge of the template will be $\frac{111}{2}$ = $55\frac{1}{2}$ inches.

```
Then 1152 inches.        28.25 inches = half the
     1152                28.25   length of the
     ----                -----   plate.
     2304                14125
    5760                 5650
   1152                 22600
  1152                  5650
  --------              --------
  1327104               798.0625
      798
  --------
  1326306(1151.65
  1
21)32                Then 1152
   21                     1151.65
   ---                    -------
225)1163                      .35 = versed sine.
    1125
    ----
 2301)3806
      2301
      ----
23026)150500
      138156
      ------
230325)1234400
```

The template may now be drawn as formerly

shown with a lath, and as the distance between the rivets is to be about 2 inches, the length of the plate, which is 56½ inches, will thus have to be divided into 28 spaces; and the breadth, which is 20 inches, into 10 spaces, which will then complete the template.

(Fig. 107.) In some cases, particularly in marine boilers, tubes of a cross sectional shape, as under, are made to pass through the boiler; the template, in this case, will be of a somewhat different shape. The mode of calculation is shown at length.

Fig. 107.

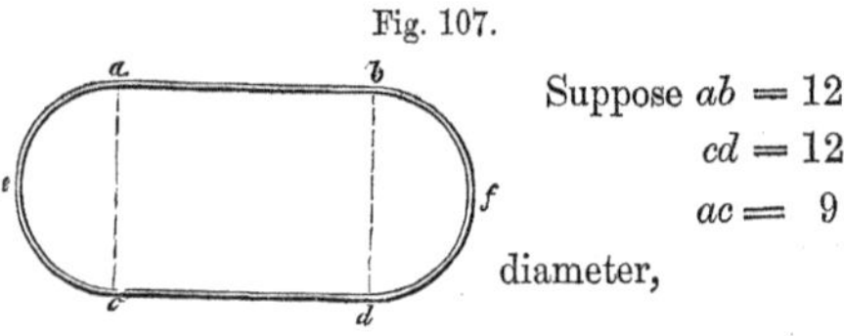

Suppose $ab = 12$
$cd = 12$
$ac = 9$
diameter,

and that the frustum is to be of one plate in length, and 18 inches in breadth, and ¼th of an inch thick, and distance between holes 2 inches.

As ¼ in. : 4½ in. : : 18 in. : 324 radius of circle of the outer edge of the template for the semicircular ends *aec*, *bfd*.

```
         4½
        ---
         72
          9
        ---
     ¼)81
        ---
        324 inches.
```

The diameter of the semicircular ends being 9 inches, the circumference of each part will be $\frac{9 \times 3.1416}{2} = \frac{28.2744}{2} = 14.13$ inches for large end.

And 324 inches radius.

```
   324                        7.06 = ½ chord.
  ----                        7.06
  1296                        ----
   648                        4236
  972                        4942
 ------                      ------
 104976 = radius squared
     49.8 = ½ chord squared  49.8436
 ------
```

```
   104926.2(323.9 inches
   9
  ---
 62)149
    124
   ----
 643)2526
     1929
    -----
6469)59720
     58221
    ------
     149900
```

Then 324—323.9 = .1 versed sine.

The diameter of the small side of semicircular ends will be 8½ inches, consequently, circumference of the half will be $\frac{8\frac{1}{2} \times 3.1416}{2} = \frac{26.70}{2} =$ 13.35 inches.

Fig. 107*.

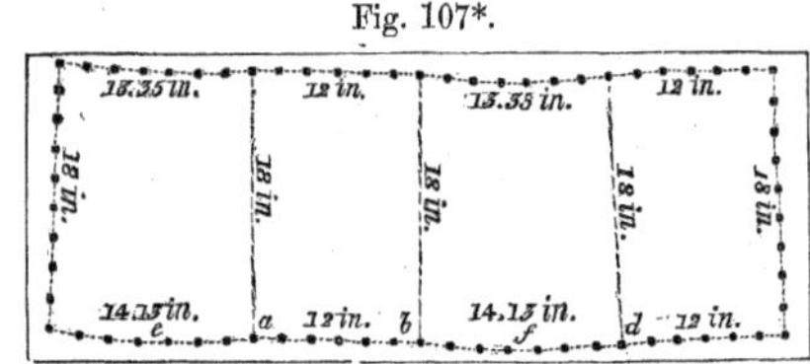

(Fig. 107*.) The template may be drawn as above from the calculations, and will, when bent round, form a frustum, same in shape as Fig. 107.

In the foregoing examples, it will be perceived that, when calculating the versed sine, the length of the *chord* was assumed to be the same as the length formed for the plate measured on the *curve;* this, strictly speaking, is not mathematically correct, as the chord will, in fact, be a little shorter; but in cases such as in the examples where the radius is very great, the difference is so small as to cause little or no error in the result: in none of the examples given, does the curve exceed the chord in measurement more than two-tenths of an inch, thus causing no difference whatever in the length of the versed sine. The calculation for finding the true length of the chords by trigonometry is tedious, and would be uninteresting to the mere practical man.

GEOMETRICAL PROBLEMS BY THE COMPASSES ONLY, AND WITHOUT THE USE OF A RULER.

For this ingenious department of construction, which will be often found of considerable assistance to architects, engineers, and draftsmen, we are indebted to Signor L. Mascheroni.

To find the centre of a given circle.

(Fig. 108.) Take for a centre any point 1, in the circumference, and with a radius 1 2 at plea-

Fig. 108.

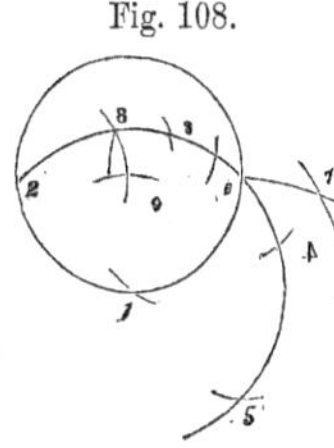

sure, which must be less than the diameter of the given circle, but greater than one-fourth part of that diameter. Describe the arc 2 6 5, and make 1 2 = 2 3 = 3 4 = 4 5; then will 2, 3, 4, 5 be a semicircle. Let 6 be the point where this circle cuts the given circumference. Then from the points 1 5, with the radius 5 6, describe two arcs intersecting in 7; and from the centre 7, with the same distance 5 6, cut the semicircle in 8. Lastly, from 1 and 2 as centres, with radius 2 8, describe two arcs which will cut each other in 9. The point 9 will be the centre of the given circle.

To divide the circumference of a circle into four equal parts without the use of a ruler or straight edge.

(Fig. 109.) Make 2 3 = 3 4 = 4 5 = 1 2 =

Fig. 109.

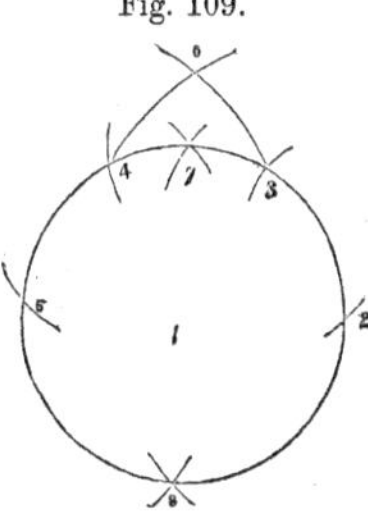

the radius. From 5 and 2, as centres, describe 3 6 and 4 6. With 1 6 as radius, and 5 and 2 as centres, determine the points 7 and 8. 2 7 = 7 5 = 5 8 = 8 2 = one-fourth the circumference.

To divide a given distance into two equal parts.

(Fig. 110.) Let 1 2 be the given distance; with

Fig. 110.

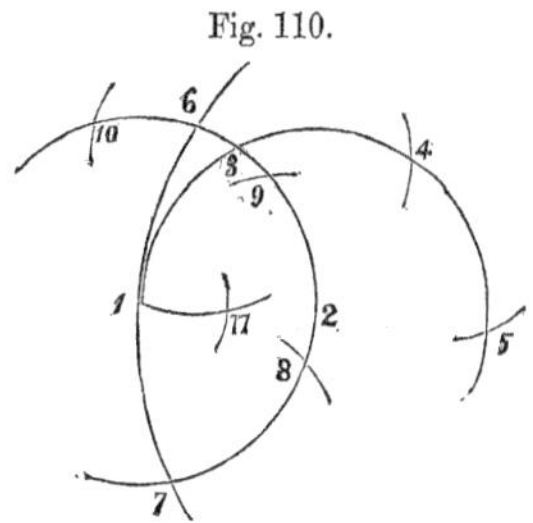

1 2 as radius, describe 1 3 5. Make 1 2 = 1 3 = 3 4 = 4 5. Describe 7 1 6, with 5 1 as radius, and 7 2 6, with 1 2 as radius. Make 7 8 = 8 9 = 9 10 = 1 2, the radius. From 1 describe an arc, with 10 6 as radius, and from 6 describe an arc, with 6 1 as radius, to cut in 11; the point 11 is in the middle between 1 and 2.

To construct a square on one of its diagonals, with compasses only.

(Fig. 111.) Let 1 2 be the given diagonal, with

Fig. 111.

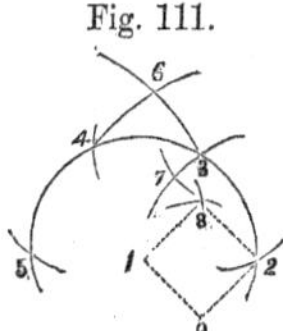

which as radius describe 2, 3, 4, 5. Make 2 3 = 3 4 = 4 5 = 1 2 = radius. With 5 3, and 2 4, describe arcs intersecting in 6. With 1 6 as radius, and 5 as centre, describe an arc cutting 3 7 in 7. Lastly, with 1 and 2 as centres, and 1 7 as a distance, describe arcs cutting in 8 and 9; then 1 8, 2 9, will be the angular points of the required square.

To divide an arc into two equal parts, by compasses only.

(Fig. 112.) Let 1 2 be the circular arc, and 3 its centre. Describe 3 4 and 3 5, with 1 and 2 as centres, and 1 3 as radius. Make

1 2 = 3 4 = 3 5.

With 4 and 5 as centres, describe 1 6 and 2 6. Lastly, with 3 6 as radius, and 4 and 5 as centres,

Fig. 112.

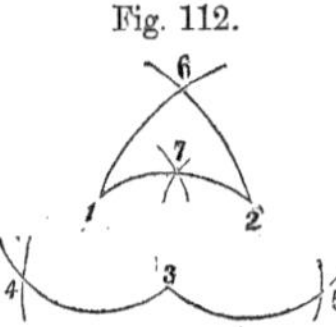

describe the arc 7; then the arc 1 2 is divided into equal parts in the point 7.

Given two points 1 2 *to find a third* point, from which, if a right line be drawn, it will be perpendicular to 1 2, at one of its extremities 2, *and equal to a given distance* 3 4.

(Fig. 113.) From 2 with 3 4 as radius, describe

Fig. 113.

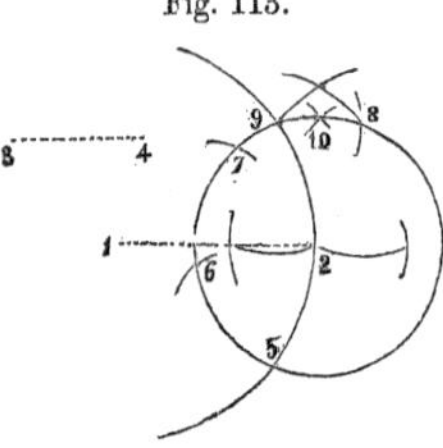

5 6, 7 8. With 1 2 as radius describe 5 2 9; divide the arc 8 9 into two equal parts by the last problem in the point 10; then is 10 2 perpendicular to 1 2 and equal to 3 4, 56 = 67 = 78 = 25.

To divide the circumference of a circle into five equal parts, by compasses only.

(Fig. 114.) Apply the radius 1 2, and divide the

Fig. 114.

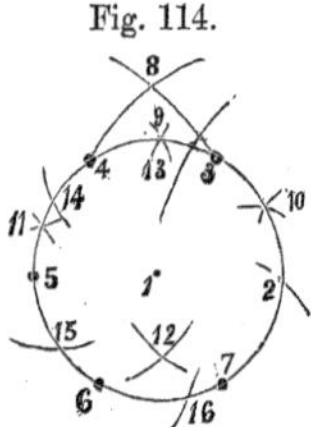

circumference into six equal parts by the points 2, 3, 4, 5, 6, 7. With 2 and 5 as centres, describe 4 8 and 3 8. Then, with 1 8 as radius, and 5 and 2 as centres, divide the arc 4 3 into two equal parts in the point 9. With the same radius, and 4 and 7 as centres, divide the arc 2 3 into two equal parts in the point 10. And, again, with the same radius, and 3 and 6 as centres, describe the arcs 11, dividing 4 5 into two equal parts. With the same radius 1 8, describe the arcs 12, with 10 and 11 as centres. Then the distance from 12 to 2 will go round from 2 to 13, from 13 to 14, from 14 to 15, and from 15 to 16, and divide the circumference into five equal parts.

To describe a five-sided, regular polygon on a given line 1 2.

(Fig. 115.) Describe the circle 1, 3, 4, 5, 6; make 1 3 = 1 2 = 3 4 = 4 5 = 5 6.

Fig. 115.

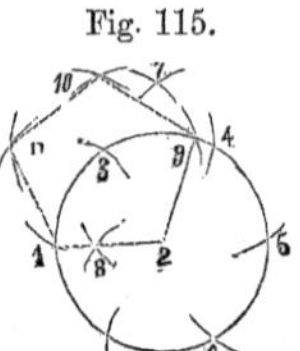

With 1 and 5 as centres, and 1 4 as radius, describe the arcs 7; then, with 2 7 as radius, and centres 4 and 6, describe the arcs 8. With radius 8 5 and centre 1, describe arcs 9 and 10; with the same radius and centre 2, describe 11 and 10; with the same radius and centre 9, cut 11; then 1, 2, 9, 10, 11 is a regular pentagon.

To describe an eight-sided regular polygon on a given straight line 1 2, *by the compasses only.*

(Fig. 116.) Describe the arcs 1, 3, 4, 5, and 2, 3, 6, 7, with radius 1 2.

Fig. 116.

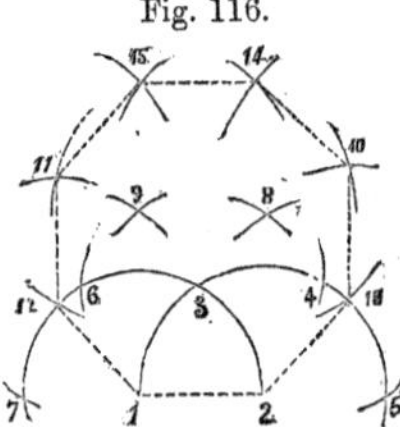

Make 1 3 = 1 2 = 3 4 = 4 5 = 3 6 = 6 7. With 1 4 as radius, and 1 and 5 as centres, describe the arcs 8. With 1 4 as radius, and 7 and 2 as centres, describe 9. With the same radius, 1 4, and 9 as a centre, describe an arc through 10; and with the same radius, and 8 as centre, describe an arc through 11.

With 1 2 as radius, and 9 as centre, describe 12; and with the same radius 1 2, and 8 as centre, describe 13. With the same radius 1 2, and 12 13 as centres, cut 11 and 10; and with 10 and 11 as centres, and radius 1 2, describe arcs at 14 and 15. With 8 as centre, and 8 2 as radius, cut 15; in the same way, with 9 as centre, and 9 1 as radius, cut 14. Then will 1, 2, 13, 10, 14, 15, 11, 12, 1 be a regular octagon.

To describe a ten-sided regular polygon on the line 1 2.

(Fig. 117.) Describe the circle 1, 3, 4, 5, 6 with

Fig. 117.

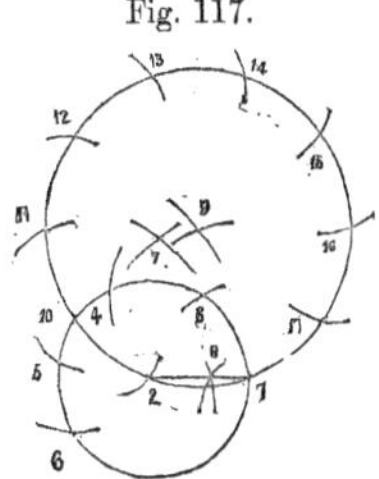

radius 1 2. With 1 4 as radius, and centres 1 and 5, describe 7. Then with 4 and 6 as centres, and radius 2 7, describe 8. With 8 5 as radius, and 1 and 2 as centres, describe 9; with 9 as centre, and 9 1 as radius, describe the circle 1, 2, 10, 11, &c., and lay off 1 2 = 2 10 = 10 11 = 11 12, &c. If the points 2, 10, 11, 12, 13, &c. be joined, we have the decagon required.

(Fig. 118.) Given the five points 1, 2, 3, 4, 5 of the American star, or, found by problem Fig. 115, to find the other points 6, 7, 8, 9, 10 in the diagonal.

Fig. 118.

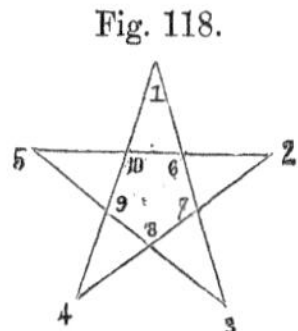

With 1 2 as radius, and the points 3 and 5 as centres, describe the arcs 6; in the same manner the points 7, 8, 9, and 10 may be readily found.

The young draftsman, when he becomes dextrous in drawing geometrical figures and diagrams, and can use his compasses and squares with freedom, must next attempt to draw the outlines of small details which it may be necessary to give at the commencement, elevations, plans, and sections. We add some exercises of the simplest kind, and show how they are made in the shop as well as on paper.

BRACKETS AND PILLOW-BLOCKS.

We shall first give views of a number of forms of brackets and pillow-blocks, adapted to various positions and purposes in mill-work and engineering.

Fig. 119 is an elevation of a pillow-block, or pe-

Fig. 119.

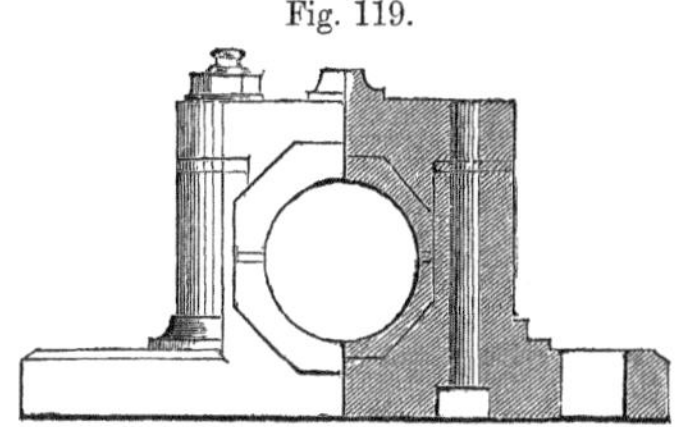

destal, of which Fig. 121 is an end view, and Fig. 120 a plan.

Fig. 120.

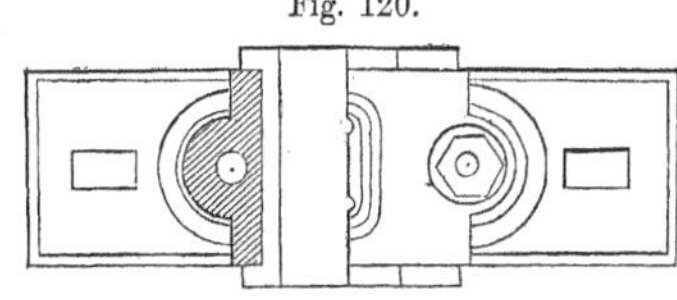

The pillow-block is commonly made of cast-iron, and in size proportioned to the diameter of shaft

Fig. 121.

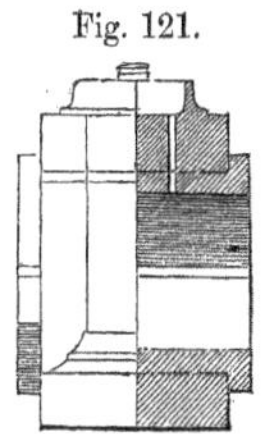

which it is intended to support. In machine-making, the pedestal is sometimes cast on the frame of the machine; but in mill-work this is rarely practicable, and seldom desirable. The usual form is that shown in the figures referred to; the pedestal being bolted to a sole plate, beam, or other part, by bolts passing through its own sole. Two bolts again, passing upwards from the sole, into which recesses are made to receive the heads, serve to hold on the cover into which is the upper half of the brass. The brasses form together rather less than a complete cylinder, the deficiency being made up by slips of wood placed between their edges; this allows of subsequent adjustment; for when the brass sustaining the pressure has been to a certain extent worn by the journal, the slips of wood may be removed and reduced in thickness, so that the two halves will be brought closer together and embrace the journal more tightly.

Fig. 122 is an elevation of a pedestal, such as is used when the axle that it carries is a considerable

Fig. 122.

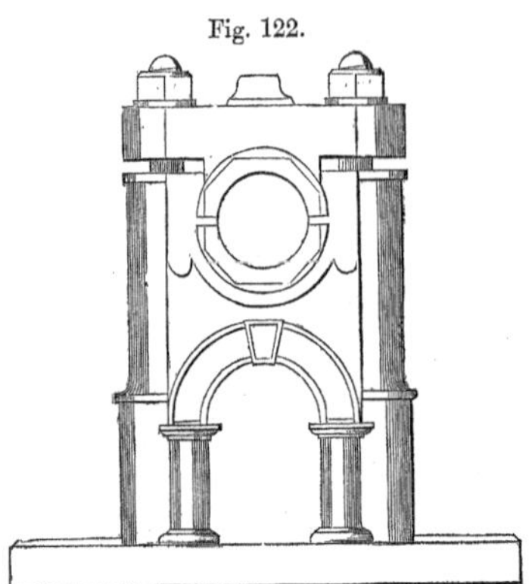

height from the base on which the pedestal stands. Pedestals of this form are very common as main-centre supports of the beam in steam-engines. They are of various patterns, according to the taste of the engineer.

(Fig. 123.) The elevation of pedestal and saddle-plate for a water-wheel. In this case no cover is

Fig. 123.

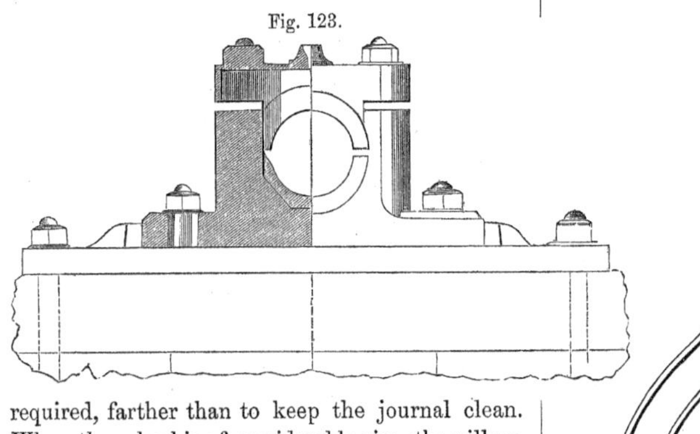

required, farther than to keep the journal clean. When the wheel is of considerable size, the pillow-block is generally fitted on to a plate of metal, termed a saddle-plate, which is accurately bedded and fixed to the building upon which the whole rests.

When a false cover is applied, it is sometimes retained in its place by fitting within the cheeks of the pedestal; and, for appearance, the cover is sometimes cast with the same size and form of flanches as the brass; and these retain it in its place. At other times it is holden on by pins, in the same position and relation as the cover-bolts of the pedestal, Fig. 119.

(Fig. 124.) A wall-box and pedestal. The box is supposed to be built in the wall, and in many

Fig. 124.

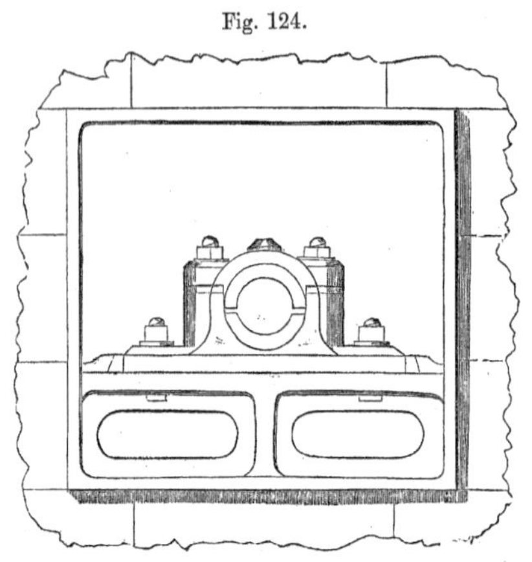

cases is a very convenient mode of supporting a shaft.

(Fig. 125.) An elevation of a frame suitable for a portable crane, or crab, as it is often styled.

Fig. 125.

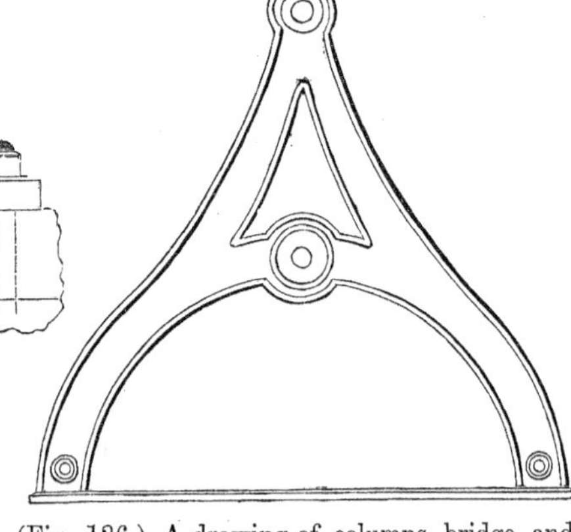

(Fig. 126.) A drawing of columns, bridge, and pedestal for supporting a horizontal shaft. This mode is sometimes adopted when it is requisite to carry a line of shafts into the middle of a flat, at a less height than would be convenient to employ brackets, and where the columns are requisite for supporting the floor above. This arrangement is sometimes adopted in flour mills, and frequently in the framing of machines.

Fig. 126.

Figs. 127, 128, 129, 130, are specimens of hanging brackets, or gallowses, for carrying light

Fig. 127.

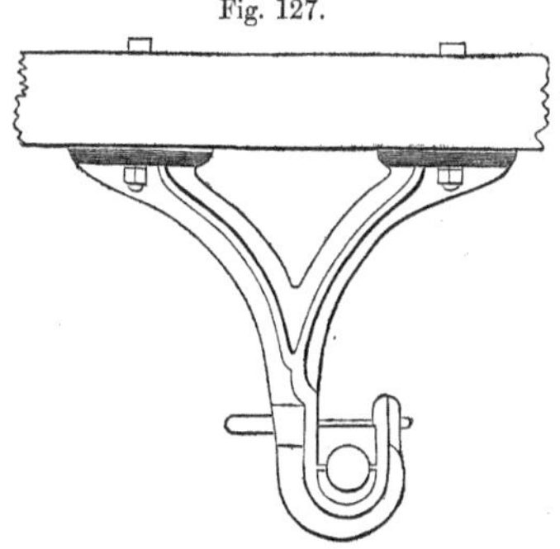

shafts, and are generally hung from a beam, as shown in the figures. These are frequently pro-

Fig. 128.

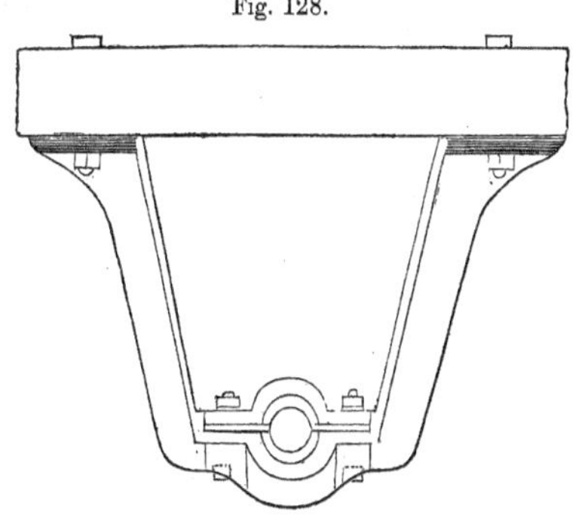

vided with shells or hollow covers, when the pressure is entirely downwards; but this should be avoided when the shafts are drivers acting upwards.

7

Fig. 129.

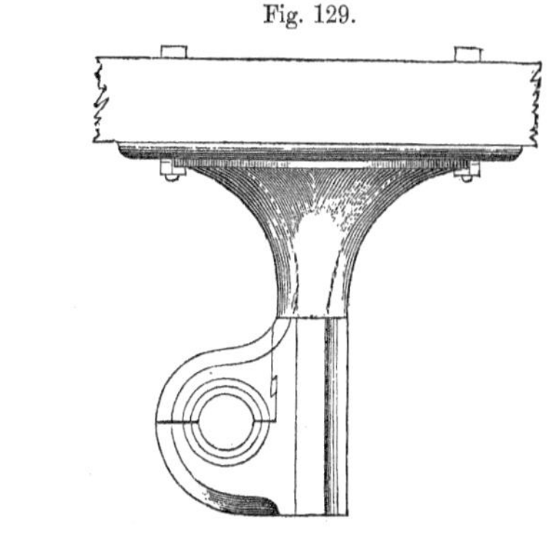

Fig. 130.

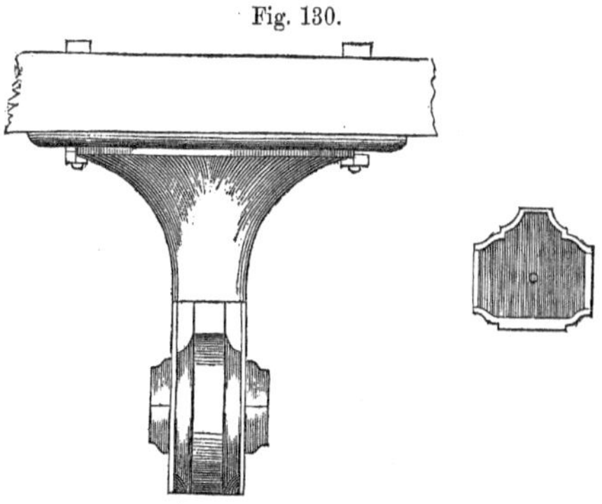

Fig. 131 is a specimen of a bracket with pedestal attached. This form of bracket is useful for bolting to a wall, at the termination of a shaft.

Fig. 131.

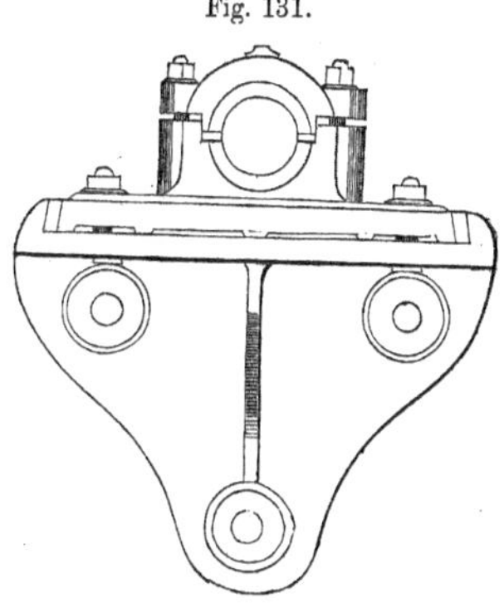

(Fig. 132.) A bracket, supposed to be fixed to a wall or column. When a line of light shafts is required to run parallel to a wall, and at no great distance from it, or through the middle of a flat, where columns are also necessary, such a mode of carrying them is usually adopted.

Fig. 132.

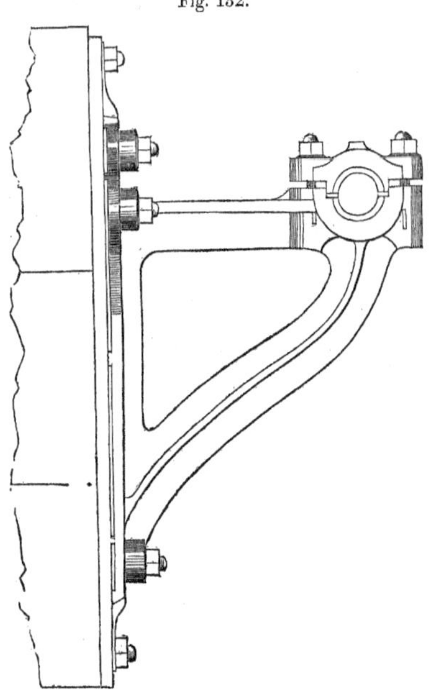

Fig. 133 is an elevation of a bridge carrying an upright shaft. This arrangement is generally adopted when the upright shaft receives its motion from a *lying* or horizontal shaft by means of bevel-wheels. The lying shaft passes underneath the upright shaft, and should have a bearing in a pillow-block, keyed and bolted on the same bed-plate with the bridge, in order to secure the accurate and steady working of the bevel-wheels. When the upright shaft is of any considerable size, the brasses guiding it laterally are made in two pieces to admit of their being tightened, and have a hollow in their upper edges to retain oil. The shaft is supported on a plate of brass or hard steel. The box, into which the brasses are fitted, is cast open on one side and fitted with a door, having pinching screws through it to tighten the brasses. The brasses are carried on a block which may be removed in order to admit of the shaft being lowered. —These arrangements are more particularly illustrated, and their uses and advantages treated of, in the article on geering.

Figs. 134 and 135 are front and side views of a bracket B for carrying guide-pulleys. This sort of bracket, usually termed an universal guide, is useful when the direction of motion by a strap has to be carried at an angle. It will be observed that the bracket is fixed to the beam D, by two bolts which pass through circular slits cast in the bracket; so that the latter can be set at any angle. The pulleys are supported by the studs, which pass through slits in the bracket, and are fastened by means of nuts on the ends of the studs; these pul-

Fig. 133. Fig. 134.

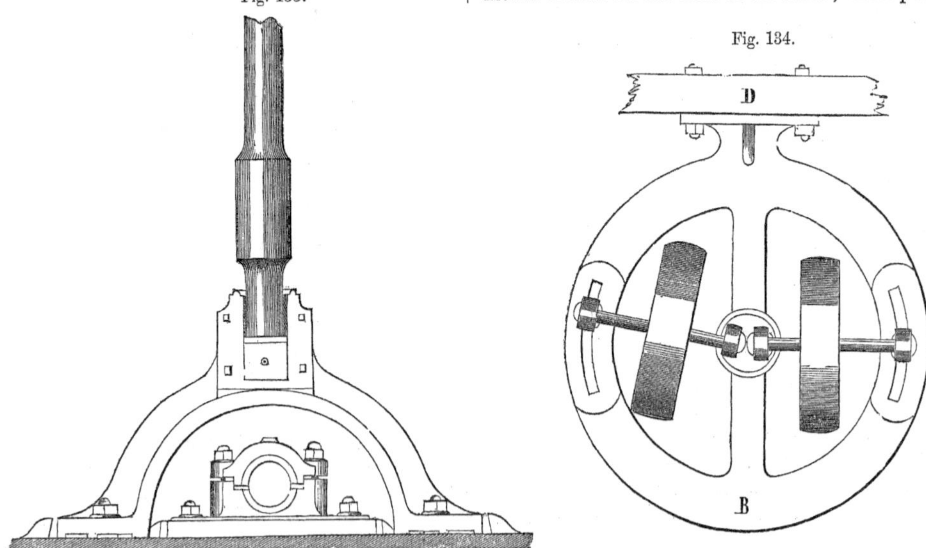

leys can thus be set at any angle required, for conveying the motion to the proper place.

Fig. 135.

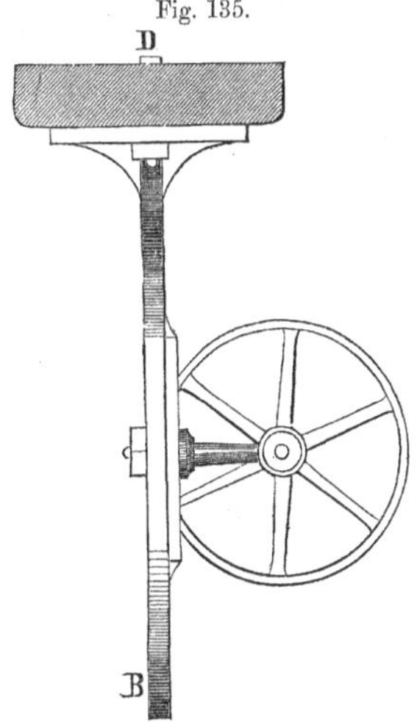

Fig. 136.

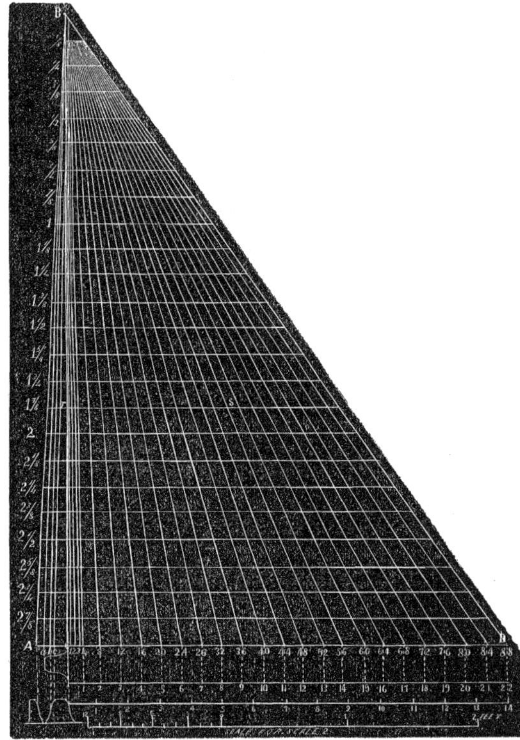

SPUR MORTISE-WHEEL.

PLATE II.

The Figs. of this plate give two views in elevation, and a section of a mortise spur-wheel of 34¼ inches diameter, and containing 48 cogs; pitch 2¼ inches.

Fig. 1 is a section of the wheel where *aa* represents the cogs; *rr* the ring; *cc* the face arms; *bb* the feathers of the arms, and SS the socket or eye of the wheel.

Fig. 2 is a view parallel to the axis of the wheel, and Fig. 3 is a view of the same wheel in the line of its centre.

These Figs. are intended to illustrate the mode of drawing the wheel. The pitch and number of cogs being given, the first part of this operation is to determine the diameter of the pitch circle. This may be done by multiplying the pitch of the teeth by their number, and dividing the product by 3.1416; or it may be directly found from the rules and tables usually given; or the compasses may be at once set to draw the pitch circle from a proportion-scale for geering, as Fig. 136. This scale, and Figs. 1, 2, 3, in the plate, being drawn to $\frac{1}{12}$th the size, the dimensions of the drawing will correspond with those marked in the scale, as explained thus. The pitch being 2¼ inches, the radius of the pitch circle will be found in the line which runs parallel with AD, and which is marked 2¼; and the distance C to 48 in that line being the radius for a 2¼ inch pitch with 48 teeth, one point of the compasses placed in the intersection of the line 2¼ by CB, and the other in the intersection of the line terminating in 48, will be that radius. The other required dimensions will also be found in the line 2¼; the distance AC = the pitch; *ac* = the length; *bc* = the thickness; *ac* = the length from the pitch line to the point; and twice this is the working depth; the width of space is A*b*, and their lateral clearance is A*b* — C*b*, and the bottom clearance *a*C — 2 *ac*.

The same scale may be used in finding the proportions of parts in making out reduced drawings of wheels to different scales. If the compasses be set to the required pitch, and moved up the line CB, keeping one point in CB until the other point meet the line AB, the points running parallel to

AC, then in a line drawn parallel to AD, and passing through the points in which the compasses meet the converging lines, will be found all the other required dimensions in accordance with that scale.

Fig. 2, Plate II., shows the method of finding the shape and position of the teeth, by the application of the T square to Fig. 3, as indicated by the dotted lines *eeee* at 2, 2, 2. The lines forming the outline of the shaft are found in a similar manner from Fig. 3.

The mode of drawing the curves of the top and bottom of the teeth is shown by the dotted circles, marked *ffff*, and which are drawn from the centres of the teeth *aa*. This curve is, however, very variable, and depends much upon the size of the pinion intended to work in the wheel.

Construction.—Wheels of this kind were formerly constructed entirely of wood; but in the example given, the teeth or cogs only are of that material, the body of the wheel being iron, with mortises cast in the rim to receive the ends *aa* of the cogs. The cogs are formed of hard wood, as hornbeam, beech, hickory, or the like; their inner ends are slightly dovetailed to receive between every pair a wooden key, V, which holds them in their places.

The eye of this wheel is cast square, to receive the square boss of the shaft, on which it is fixed by four iron keys.

UNDERSHOT WATER-WHEEL.

PLATE II.

This plate exhibits two views of an undershot water-wheel containing thirty floats SSS.

Fig. 4 is a view of the wheel in the line of its centre of motion. The ring R and the arms are supposed to be of cast-iron, having cast mortises *mm* for the insertion of the wooden starts FF. The float-boards SS are intended to be wood.

The manner of proceeding in the drawing of this plate, is to draw the diameter AB equal to the proposed size of the wheel; bisect it in the point E, and from E as a centre describe the circle ASSB, which divide into fifteen parts, being half the whole number of floats; through these points, draw radial lines, which will form the face of the float-boards; the size of the ring, arms, and starts, may then be set off as in the plate, the manner of drawing which will be obvious without any explanation.

Fig. 5 is a plan of the same water-wheel, showing the breadth of the floats S, ring R, starts F, &c.; and also the position and appearance they present to the eye. In finding these, the application of the T square to the various points in the elevation Fig. 4 is necessary, as indicated by the dotted lines *ooo*.

The starts FFF, &c., are held in their places by cotter keys passing through them within the rim which is mortised to receive the tails *mm*. When the wheel is large it is usually cast in segments, which are joined under laps formed on the outer extremities of the arms. The centre is usually also a separate casting, into which the arms are fitted and attached by bolts.

DETAILED DRAWINGS OF A METER-WHEEL.

PLATE III.

Fig. 1 is a section, Fig. 3 a side view, and Fig. 2 a face view of a meter-wheel. This is a kind of bevel-wheel, that is used when it is required to change the direction of motion 90° without altering its angular velocity—a case which occurs very frequently in practice. It is obvious that only one pattern is required for the pair of wheels of this kind, and the method of drawing any one of them will apply to both. The following is the process:—

Draw a line AB equal to the diameter of the wheel (diameter of pitch circle); bisect AB, and produce a line at right angles to it which will represent the centre line of the shaft. The points C and D in this line (see Figs. 1 and 3), where the produced centre lines of the two shafts intersect each other, is the point to which all the lines running in the direction of the breadth of the teeth are drawn. The distance of the point D or O from the line AB is equal to half the diameter of the pitch circle; this will be evident if BC be drawn from the point B at right angles to AB. The line BC being equal to AB, will represent the proper position of the other wheel; and, if bisected in E, the line ED produced perpendicular to it will be the centre line of the shaft. The point D is therefore the position of the common apex of the two cones.

Join AD and BD, and AO and BO, and at right angles to these lines draw *em* and *ri* (see Fig. 1), passing through the points A and B. Make A*k* B*n* equal to the breadth of the teeth, and draw *kg* and *nh* parallel to A*m*, BI. Set off upon A*m*, BI the length of the teeth, as *ef*, *rs*; also the thickness

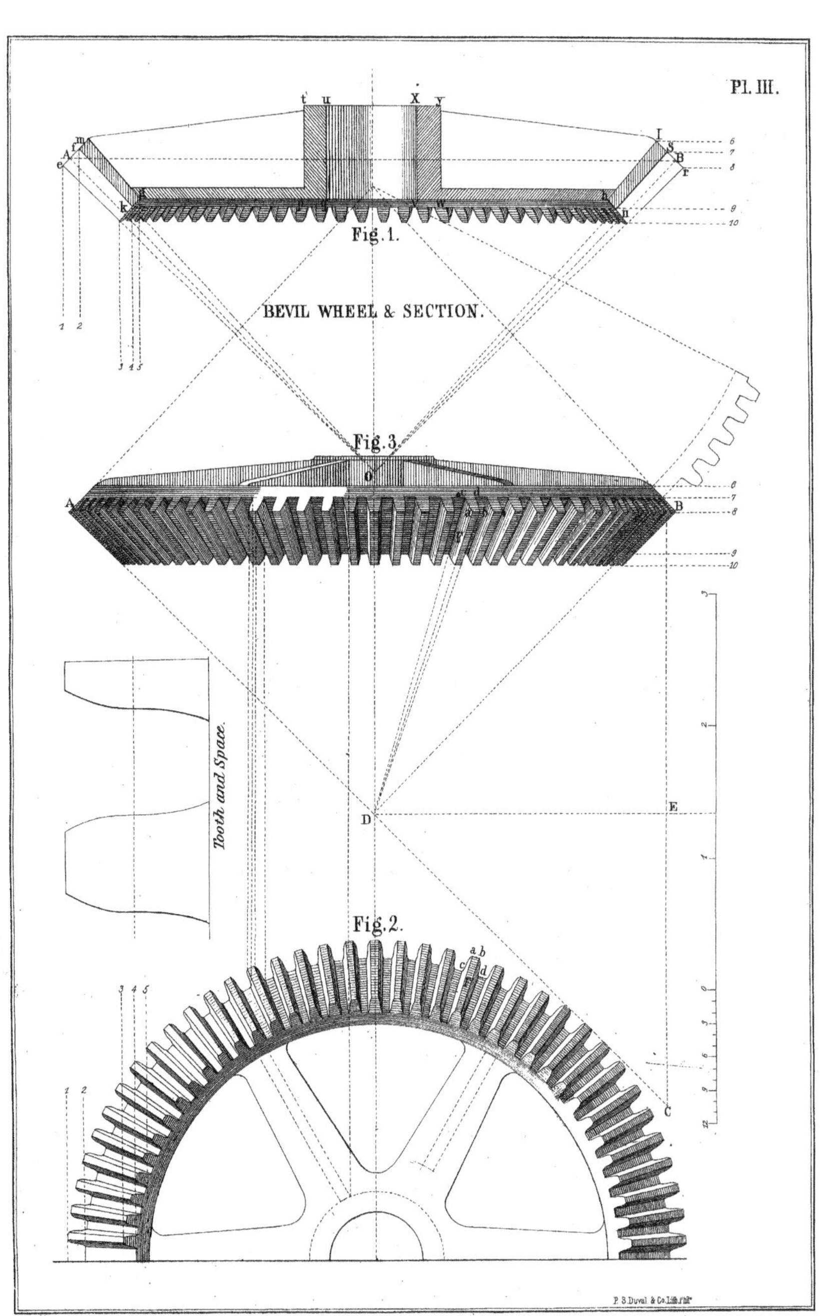
Pl. III.
Fig. 1.
BEVIL WHEEL & SECTION.
Fig. 3.
Fig. 2.
Tooth and Space.
P. S. Duval & Co. Lith. Phil^a

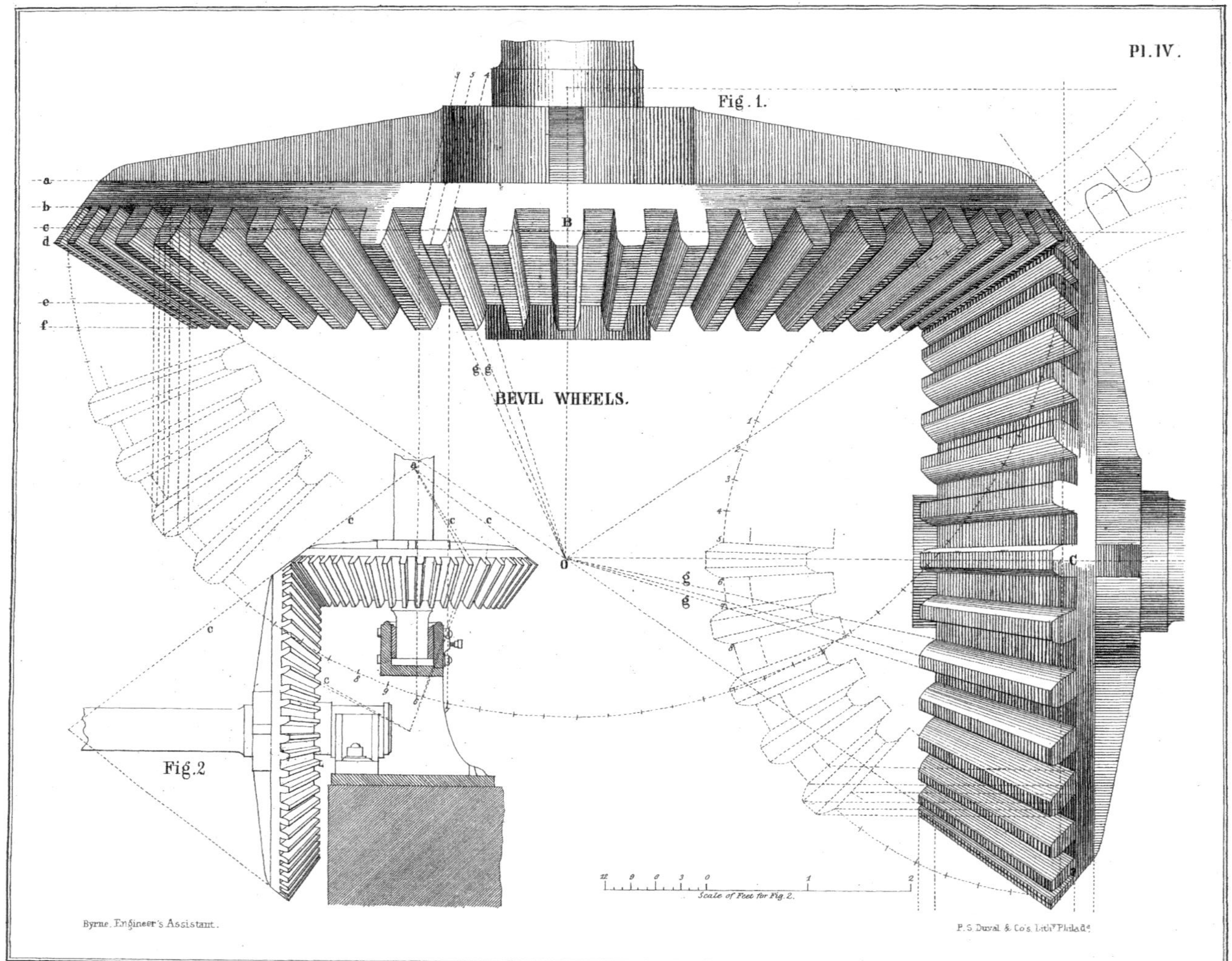

Byrne. Engineer's Assistant.

P. S. Duval & Co's. Lith. Philada.

of rim, as *fm*, *s*I; and from these points let lines be drawn to the apex of the cones, as shown in the drawing. Join *gh*, and make *qv* equal to the size of the eye; P*q* and V*w* are each to be equal to the intended thickness of the eye, and P*t* equal to the depth. Draw *pt*, *qu*, *vx*, *wy*, at right angles to *gh*, and join *tm* and *y*I, and thus a section of the wheel is determined, from which all the lines and points requisite for drawing the plan can be found.

Fig. 2 is a face view, the mode of proceeding with which is to transfer the points 1, 2, 3, 4, 5 from Fig. 1 to it by means of the T square, which determines the extremities of the teeth and rim; circles are then described passing through these points, and that passing through the point 4 is divided into the number of teeth intended to be in the wheel: the thickness of the teeth is then set off, and drawn in a similar manner to that described in Fig. 3, Plate II. The lines forming the edges of the top and bottom of the teeth are radial lines, and of course are drawn in the direction of the centre of the wheel.

Fig. 3, the side view. The elementary lines for this drawing, viz., 6, 7, 8, 9, 10, correspond to the lines in the section having the same figures, and the points forming the teeth are derived from Fig. 2, by the application of the square. For example, the two points, *ab*, forming the top of the outside of the tooth F, are transferred to the line marked 8 on Fig. 3, and the points *cd*, to the line marked 7; these points being connected by the lines *ac* and *bd*, form the end of the tooth: straight lines are then drawn from *ab* in the direction of the point D, until they meet the line marked 10, and a line in the same direction from *c* meeting the line marked 9. The terminations of these lines mark out the extremities of the inside of the tooth, which being joined, complete the tooth F. The shape and direction of the other teeth in the wheel are found by a similar operation to that used for finding F, keeping in view that the slope of all the teeth tends to the point D.

The eye of this wheel is intended for a round boss, on which it may be keyed in the usual manner. The thickness of the web is equal to that of a tooth of the wheel; the arms have a thickness somewhat less, and the thickness of the metal of the eye is equal to the pitch of the teeth.

The radius representing the circle of action of wheels of the kind described, is found by producing the line BI till it meets the centre line of the shaft.

BEVEL-WHEEL AND PINION.

Plate IV.

The pair of wheels, shown in Fig. 1 of this Plate, differs from that in the preceding Plate, in being of unequal size; and hence come under the denomination of *bevel-wheels*. Both wheels of this pair are supposed to be placed on horizontal shafts, in which they differ from the pair of bevels in Fig. 2, of which the pinion is placed on an upright or vertical shaft, having its bottom bearing in a footstep, while the wheel with which it is in geer is placed on a horizontal shaft. The mode of drawing a pair of wheels of this kind will be understood from what follows.

Fig. 1 is a side view of the wheel and pinion, drawn to full size.

When only the side view of a bevel-wheel and pinion is required, it is not necessary that the whole section, as in Fig. 1, Plate III., should be drawn farther than to determine the position of lines *a*, *b*, *c*, *d*, *e*, and *f*, and the position of the apex of the two cones, as at O, Plate IV. It should also be observed, in the example given in Plate III., that the view in Fig. 2 was requisite for drawing the side view, only so far as finding the position of the four points of the teeth *a*, *b*, *c*, *d* was concerned; but for common purposes, these points can be found with sufficient exactness by merely drawing circles of the same diameter as the wheel and pinion, and dividing them into the given number of teeth, and marking off their thickness. This will be readily understood, by examining Fig. 1, in which circles, so divided, are laid down equal in diameter to the wheel and pinion; and 6, 7, 8, &c. show the thickness of the teeth. Now by applying the T square, as at 6 and 7, and marking these points upon the pitch line *c*, the lines forming the sides of the teeth at 3, 4, are found, by drawing them parallel to the centre line 5, which is drawn to the point where the lines 1 and 2, forming the bevel of the ends of the teeth, meet. This point is not shown in the drawing, being at too great a distance for the size of the plate. The lines forming the face of the teeth are all drawn to the point O where the cones meet, as shown by the lines *gg*; and exactly the same mode is adopted in determining the shape and position of the teeth of the pinion C.

When the wheels are drawn to a small scale, as in Fig. 2, the two lines forming the sides of the teeth may both be drawn to the same point, as shown at *a*, as in such cases they will not differ sensibly from the parallel.

As a thorough understanding of the mode of drawing bevel-wheels is of the utmost importance to the young engineer, he should, before proceeding to any of the other plates, exercise himself in laying down wheels from such data, as in the following example.

1*st.* Required to draw the section, plan, and side views of two bevel-wheels, in the proportion of 3 : 2, the one being 4 feet six inches in diameter, containing 72 teeth, 7 inches broad; and the other being 3 feet diameter, having 48 teeth; the length of the teeth to be made equal to $\frac{7}{10}$ths of the pitch, the thickness to $\frac{7}{15}$ths of the same unit. The socket to be the same depth as the breadth of the teeth, the boss for shaft 8 inches diameter, and the thickness of the socket equal to the pitch. The thickness of the rim outside to be 1¼ inch, to have six arms, 5 inches broad at socket, 4 inches at the rim, and ⅞ths thick.

As wheels ought never to overhang their bearings, when the contrary arrangement is possible, it would be necessary, in the example Fig. 1, to contrive a double bracket, or other fixing, which might be contained within the angle of the wheels, and at the same time to have the bearings as near to the wheels as possible. This is often a problem to the millwright, involving much ingenuity in its proper solution. The pair shown in Fig. 2 affords an easy case of this problem; for, resting the bottom of the upright shaft upon a bridge of the same kind as that shown, Fig. 134, sufficient space can be obtained underneath the arch, and on the same base-plate which supports it, for a pedestal to carry the horizontal shaft.

By the arrangement referred to, the wheels are securely bound together, which is not the case either when they overhang their bearings or have bearings on separate parts of a wall or foundation. The true principle of geering is indeed to confine the strain arising from the action of the wheels to their fixings; if this be referred to the wall and beams of the building, the geering will work less securely, and much greater strength of building will be necessary.

BEMENT'S LUBRICATOR.

Bement's Lubricator, Figs. 137 and 138, was invented by W. B. Bement, whilst in the employment of the "Lowell Machine Shop Co.," and under the following circumstances, viz.: The Company had made some large horizontal engines, for driving cotton mills in and about Lowell, Mass., and had tried three kinds of oilers, some with two cocks, and in various other ways commonly used, but they all proved ineffectual. They were about to try another project, when the inventor suggested to the superintendent to force the oil in by means of a pump, an idea which, though new, yet occurred to him as being practical, and he gave the inventor permission to make the experiment. The first attempt was to place the pump in the centre of a disk, upon the top of the steam-chest (into which the tallow or oil was put), to suck the oil from the disk into the chamber of the pump, when, on the return of the piston, the lower valve would close, and the oil pass through the pipes into the steam-chest to the valves or into the ports, as desired. This experiment worked very well at first, but it was found that after standing awhile, with the heat of the cylinder upon it, the lower valve adhered and would not close, it being so light; the oil probably became glutinous, or thick; it did not give entire satisfaction, though it worked much better than any machine for the purpose before tried, and is still in operation. Seeing the difficulty above named, the inventor made a second instrument. (See Fig. 136, 137.)

Fig. 137.

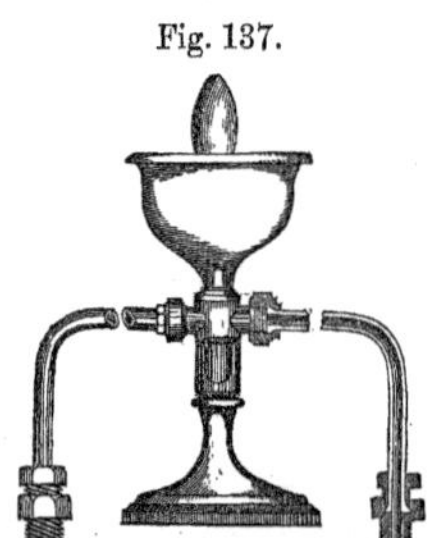

In this pump (or lubricator) the reservoir for the tallow or oil is placed on the top with an inverted

Fig. 138.

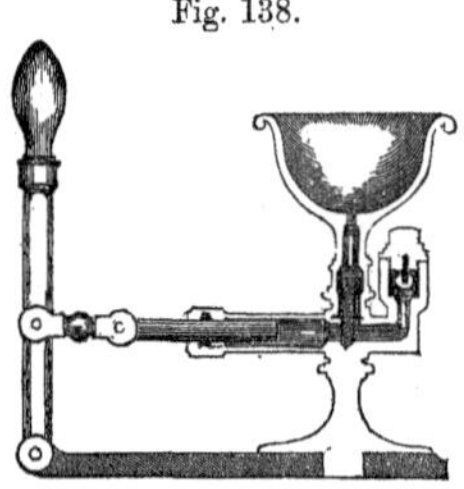

valve held up by a light spiral spring, as seen in Fig. 137, which gives the means to get at the valve in case it should stick; besides, the oil being above the chamber in the pump, it flows in more freely. This plan has worked to perfection, and is in use in the factories of Massachusetts, Connecticut, and other parts, and is spoken of by engineers in the highest terms. The engineer puts the tallow or oil in the reservoir; the heat of the cylinder soon warms it, when it is ready to pass into the cylinder, or on to the valve-seats, as directed by the leading pipes. A few motions of the lever attached to the pump, occasionally, keeps the cylinder and valves well lubricated. The action is positive; for the engineer can see the oil while pumping, and knows when the pump is operating well; while with the globe oilers generally used, the oil is put in and closed; it is then left to find its own way, which is of but little use by the time it gets into the cylinder, if it ever gets there.

It is now a settled fact that the oil invented by Patrick Sarsfield Devlin, of Reading, Pa., is the best for all sorts of machinery, and is best suited for this lubricator.

DETAILS OF LOCOMOTIVES.

Plate IV.

Details of engines and machinery have to be drawn full size by the pattern-maker and designer, on a floor, or on pine boards, planed up for the purpose. Plate IV. is given to exercise the apprentice and student in drawing the parts of engines the full size. Practical men depend much on full-sized drawings; and there is one thing certain, that, unless the young engineer is able to give a rough outline, and accurate proportions to each part that compose an engine or machine, full size, he will get through his work with difficulty, or like an automaton.

Fig. 1. Levers for moving cut-off slide and main rock-shaft that receives the motion from the eccentrics, and transmits it to the main slide-stem.

Fig. 2. Spring and pedestal boxes, in which the axles of the wheels move.

Fig. 3. Piston and packing.

Figs. 4 and 5. Connecting-rods.

Figs. 6, 7, 8, 9, 10, 11. Details of cylinder eccentric rods and hooks, whistle, steam-chest, piston-rod, piston, section through cylinder, with the view of main slide and cut-off slide, section through feed-pump, and axles of the wheels in section.

By introducing separate parts made of laths, the dispositions and proper positions of the several parts of a machine are often determined, after a full-sized sketch or drawing is produced. In this way the action and position of the combined parts in Figs. 8, 9, 10, 11 may be found. However, it must be remembered, that it is necessary for the engineer to be able to move the slides Fig. 8 independently of the motion of the axle; for this purpose the eccentric rods have hooks something like the letter V, which may hook in or out of a notch on the rock-shaft, by means of a lift-shaft, to which are attached two double-armed levers, to lift the forward and backward moving eccentrics separately into geer, or at the same time out of it. When they are taken out of geer, the slides are at liberty to move independently of the axle; then, by means of two handles connected to the slide-rods, the slides may be given the required motion. The eccentric must be placed very nearly at right angles with the crank, so that the eccentric is in full action when the piston is at the bottom of the cylinder. By this means, the slide is in its most rapid motion when it has to open and shut the passages. Let us suppose the piston to be just in the middle of the cylinder, and the crank upon which the piston acts in its vertical position above the axle, to make the engine go forward the steam must make the piston go forward, and if we wish to retrograde, the steam must arrive on the other side of the piston; hence the slide is pushed back, and the eccentric is in front, that is, as far off from the centre of the axle in front of the crank as it was in the progressive motion behind it. The lever which changes the position of the eccentrics is placed within the reach of the engineer when in his proper place. How the most compound arrangements of machinery are to be effectually geered may be determined from full-sized drawings, and drawings on separate pieces to represent the moving parts.

BOILER FOR GENERATING STEAM BY BURNING OF ANTHRACITE.

INVENTED BY F. P. DIMPFEL, ENGINEER, PHILADELPHIA.

PLATE X.

THE construction of a boiler fitted for the combustion of anthracite, without the very great injury received in ordinary constructions from the intense local heat from that fuel, the difficulty of managing the fire, and the silicious nature of its ashes, has long been a requirement, both on account of the notable economy to be thus introduced into our steam-engines, and because it appeared a sad reproach upon our ingenuity that the very locomotives which brought down the anthracite from the mines should be compelled to use wood or bituminous coal for fuel.

Many efforts have been made to solve this important problem, but with no very notable success, until the invention of Mr. Dimpfel, which appears to have been, after a sufficient trial upon the Reading Railroad, perfectly successful.

This engine has been in daily use for several months, running over six thousand miles with anthracite coal exclusively.

The fire-box is of iron, and only two inches water space (in other engines usually three to four inches) around it. There is not any perceivable evidence of the least injurious effects either on the sides of the fire-box or tubes.

The engine is provided with a patent apparatus for the purpose of returning a portion of the unconsumed gases. It retains the cinders, and with bituminous coal the smoke is consumed.

Within this apparatus is a blower, which is driven by the exhaust steam, and after it has performed this duty, it is led back into the tender for the purpose of heating the water.

The following are the dimensions of the engine:—

		Feet.	Inches.
Length of Boiler		10	8
Diameter			42
Inside of Fire-Box	56 in. long × 37 in. wide.		
Water Space around Fire-Box			2
Depth of Fire-Box		4	
Number of Tubes	99		
Average Length of Tubes		13	
Diameter of " (outside)			2
Fire Surface in Fire-Box	59¼ sq. ft.		
" " Flue Part	104⅓ "		
Heating Surface of Tubes	671½ "		
Total Heating Surface	835¼ "		
Diameter of Cylinders			15½
Length of Stroke			26
Number of Driving Wheels, connected	4		
Diameter		6	
Weight of Engine in condition	24½ tons.		
" on Driving Wheels	16 "		
" of Water contained in Boiler	1¼ "		

Cost of Running Passenger Train per Round Trip.

Wood for Fuel, 4.8 Cords, $4 25	$20.40	
157 Round Trips per year	157	
		$3202.80
Coal for Fuel, 3 Tons, $2.30	$6.90	
Wood to Kindle Coal	1.10	
	$8.00	
157 Round Trips per year	157	
		$1256.00
Difference in favor of Coal		$1946.80

The principle of the first part of this invention relates to the employment of tubes or pipes within a boiler which communicates at both ends with the body of water in the boiler, and through which the water circulates, and consists in making such tubes or pipes, with one end bent up, when such bent-up ends are attached to the crown-plate of the boiler, or the plates forming the sides or end of the fire-box or flue, at or near the junction with the crown-plate, provided the other end is attached to a water-space of the flue, and at or near the end of the same, whereby the water is caused to circulate freely through such tubes, and is freely delivered out of the bent-up ends without any counteracting effect, and the circulation of the water through the tubes is always insured in the same and required direction, the bends in the said tubes at the same time giving the required elasticity to yield to the expansion and contraction due to the changes of temperature to which they are necessarily exposed.

And this part of the invention also consists in combining such bent tubes with a water-bottom of any form whatever, or other bottom water communication which will freely supply water to the space with which the straight ends of the tubes connect, by means of which combination a full supply of water is given to insure the circulation through the tubes, and which at the same time prevents the overheating of the plate or plates to which the straight ends of the tubes are attached, and consequently avoids the evil effects which otherwise would take place; for the heating of the plates tends to repel and drive up the water, and hence prevents it from entering the tubes freely. But, by the arrangement herein specified, the water is supplied to this space freely, and by the rapid circulation prevents, in a great measure, the heating of the plate to which the ends of the tubes are attached, and hence admits of the more free circulation of the water into the tubes.

This part of the invention also consists, in connection with the bent tubes attached at one end and within some part of the flue, in attaching the bent-up ends of the said tubes to the crown-plate or roof of the fire-box, that the current of water through the tubes may be discharged over the said crown-plate or roof, and thus prevent the overheating thereof; for the heat in the fire-box acts upwards, and impinges on the under surface of this plate, and tends to heat it to a high degree; and if by accident the water be suffered to sink below, it soon becomes overheated, and endangers the safety of the boiler. But by attaching the bent-up ends of the tubes to this plate, the current of water discharged by them will flow over the upper surface of this plate, and thus keep it covered with water even after the level of the body of water in the boiler has fallen below it. In this way, the parts of the boiler most exposed to the effects of intense heat are fully protected.

The second part of this invention consists in combining with the bent-up tubes attached to the crown-plate of the fire-box, the making of such crown-plate with a ring or projection around the edges thereof, the better to retain on its surface the water discharged into it by the circulation through the tubes.

The third part of this invention consists in extending the bent-up ends of the tubes above the surface of the crown-plate or other plates, on one side of which the fire or products of combustion acts, to which they are attached when the other end of the tubes communicate with a water-space or body of water below or further from the fire-box than the said bent-up ends, whereby the disturbance of the water above the crown-sheet, or other plate to which the bent-up ends of the tubes are attached, is avoided.

And the fourth or last part of the invention consists in giving a forced circulation to the water in steam-boilers, or generators, by mechanical means, whereby the water is caused to pass with greater velocity over the heated surface, and thereby to take up the heat more rapidly.

In Figs. 139, 140, 141, *A* represents the external shell of the boiler, which may be of any desired

Fig. 139.

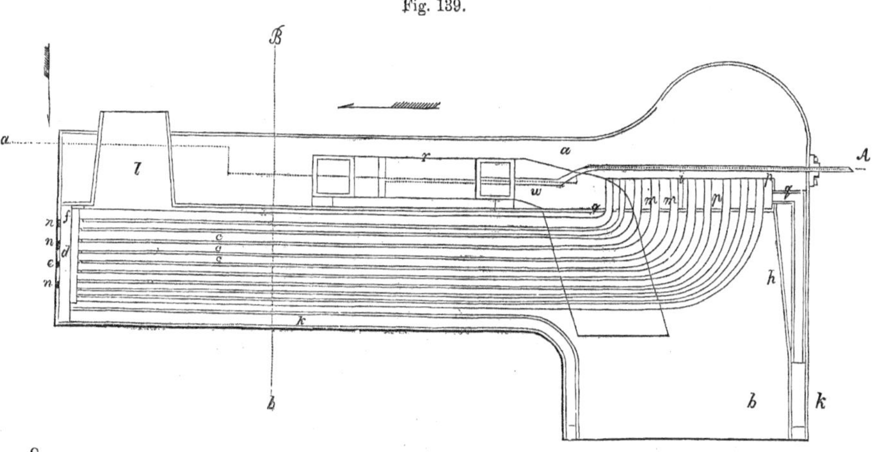

form, and *B* the fire-chamber. Within the shell is arranged a series of water-tubes, or pipes, *c*, which

Fig. 140.

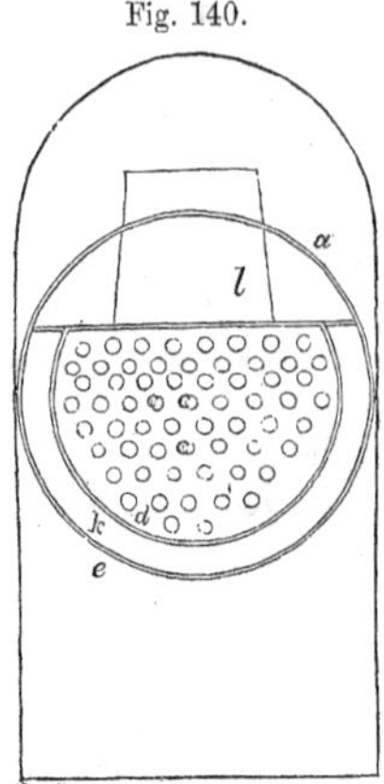

act on and impart heat to external surface of all the water-tubes, or pipes, the most intense heat being applied to the curved or bent ends of the tubes, which first receive the action of the heat. The products of combustion also heat the plate *i*, which is the inner shell of the water space surrounding the flue, and which constitutes the water bottom. The tubes being bent or curved upwards as the water in them is heated and rarefied, it will tend to rise in the curved end, and thus establish a rapid circulation through the entire length, and as their other end is connected with the body of water at the back, and where the water is not heated to so intense a degree, the circulation in the tubes or pipes will be fully supplied. The water space *j*, between the plate *i* and the outer shell of the boiler, as well as the space *f* at the back, are closed at the top from the back to the space *k*, around the furnace or fire-box, and the crown-plate

Fig. 141.

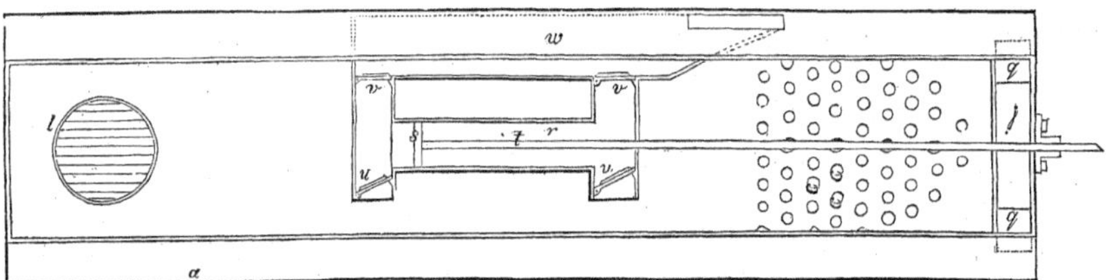

are secured at the back end to a vertical plate *d*, which plate *d* is at such a distance from the end plate or head *e* of the boiler, as to have a space *f* for the free admission of water to this end of the tubes or pipes.

The other ends of the said tubes or pipes are curved or bent upwards, and attached to the roof or crown-plate *g*, which runs back to and is connected at the back end with the plate *d* before described, and at the front end with a vertical plate *h*, or lining of the furnace, and at the sides with the upper edges of a plate *i*, within the boiler, and at such distance from it as to leave a water space *j* all around, and communicating with the space *f* at the back end, and with the water space *k* surrounding the furnace. This plate *i*, together with the roof or crown plate, constitutes the fire-flue, which leads from the furnace to the chimney *l*, so that the flame and other products of combustion, in passing from the furnace to the chimney, act first on the curved or bent-up part of the tubes or pipes, and then, in passing towards the chimney,

or fire-roof, to which the bent-up ends of the tubes are attached, is surrounded by a rim *p*. Two or more tubes, *q*, form communications between the space above the crown-plate and the lower end of the space *k*, around the fire-box; and this space *k* in turn communicates (as indicated by the arrows) with the space *j*, which, as, stated, constitutes the water-bottom.

The effect of this arrangement will be that, as the water above the crown-plate or fire-roof cannot pass down the side or back spaces *j* and *f*, it will run down the tubes *q*, to the bottom or lower part of the spaces *k*, surrounding the furnace or fire-box, and thence through the water-bottom to the space *f*, to supply the circulation in the tubes. The current thus supplied to the space *f*, which cannot rise above the covering of the said space *f*, by reason of its being closed up at top, will effectually supply the tubes; for if the said space *f* were open at top, and not connected with the water-bottom, the heat which the plate *d* receives from the impingement of the products of the combustion in passing through the flue, would have the effect to repel the water from the surface of the plate, and to induce an upward circulation in the said space *f*, so rapid as not to give an adequate supply of water to the tubes.

And as the curved and bent-up ends of the tubes are either directly over or nearest the fire-chamber, they will be more highly heated than the rear ends; so that the water, by its circulation through the tubes or pipes, will move in a direction the reverse of the current of heat, as it passes from the fire-chamber to the chimney, thus increasing the absorption of heat by the water.

The bent-up ends of the tubes are extended above the roof or crown plate, as at *m*, which will induce a more rapid circulation, and avoid the agitation of the water on the surface of the roof around the tubes.

The shell of the boiler at the horizontal end of the tubes or pipes may be perforated, as at *n*, with a series of holes, corresponding with the bore of the tubes, for which one large hole for the whole series, covered with a plate in the manner of a man-hole, may be substituted, for giving access to the tubes or pipes, for cleansing or repairing them.

A short distance above the top flue-plate there is a cylinder or case *r*, provided with a reciprocating piston *s*, the rod *t* of which passes through the head of the boiler, that it may be connected with any moving part of the engine, or any other first mover, to give it a reciprocating motion. The said cylinder is provided on one side with two induction-valves *uu*, one at each end, and on the other side with two eduction-valves *vv*, discharging into a pipe *w*, leading down into one of the outer spaces. It will be obvious from this, that the reciprocating motion of the piston will produce a current of water down the water space in which the pipe is located, and that this will induce a circulation through the boiler, to return the water to the induction-valves of the cylinder, and in this way establish a circulation of the water over the heating surface of the boiler with a velocity dependent on the capacity of the cylinder and the motion of the piston.

BOILERS AT THE MERRIMACK PRINT WORKS, LOWELL.

Plate X.

This boiler was constructed by H. N. Hudson, C. E. of Lowell, Mass., and except the boilers of the cotton factory at Newburg, on the Hudson, I know of no better arrangement, or disposition of parts; the engineer's name I do not remember, but the Newburg boilers were shown to me by Mr. Wilkinson and his son, who work in the machine-shop near the factory; we allude to this boiler here, for the purpose of showing the young engineer how the tubes are hung, and how the heat is conveyed to the water and steam in the tubes and to the surrounding brickwork. Fig. 1 Plate X. is a section showing the hanging, Fig. 2, a front elevation, and Fig. 3 is a section through one of the supports. The great improvement in this boiler is the back heaters, which are not shown, and although they are essentially different from the means employed by Dimpfel, they have the same effect. This boiler is well constructed for the application of Dunn's safety-gage, of which we will speak presently; it is given in Fig. 4. One row of two boilers are set above another row of three boilers, the fires being under both tiers; and when reflected from the covering arcs, the disposition of the heat is complete. The two great evils of boilers are not created by this; first, the prevention of a sufficiently rapid transference of the heat of the plate to the water, excepting only at the lowest points of the effective heating surfaces, where the fire is in immediate contact with the plate, thereby diminishing the evaporative power of the boiler; and secondly, the effectual prevention of all proper excess of the water, to those portions of the generating surface, immediately above the heated points. By this means, the plates in other boilers, in these parts, are sure to get overheated and burnt out in a comparatively short time.

SAFETY-VALVES.

OBSERVATIONS BY HENRY HOWSON, C. E.,
AND MECHANICAL DRAFTSMAN.

Whatever may be the ultimate causes of explosion in steam-boilers; to whatever defect of construction, workmanship, or management these disastrous occurrences may be individually traced; it is certain that, in all cases where violent disruption has taken place, the approximate and immediate cause has been pressure, and nothing but pressure. Ingenuity has been taxed, and experimental science has been ransacked, to deduct from ascertained facts in connection with steam, the means of remedying the results of its dangerous properties; while, with the same laudable intention, theories without number have been advanced, seeking to throw a light on mysterious agencies, other than experiment has confirmed, and to expound hidden properties which never existed. Although, however, nothing comparatively has been effected, although explosions still take place, and in all probability will continue to take place, it is not too much to affirm that the present state of our knowledge on this subject, limited as it may be, is nevertheless amply sufficient to obviate even the chance of danger; that even the simple knowledge of the fact that pressure alone, from whatever cause evolved, is the immediate forerunner of every explosion, ought to be in itself a sufficient guarantee for its prevention. Precaution, under our existing knowledge, is the only preventive, but it is a safe one; precaution in construction, precaution in workmanship, and precaution in attendance. As, however, this latter is not always to be depended on, and the most careful engine-tender may sometimes be at fault, it follows that, in the construction of boilers, combined with sound workmanship, too great attention cannot be paid to the means of rendering them so perfect in their self-adjusting action, as to defy the consequences of the most reckless carelessness.

Since, therefore, it is an axiom not to be controverted, that a boiler cannot burst or explode in the ordinary manner without internal pressure, it may be fairly submitted, that if we can devise any precautionary method, whereby it can be relieved from that pressure as fast or faster than it is evolved from any undue cause, the means of perfect security will in all cases be attained, except when some most inordinate and preposterous defect exists.

To effect this desirable purpose, the ordinary safety-valve has been devised; and as it is a most obvious and simple contrivance, so it would appear at first sight to be most effective; but it is not too much to believe that, for the very reason of its being obvious and simple, it has not sufficiently claimed the attention of engineers; and that it is not so effective as is generally supposed, but is capable of very great improvement, we shall now attempt imperfectly to show.

(Fig. 142). The most common safety-valve now

Fig. 142.

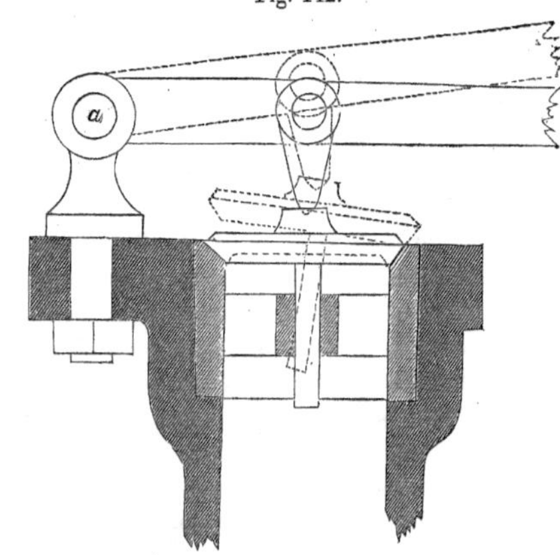

in use for boilers working much above atmospheric pressure is the one shown in Fig. 142, being the ordinary weighted lever-valve. In some cases, however, the lever is discarded, and weights are perpendicularly placed over the valve, a preferable mode in all respects, where compactness and steadiness can be obtained.

In both cases, the valve itself consists of a flat plate (frequently hollowed out on the under side), having a tail or guide-spindle, and bearing with its edges a brass seat to which it is ground conically.

With such a valve or valves, or others similar in their important features, has every boiler been furnished, which has exploded since the use of steam-engines became general; a fact which would alone prove that, where real danger exists, and when they ought to fulfil their intention, to most purposes they are of little or no use.

Indeed, it may be confidently asserted that their utility as safety-valves does not in any great degree extend beyond that of indicating to the attendant any increment of pressure that may take place, and giving him the power of blowing off at intervals what amount circumstances may require.

Their inutility, as self-acting protectors at the critical injunctions of neglect and danger, would appear evident, and the fault lies most probably in some defect in their construction. It may be said that, by making them of larger diameter, greater security might be afforded; but this is inconvenient; and it is, moreover, quite possible that a defect may exist which is common to large ones as well as small.

Now it seems highly probable that a most serious defect does exist, and lies in this simple fact, that the plate constituting the valve is made flat or hollowed out on the under side. It cannot be doubted, on due consideration, that this form of valve is bad; for this simple reason, that any fluid in motion, meeting with an obstacle at right angles to its course, must reverberate upon itself, as is exemplified in Montgolfier's hydraulic ram, and in the bursting of pipes by the reaction of water on sudden stoppage; thus it is evident that, when the valve is open, the greater part of the steam, rushing to its exit, will strike against the under side of the valve-plate, and be thrown back in an opposite direction, forming thereby an opposing current to the particles of steam which immediately follow.

Now that the evil effects of this action are more serious than might be at first imagined, may be shown on reference to a small well-known philosophical curiosity, first noticed by Clement des Ormes. Fig. 143 represents a small tube A, having attached to one end a flat plate B, C being another loose plate of the same diameter. The top side of B and the under side of C, ought

Fig. 143.

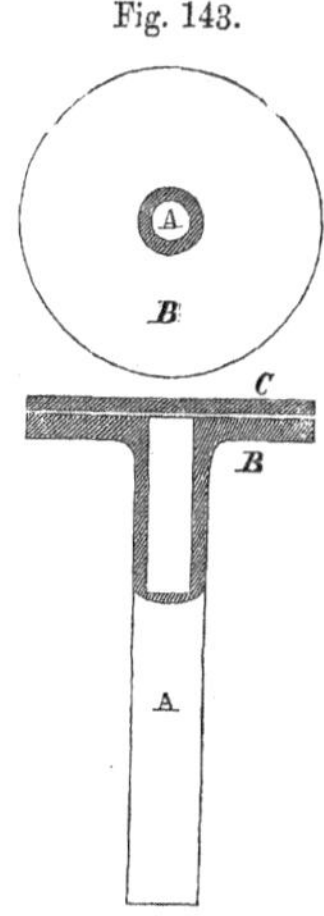

to be both level and somewhat accurately fitting when placed together. If we now hold the instrument perpendicularly, having placed the plate C on the top of B, and blow through the lower end of the tube, no force of blast which can be exerted will be able to move the plate C from its position. The fact is certain, the reason has been variously explained. Although, however, a true and exact solution is difficult to arrive at, it seems most likely that the action which takes place is very nearly allied to the following.

The air being projected up the tube A, strikes forcibly in the first instance against the top plate C, tending to lift it from its state of rest, which it certainly does to some extent; no sooner has this taken place, however, than the air recoils upon itself, and prevents the escape of any but a very small quantity. This action of the air in the tube is either then repeated by a series of pulsations, or it resolves itself into two opposing currents, the downward one of which, having only slightly less velocity than the upward, stops the passage into the annular space between the plates of any except a very minute portion of air. In the mean time, the plate C, when first struck by the air in the tube, rises from contact with B, with so great suddenness that the air from the exterior has not time allowed to rush in between the plates to fill up the vacuum; so that the pressure of the atmosphere on the top forces it immediately back to its former position, or rather till it meets with an elastic stratum of air, and the combined force of the upward blast: it then rebounds as suddenly as before, and continues to repeat this action by a series of minute and almost entirely imperceptible pulsations. It would seem, then, that the quantity of air escaping into the annular space, by even the most forcible blast, is so extremely minute, that the plate cannot rise far, before the pressure of the atmosphere on the top becomes greater than the pressure in that space, and the force of the upward current on its limited area, combined. Precisely similar in all respects is the action of a safety-valve, except that its tendency to ascend on pressure being exerted below, is not retarded to the same extent as in the instrument described, by reason of its annular space bearing a much smaller proportion to the whole area of the plate.

That it is, however, in some degree retarded and prevented from rising to its due height may be gathered from analogy; and I think this is also confirmed by experience.

It would not be easy, from the data of which we are possessed, to fix the point at which a valve of a given area and configuration ought to stand under a given pressure, but it is certain that observation points out that they never rise very high, even under the greatest pressures. Granting, however, that they rise to a sufficient height (which they seldom or never do) to give an annular area for the escape of the steam equal to the area of the passage leading thereto; still, the effect noticed with regard to the pipe, must hold good here also; in fact, the amount of steam which the area of the passage ought to give does not escape. The fury of the steam is expended by being thrown back in antagonism to itself, and in forming an effectual barrier to free egress, those particles which are so successful as to find a passage out, making their escape into the atmosphere with a loud and intolerable noise. We are well aware, as has been before stated, that the recoil of water in a pipe, on an obstacle at right angles to its course, exercises a very great retarding influence on its flow, and it is much to be apprehended that the more elastic the fluid the greater the evil. Having thus pointed out a defect, which, simple as it may appear, there is every reason to believe results in rendering the safety-valve no safety-valve at all, it remains to find a remedy. This is so simple and so obviously efficient that it needs no further recommendation than merely to state that it consists of making the under side of the valve of such a shape, as that the particles of steam, on striking it, shall be directed in their recoil immediately towards the opening. Fig. 144 will give a rough idea of such a valve; and it may be stated, in confirmation of the self-evident superiority of such a construction, that pump valves of this description, which the writer has tried, are, so far as may be judged from practical and inaccurate experiment, more effective in their delivery, less noisy, and better in all respects than the ordinary plate valves. There are, however, other minor defects in safety-valves. One of these frequently prevails in the weighted lever-valve, and is illustrated with some exaggeration by the lines in Fig. 142.

In consequence of the point at which the lever here bears upon the valve, being placed so much

Fig. 144.

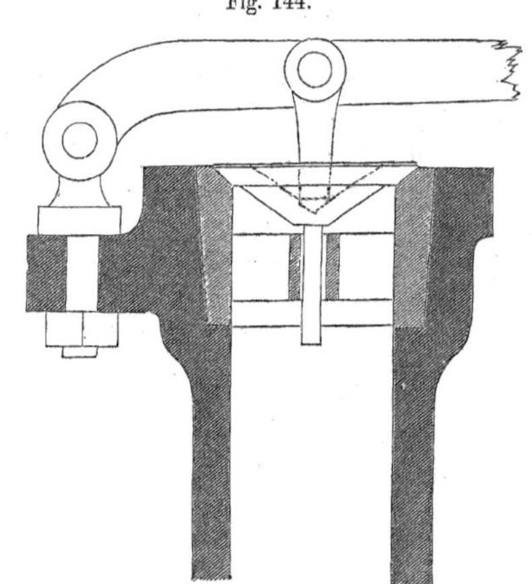

above the part which guides it, and the often ill-considered position of the fulcrum *a*, it is evident that, before the valve can rise any reasonable height, a large amount of resistance must be given to its further progress, by its being forced into an angular position, thereby jamming the spindle in its guide, and adding an undue amount of friction.

Some valves, it is true, being carefully constructed, and with due attention to their proper action in this respect, are not open to this objection, but it is to be feared that this applies only to the minority of cases. The risk, however, if not entirely removed, is very greatly diminished by the arrangement which results from the form of the valve, Fig. 144, where the bearing point of the lever is considerably lower than the seat of the valve.

Another imperfection may be noticed in a common application to this species of safety apparatus, namely, the ordinary spring balance. Although this is in other respects a neat and convenient contrivance, it has the serious defect of giving no clue to the actual pressure in the boiler at the time when steam is blowing off.

For instance, supposing the valve to have been screwed down to a given pressure at the instant of the valve's first rising, that pressure will be indicated on the scale with tolerable correctness, but on its rising, and thereby lifting the lever to the smallest extent further, the spring becomes immediately stronger, by tension, while inversely (from the before-mentioned causes) the tendency of the valve itself to rise becomes weaker, and that to an unknown amount. The deceptive consequences of this are obvious, and need no further explanation; but, although the matter may be made light of, as it is certain that a boiler may explode when its safety-valves are blowing to their utmost, so it is possible that, under these circumstances, a spring balance, instead of acting as a protector, becomes the very reverse.

Having thus endeavored to trace some of the principal causes of the imperfect action of safety-valves, and being bold to assert that, in cases of real danger, they are little better than useless, as ordinarily constructed, I would also again press the assumption that, if constructed on sound principles, they are capable of being rendered at once the most natural and most effectual means of protection.

Let us see, then, what are the requisites of a good safety-valve. They may, I think, be stated to be simply these: 1. That it should be of such a form as to allow of the most free egress of the steam. 2. That it should be capable of rising (by pressure) any limited height, freely, without sticking. [NOTE.—It has been asserted that cases have been known of valves getting fixed in their seats by oxidation. It is beyond belief, however, that a brass valve can, from this cause, become set so firmly, as to resist pressure with greater obstinacy than even the boiler itself. It is much more likely the assertion has been invented as an excuse for some gross neglect or abuse. Besides, a properly constructed valve will be too frequently on the move, to run the chance of rusting fast.] 3. That it should be of dimensions large enough to relieve the boiler of its pressure, even under the most unlooked-for rapidity of evolution. The first requisite is in some degree fulfilled by the arrangement shown in Fig. 144; the second also partially, although it would be better to discard the lever altogether, and substitute weights placed immediately over the axis of the valve; as this, however, would be inconvenient and awkward in high-pressure boilers, and as, in order properly to fulfil the last requisite, any method of weighing would be extremely clumsy and intractable under ordinary construction, I would submit the contrivance shown in Fig. 145, for consideration, as one likely

Fig. 145.

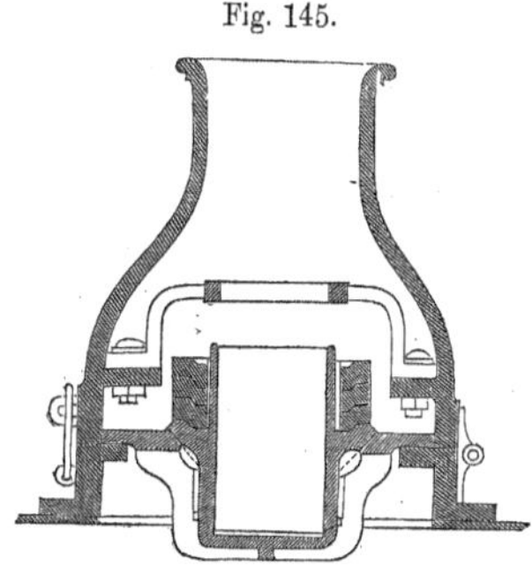

to answer the purposes of a safety-valve to a fuller extent than any that has yet been in use.

It will be seen on reference to the sketch (Fig. 146 being a plan of the seat), that this valve is annular, and has two concentric bearing surfaces, so that when lifted it allows the steam to escape through two openings. The inner opening may be made of any diameter, and the annular area on

Fig. 146.

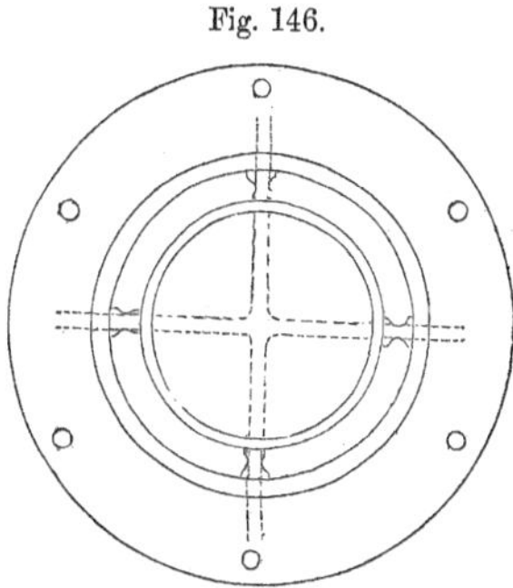

which pressure is exerted thus limited to any amount, by which means the whole can be weighted in the manner shown, conveniently, and without occupying much bulk.

Its advantages in this respect are very great, inasmuch as a greatly increased diameter may be used without injuring its sensitiveness or increasing its unwieldiness. Exclusive of this, moreover, it enables a much greater amount of steam to escape for a given diameter than an ordinary one, and none of the phenomena noticed as appertaining to the latter can here take place, provided a proper form be given to the under side, between the outer and inner seats. This form is perhaps shown imperfectly in the sketch, that marked by the dotted lines being better.

Fig. 147 is also a valve of the same construction,

Fig. 147.

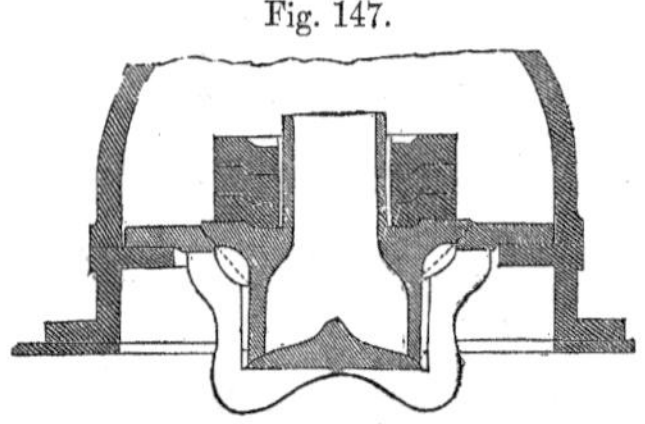

but possessing this difference, that the central opening instead of having straight sides, is contracted towards the mouth; the purpose of this modification being that, besides allowing more room for weight, it gives the valve a tendency to rise more freely under great pressures, by presenting an additional area to the action of the escaping steam when the valve is partially raised from its seat.

Fig. 148 is also another modification of the

Fig. 148.

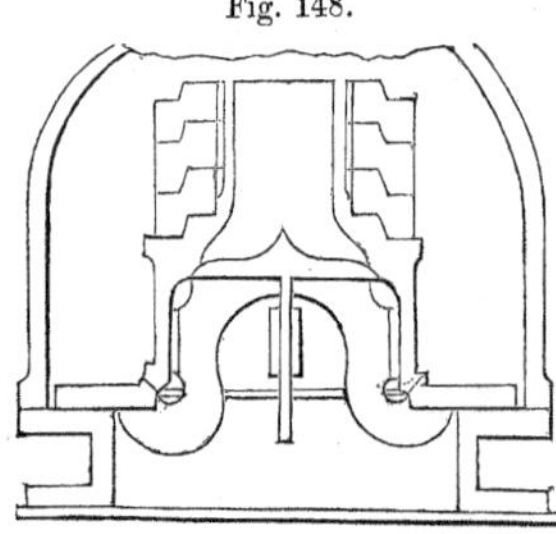

same valve, the position of the seats relatively to one another being reversed. This form is perhaps the most convenient, and the section of the upper plate may advantageously form a curve downwards, as shown by the sketch. This form, however, may be modified to some extent, and the best form must be the result of experiment; but I would draw attention to the fact that with this construction there exists apparently no objection whatever to the employment of valves of such increased dimensions as to discharge rapidly even the most dangerous evolution of steam, or by whatever other name the gaseous originator of pressure may be designated.

I may be allowed, in conclusion, to suggest a combination and application of the principles above described, constituting a safety apparatus which, however imperfect, may be confidently asserted to be superior to that commonly used in locomotives, and may be applied with advantage to all boilers.

It consists of an arrangement of two valves (Fig. 150); one, A, is of ordinary dimensions, while

Fig. 149.

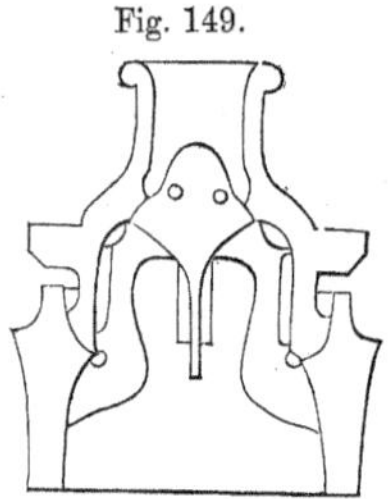

the other, B, is much larger, and regulated by its weights, so as to rise under a somewhat greater pressure than A. The two valves are similar in their principle of construction, being the same as that shown in Fig. 149, but have this difference, that the smaller one, A, which is also shown in enlarged section in Fig. 150, has the edges of its two seats at *a* and *a′* raised upwards and slightly inclined, the intention of this addition being that when the valve is first lifted only a small portion of steam may escape, in order to insure its rising higher as the pressure increases.

The larger valve, B, is weighted by a series of metallic rings, as before described, and the smaller one, A, by a combination of levers; of these, the upper one, C, having its fulcrum at *b* beyond B, and resting on knife-edges *c* on the valve A, is connected by links with the lower one, D, the latter being graduated and weighted in such a manner that the weight can be traversed backward and forward by a screw, so as to indicate any pressure required. The valve B has also knife-edges *d*, but reversed and placed so that the lever C may bear upon them only when the valve A has risen a given height.

It will be understood, then, that on the pressure in the boiler becoming greater than circumstances

Fig. 150.

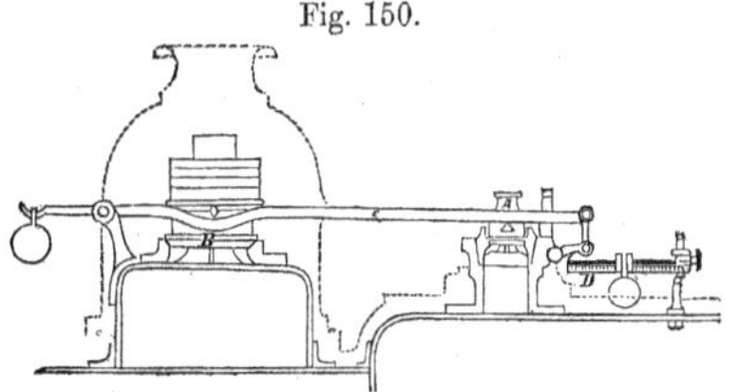

require, the steam first escapes at the valve A, B never rising till it becomes dangerously strong; but the more effectually to insure the proper action of the latter, when this does take place, the valve A rising higher under the increasing pressure, lifts the lever C till it bears upon the knife-edges *d* and relieves B of a portion of its weight. Thus, when the attendant desires to ascertain that the valve B is in proper working order, all he requires to do is to screw the weight back, until the valve A communicates sufficient pressure to the knife-points *d* when the valve B begins to move, and he sees that all is right by the escape of steam. This can be done although the valve B should be locked up and out of reach of the attendant, while at the same time it cannot be affected by any undue weighting of the levers C and D.

For knife-edges in this apparatus may perhaps be substituted with advantage small steel rollers, and additional delicacy of action might be secured by counterbalancing the weight of the two levers as shown.

More important improvements might also possibly be suggested, more especially such as tend to simplification, which would render the apparatus more complete and effective; in the mean time, if it be allowable to decide *à priori* that the foregoing principles are correct, there seems little reason to doubt that safety-valves may yet be constructed which shall be worthy of their name, or, in other words, that steam-boilers are capable of being rendered as harmless as a tea-kettle that is not soldered hard and fast.

ELECTRIC STEAM-GAGE.

Plate X.

This gage was invented by Arthur Dunn, and is now attached to several steam-boilers, in this country, by A. M. Eastman, of Boston, the proprietor of the patent. The action of the instrument represented in Plate X. Fig. 4, depends entirely on the temperature within the boiler EED, which is indicated by a mercurial thermometer ABD, of peculiar construction. The part CD, within the boiler, consists of an iron tube, filled with mercury, and placed in contact with the flues. This tube passes through the top of the boiler EE, at which point a glass tube is fitted to it, in which the mercury is seen at different heights, as in a common thermometer. Through the top of this glass tube the end of one of the wires A, of a galvanic battery is inserted, and the wire A is connected with an alarm-bell, which may be placed in a counting-house, or in the cabin of a ship, at any distance whatever from the boiler. The relations between the temperature and the elastic force of steam has been fully investigated and determined by that great French experimentalist and chemist, M. V. Regnault. The following table is calculated from Regnault's experiments, the heat is given in Fahrenheit degrees and American inches.

For example, 2.671 atmospheres, or 79.9321 inches of mercury, or $79.93 \times .491 = 39\frac{1}{4}$ lbs. nearly on the square inch is equal to 266° Fahrenheit, or 130 Centigrade; 6.12 atmospheres pressure is equal to 320° Fahrenheit; 10 atmospheres is nearly equal to 356° Fahrenheit. Then if the required pressure in the boiler be 40 lbs. to the square inch, the end of the circuit wire B, within the glass tube, must be placed at the point marked 266° upon the graduated scale attached to the tube CB. The action of the instrument is this: As the mercury expands and rises in the glass tube, it comes in contact with the end of the wire B, then the electric circuit is closed, and the alarm-bell rings. The opening and closing of the circuit by the metallic contact of the point B, and the mercury in the tube, and the entire action of the instrument depend upon the same principles as the electro-magnetic telegraph. A bar of iron wound with insulated wire, so as to be inclosed in a helix, termed an *electro-magnet*, and during the passage of an electric current along the wire and through any metallic things that are in continuous contact, the bar of soft iron exhibits a remarkable degree of magnetic power, which ceases to act when the circuit is broken. When such circuit is formed, we are able to ring bells, raise weights, and let them fall again, by breaking or closing such circuit. In House's Printing Telegraph the magnet is straight, but in Morse's it is in the form of a U.

Temperature of saturated steam; that is, the vapor of water at the point of condensation.	Centigrade degrees of heat of the vapor of water at the point of condensation.	CORRESPONDING ELASTIC FORCE.			Total heat, or the latent heat added to the sensible heat above 0° Fah.
		In inches of mercury.	In atmospheres.	In millimetres of mercury.	
F. 32°	C 0°	0.1811	0.006	4.60	1123.70
50	10	0.3606	0.012	9.16	1129.10
68	20	0.6846	0.023	17.39	1134.68
86	30	1.2421	0.042	31.55	1140.16
104	40	2.1618	0.072	54.91	1145.66
122	50	3.6212	0.121	91.98	1151.06
140	60	5.8578	0.196	148.79	1156.64
158	70	9.1767	0.306	233.09	1162.04
176	80	13.9621	0.466	354.64	1167.62
194	90	20.6869	0.691	525.45	1173.02
212	100	29.9212	1.000	760.00	1178.60
230	110	42.3374	1.415	1075.37	1184.00
248	120	58.7116	1.962	1491.28	1189.58
266	130	79.9321	2.671	2030.28	1194.98
284	140	106.9930	3.576	2717.63	1200.56
302	150	140.9930	4.712	3581.23	1205.96
320	160	183.1342	6.120	4651.62	1211.54
338	170	234.7105	7.844	5961.66	1216.52
356	180	297.1013	9.929	7546.39	1222.56
374	190	371.7590	12.425	9442.70	1227.92
392	200	460.1943	15.380	11688.96	1233.50
410	210	560.9673	18.848	14324.80	1238.90
428	220	684.6584	22.882	17390.36	1244.48
446	230	823.8723	27.535	20926.40	1249.88

I have no hesitation to state this is the best gage or safety-alarm ever invented. Out of repair it cannot get; it requires no attention; it will cost little, and cannot be disturbed by unthinking or careless hands. I may add that, with a thick and rather short wire, a battery of one or two pairs of cups is best, but with a long and fine wire a number of pairs of cups should be employed. A small electro-magnet will hold up a large weight of iron about its poles, which will fall when the flow of the current is stopped. All other safety-valves and gages are well-adapted to show the elastic force of the steam, but do not show its heat—the most important element. After a very short time, and having observed any other gage standing at its ordinary working pressure, a degree of force may be developed by heat to cause an explosion. An engineer cannot be all the time watching the safety-valves and gages. Dunn's gage remedies all these defects. Indeed, a series of points might be introduced into the tube, like the point B, so that the alarm-bell may ring at different stages of the pressure; then there must be more wires than one. The author of this work, Mr. Oliver Byrne, has invented a new arrangement that indicates every degree at any distance; he has also discovered that the true cause of the explosion of boilers is the introduction of *the medium of space.* The theory of this *medium* was first made known in the *London Polytechnic Journal,* by Mr. Pasley, of the Island of Jersey, on the coast of France. The lightest of all the gases is hydrogen, and when it is highly heated, the *medium of space* is admitted and an explosion follows. When the steam from the upper cock has a blue appearance, there is danger, for the blue appearance shows the presence of hydrogen gas sufficiently heated to admit the *medium of space.* The flame of this gas is light blue, and is said to burn when it comes in contact with oxygen. Lieut. W. D. Porter, U. S. N., rightly observes that, as it is the lightest of all the gases, and rises to the upper part of the steam-jacket, a pipe could be introduced to conduct it to the engine-room, where the fireman or engineer could occasionally try the cock and ascertain its formation by the color of the jet. Should the jet appear of a blue cast, or should our bell sound the alarm, by having this pipe continued overboard, and under the water line, the gas could be allowed to escape through this tube, and then steam would take its place in the boiler. When the boiler is supplied with an insufficient quantity of water to compensate for that which is converted into steam, the water within is lowered, and the steam takes a temperature that has not a corresponding elastic force, as the moisture sufficient to supply the proper density is denied. Of this, the ordinary safety-valve gives no indication, and if it be opened it will produce an explosion; the steam rushes out in a conical form, the base uppermost; this leaves a space in the centre of the cone, through which the *medium* of space enters, by supplying the required oxygen, and when the medium of space enters, no known strength can prevent an explosion. An explosion may be produced without raising the safety-valve, for a supply of water suddenly introduced will produce the same effect.

WRIGHT'S ROTARY ENGINE.

PLATE VII.

THE engraving, Plate VII., represents a rotary engine recently invented by Benj. H. Wright, Esq., of New York, and by him denominated "The Revolving Piston Engine." The scientific arrangement, together with its simplicity and compactness, impresses us so favorably, as to lead us to introduce it to the patrons of this work.

Fig. 1, is an end view. Fig. 2, also an end view, but of the opposite or reverse end. Fig. 3, a side view. Fig. 4, a middle section at right angles to the shaft. Fig. 5, exhibits the fixtures, on an enlarged scale, designed to regulate the velocity of the pistons. These several views will give a clear idea, without an extended description.

The inventor has certainly devoted much study to the subject, thus to have avoided many difficulties, which attach to previous inventions of the same class. He begins by adopting, as an essential element, a limited height for the annular chamber; since this has to be rapidly traversed by the steam-stops, or abutments. The floats or pistons (using analogous terms) are two in number, placed diametrically opposite each other, to preserve a due equilibrium under the action of the steam.

The pistons may be attached to a drum, which extends the entire width of the annular chamber, or else they are firmly fixed to a centre wheel of limited thickness, and the remaining surface, which constitutes the inner surface of the chambers, is formed by two cylinders cast with the heads respectively, and projecting so as to reach the centre or piston-wheel. Hitherto, it has been found necessary to insert metallic packing-rings in the cylinder ends, these rings being forced by springs against the wheel. The inventor of the present engine makes use of a different method. He employs a double cylinder on one or both sides of the centre wheel, the larger concentric, and sliding on the smaller, is, by means of set screws, placed in the heads or some equivalent manner, made to close in upon the piston-wheel sufficiently to prevent the egress of steam, and yet allow the latter to revolve in easy contact. The cylinders, stationary as they are during the operation of the machine, sustain the pressure of the valves so completely, that the piston-wheel is not retarded in its movement, the surface of the latter and the valves promptly adapting themselves to each other.

In order to show how the equilibrium is maintained by double pistons, and placing them diametrically opposite, we will illustrate it by reference to the action where only one is used. Like many other improvements, that appear most simple when pointed out, the previous impediment has been singularly overlooked, for, in the descriptions of the whole genus tribe of rotary engines, we have never seen the least allusion to this obvious defect, where the equilibrium is not so maintained. We will take the most favorable case, that of the centre wheel; we will give to this a supposed thickness of one inch and a half. Now the steam being "let on," the latter is of course confined between the piston and an abutment. Suppose the piston to have attained a distance of 12 inches from the abutment, measured on the chord of the arc. There will then be a surface of the wheel equal to 18 square inches, exposed to the action of the steam. Calling the pressure 60 lbs. to the inch, gives a total of 1080 lbs. weight of steam inevitably on to the shaft, or some equally objectionable part of the machine, and, as a consequence just so much more friction to be overcome. The use of opposite pistons and contemporaneous action removes the difficulty in an easy and scientific manner.

The valve employed is described by the inventor as the double oscillating, having two opposite wings, nevertheless retaining the advantage of a single wing by the use of a cylindric surface between the wings on the side adjacent to the piston channel. A like cylindric surface on the opposite side facilitates the introduction of a partition and separate chamber adjacent to the outer wing. The valves are hollow, forming a steam passage, the entrance of which is near the periphery, and leading from the annular chamber. The operation is in this wise. The pistons having passed the valves, the passage through the latter becomes uncovered, so that the steam which has been following the piston finds its way through the valves, and, the place of issue being opposite to the plane face of the cylinder, or valve-seat, this force comes in aid of the entering steam, acting on the opposite wing, to produce the revolution of the valve athwart the piston channel, promoted, moreover, by the removal of the resistance in the detached chamber, either vacuum or air-chamber. Just as the valve terminates its movement, the exhaust passage is uncovered, as will be readily comprehended.

The additional pair of valves is designed, as will have been comprehended, to work alternately and maintain the pressure on the piston. And the utility of the combined action on the valve which we have described, will be rightly estimated when it is perceived that the valves in the present arrangement make their revolutions in a full cylinder (technically speaking), and not in an exhausted one, as has been hitherto almost invariably the case. As each pair of valves comes into position athwart the channel, the alternate pair is relieved, and having an exhaust passage open on either side, becomes equipoised and is withdrawn from the channel by means of tappets and friction rollers, riding easily up the inclined surface of an exterior cam wheel.

The cut-off valves are hollow cylinders, the steam from the boiler having free ingress. Slits or apertures are cut to correspond with the steam-ports in the valve-caps. The inner cylinders are nicely fitted to outer concentric ones, in contact with which they rotate, actuated by means of their axis and eccentrics attached to the main shaft. We here discover a new feature, which constitutes this the most simple and effectual balance-valve; inasmuch as before any openings are made in the cylinder, the pressure of the steam is alike on all sides; when a portion of the surface is removed, the pressure becomes unequal. To restore the equilibrium, the inventor takes from the point directly opposite the same extent of surface; and then the valve will again rotate perfectly free and easy.

A wide aperture and considerable angular movement of the lever of the valve, will permit the steam to be passing in, to any desired extent, of the movement of the piston; and *vice versa;* a short throw enables the engineer to use steam to any degree of expansion, precisely analogous to the common reciprocating engine. In connection with this portion of the machine the inventor has arranged a simple self-adjusting cut-off.

This is a sliding eccentric disk moving between two stationary hubs, the disk being operated by two rods, the plane of which is inclined to the shaft, fixed at their extremities to two sliding collars. The remaining details will be readily comprehended without farther description.

The foregoing is all the space we can conveniently devote to the description of this machine. It is evidently an advance in the numerous attempts to procure a direct rotary motion, and we hope, as successful as it promises; for, we repeat it, it is the best combination of principles aiming at this result that we have seen.

Although the rotary steam-engine is as yet greatly inferior to the common reciprocating crank engine, yet many talented men, like Mr. Wright, have persevered in their attempt to perfect, and successfully to apply, the rotary principle of the steam-engine; and we are of opinion that such attempts should be encouraged and hailed with approbation, rather than treated with abuse and contempt. The experience of human life has shown that, however defective a theory may appear at one epoch in the short existence of man—sometimes by chance, and sometimes by perseverance—inventions have attained maturity, and come into extensive use, which were perhaps at first all but condemned.

LOCOMOTIVES.

Plate IX.

The locomotive, Plate IX., by Baldwin, is designed for heavy draft. It is constructed with eight driving-wheels, and its improvement consists in having a flexible truck arrangement under the front part, composed of a beam under each of the side frames. These are secured to the frames by pins with spherical ends, resting in dies, or cups, that are supported by springs suspended within the beams. In the ends of these beams are fitted vertical cylinder-boxes, in which the journals of the axles are confined and revolve. The axles and the beams form a hollow square, jointed at the corners by the cylinder-boxes in the beams, on which the beams turn. By this arrangement, the axles are at all times at right angles to the centre line of the engine, and constantly parallel to each other; whilst, by drawing the wheels back and forth across the track, the truck changes from a square to a diamond form.

Thus it will be seen that this truck does not turn on a centre pin upon entering a curve (as in the common car truck), but operates precisely on the principle of the parallel rule, the centres of the beams being held secure by the pins in the frames, whilst the ends vibrate with the wheels as they move laterally to fit the curve. These beams act as equalizers of the weight on the wheels, and of the lateral strain while curving, and, not being connected (except by the axles), are left independent in their vertical action, so that either of the wheels can freely rise and fall as the occasion may require.

To the ends of the connecting-rods are also provided cylindrical boxes, with sliding gibs suited to the curve, and keys to take up as they wear. This arrangement enables the engine to conform freely to the curvatures of the road, and distributes the lateral strain equally on the truck wheels. Thus, if the engine enters a curve, the flanges of the outer wheels of the truck come in contact with the rail, while the centrifugal force of the engine is exerted on the pins in the centre of the beams, and is divided equally on these two wheels instead of on the one forward wheel, as in the common mode.

This is an important saving of the wear and tear of the road, for, by a calculation it will be seen that an engine weighing twenty tons, and running at a velocity of fifteen miles per hour, through a curve of five hundred feet radius, will produce a strain on the outer rail (caused by the tendency of the engine to proceed in a straight line) of three thousand pounds; this, added to the force of about thirty-five hundred pounds, necessary to slide the wheels crosswise on the rails, while curving, make a total lateral strain of six thousand five hundred pounds, which, by this arrangement is resisted by two wheels against the rail, whereas, in the common mode of construction with fixed pedestals and slip journals, or flat wheels on the intermediate shafts, the whole of this strain is resisted by the one forward wheel against the outer rail, being very destructive of the road, and producing a great tendency on the part of the wheel to mount the rail.

This arrangement, it will be perceived, reduces this strain fifty per cent., and obviates the tendency of the wheels to get off of the rails, while the running geer being perfectly flexible, will accommodate itself to every inequality of the road.

These engines, and others, with six driving-wheels, built by M. W. Baldwin, of Philadelphia, on the same plan, were the first locomotives ever built, wherein the adhesion of the whole weight of the engine was used for traction, without the use of geering, and in durability and simplicity they have never been surpassed.

Thirty of these engines were placed on the Philadelphia and Reading Railroad, in 1843, 1844, and 1845, most of which are still in use there, and they have done more labor and with less cost for repairs than any other plan of engines now in existence.

HIGH PRESSURE STEAM-ENGINE,

WITH

SIXTEEN INCH CYLINDER AND FOUR FEET STROKE.

BY J. T. SUTTON & CO., FRANKLIN IRON WORKS, PHILADELPHIA.

PLATE VI.

THE form of engine delineated in Plate VI., was introduced by Messrs. Sutton & Co., about eight years ago, and has since that time, become very popular among the manufacturers of Philadelphia and the neighborhood, on account of the simplicity and elegance of its general arrangement, as well as the uniform steadiness with which it performs its duties.

The distinctive feature of this kind of engine is the single column employed to support the pillow-blocks for the main centre of the beam. The single column here performs the whole work usually devolved upon a framing composed of six columns, and having thus to receive and sustain both longitudinal and lateral pressures, it is consequently of a massive character, and thus communicates to the engine a compact and solid appearance.

This increase of bulk in the column is made available as a heater for supplying the boiler with water at a high temperature, thus dispensing with the unwieldy plate-iron appendage attached to engines of the ordinary construction.

The cylindrical form not being best adapted to withstand the strains to which the column is subjected, the latter is connected to the cylinder by means of a neat diagonal stay, or bracket, which, besides strengthening the framework, serves as a guide for the upper end of the governor spindle.

As a means of further steadiness, the entablature is extended towards the cylinder, to which it is again connected by the two crosshead guides.

An experience of eight years has fully proved this arrangement of framework to be free from all jarring or tremor, so common to most beam engines, being even more steady than the elaborate and expensive frame composed of six columns.

Reference to Plate.

Fig. 1 is a side elevation.
Fig. 2, an end view looking towards the cylinder.
Fig. 3 is a section on the line *a* B, Fig. 1, looking from the crank end of the engine.
Fig. 4 is a sectional view of the cylinder and valves.
Fig. 5 shows the face of the valve chest, with the openings for the admission of steam.
Fig. 6 is a section of the piston.
Fig. 7, a plan of the piston with the cover removed, to show the internal arrangement of screws, springs, &c.
Fig. 8, a front view of the governor to an enlarged scale.
Fig. 9, a side view of the same.

The same letters on each figure refer to similar parts throughout.

The base-plate A is a box-shaped casting with two cross-ribs near the centre, where it is enlarged in width for the reception of the column B. Eight bolts, *a a*, pass through the lower flanch of the column's base, through the foundation-plate A, and thence through the masonry, or brickwork, which forms the foundation, to the lower course of which they are secured by means of suitable cast-iron washers. Thus the bolts serve the double purpose of securing the column to the foundation-plate, and of holding down both firmly to the masonry. The cylinder C rests with its bottom flanch (which is square) on the top of the foundation-plate, and is attached thereto by means of the foundation-bolts, *b b*, which likewise pass through the masonry. On referring to Fig. 4, it will be seen that the cylinder is inclosed at the bottom by a cover totally independent of the foundation-plate, against which the square bottom flanch alone of the cylinder comes in contact.

At the crank end of the engine a projection extends outward from the foundation-plate on which rests the crank-shaft pedestal D, which has four bolts, *c c*, passing through it, through the foundation-plate, and through the masonry. The bolts *c c* have a double set of nuts, one set immediately below the pedestal cap, and another above, so that the pedestal and foundation-plate may be screwed firmly to the masonry without interfering with the cap. At the corners of the crank end of the base-plate are two additional holding-down bolts, which, with those already referred to, form ample security for attaching the whole engine to the masonry.

The two entablatures D^1 and D^2 to which the main centre pedestals E are cast, are secured to the top flanch of the capital B^1, which is cast in one piece with the column B, by means of the bolts *d*, as well as by the pedestal bolts, *e e*. A continuation F of the entablature is attached to D^1 by an internal flanch, and, passing round the end of the beam (so as to allow the latter to work freely), is similarly secured to D^2 on the opposite side. This projecting portion of the entablature is supported by the two crosshead guides G and B^1, which are bolted at the top to the inside of F, and at the bottom rest on, and are so secured to lips cast on the top flanch of the cylinder.

The diagonal brace or stay H is connected at the bottom to a preparation cast on the top of the cylinder, and to a similar preparation on the column, and at the top to the capital, thus tying the whole together in a firm and substantial manner.

The beam consists of two plates, I and I^1, of cast-iron, with recesses in their faces, as shown in the drawing. Round the outside edges are shrunk on endless wrought-iron bands, to give the beam additional strength. The two plates are maintained at the required distance apart by means of two cast-iron stays, which fit true to facings inside the plates, and through both pass the rivets, *ff*, which secure the whole firmly together. At the centre, and at each end of the plates, are raised bosses or hubs for the reception of the main centre shaft J, and the link and connecting-rod pins K and K^1. The holes in these hubs, as well as that at L, which receives the pin for working the feed-pump, are octangular, and that part of the different pins which pass loosely through their respective holes has flat sides filed on their circumference, so that keys may be driven between the sides of the octangular holes and the pins. This plan is adopted on account of the facility which it affords for setting the pins true after the two plates of the beam are riveted together.

The openings in the sides of the beam and the ends of the pins are covered by polished brass plates.

The cylinder C, shown in section at Fig. 4, is furnished with the ordinary short slide-valve *m*, round the back of which passes a wrought-iron strap; into the top of the latter is screwed the valve-spindle *l*, which passes through a stuffing-box in the valve-chest O. Attached to this valve is the casing or nozzle P, which is in immediate communication with the steam-pipe.

Inside the casing P, and against the outside facing of the valve-chest O is the valve *p*, which is constructed to cover or expose the openings in the face of the chest, as shown in Fig. 5, as the steam may require to be admitted to, or cut off from the cylinder.

The valve *p* is operated upon by the handle *q*, which works in brass guides secured to the top of the casing: this handle is connected to a small spindle, which passes through a stuffing-box in the casing, and has its end, which is let into the valve *p* square, so that while the pressure of the external steam has a tendency to keep it pressed to the face of the valve-chest, the square portion of the spindle allows it to be turned partially round with facility.

The piston, shown in Figs. 6 and 7, is in construction somewhat similar to others extensively used in this country and in Europe. It consists of a metal disk with four projections on its face to receive the screws which attach it to the cover. These projections are connected to the central hub *u*, which receives the end of the piston-rod R, by four arms, and between these arms are four screws *v*, which have square ends let a little distance into similar-shaped holes in the hub, to prevent them from turning; two nuts on the screws *v* press against the hub, one nut serving to extend or withdraw the screw, and the other for jamming the former when required. The ends of the screws are partially let into and press against the backs of the elliptical springs *w*, and these again force outwards the two cast-iron internal rings, which likewise carry with them the three brass external rings.

Both brass and iron rings are cut entirely through at one place, so as to allow them to expand, care being taken, on placing the rings, that the opening caused by this cut in one ring does not coincide with a similar opening in a neighboring ring; otherwise steam might be admitted into the interior of the piston.

It will be at once seen that when the piston-rings do not bear sufficiently hard against the interior of the cylinder, all that is requisite is, to remove the cover and turn the nuts, in such a manner as to force the springs flatter, which will naturally expand the separate piston-rings.

The eccentric S is a plain metal disk keyed on to the crank-shaft, with ledges on its periphery, to confine the eccentric straps T and T^1; the latter are of cast-iron, one of them T, having a hollow projection for the reception of the eccentric rod U, with a key passing through both and securing them firmly together.

The straps T and T^1 have two lugs, through which the ends of the stays V pass, a nut being on the outside of each lug to keep the straps together. The stays V^1 extend to the middle of the rod, and are secured thereto by means of a bolt passing through both.

The end of the eccentric rod is furnished with a hooked bearing, in such a manner that, by the assistance of the handle *y*, the rod may be in a moment unshipped from the pin on the lever W; the latter is secured to the rock-shaft X, which has two small levers with pins attached, and to these pins are connected the lower ends of the valve-rods Y, the upper ends working on the crosshead to which the valve-spindle is secured.

The rock-shaft X has an oblong hole at the middle for receiving a starting-bar, when it is necessary to move the valves by hand, and to bring the eccentric hook into gear with the line on the lever W.

The governor (enlarged views of which are shown in Figs. 8 and 9), has its spindle, 1, resting on a small column fastened to the foundation-plate; in the same column a horizontal shaft, 2, has its bearing, the two shafts being geered together by means of the mitre-wheels 3. The shaft 2 has another bearing near the edge of the foundation-plate, outside of which it has a pulley 4, which is driven by means of a strap from a similar pulley, 5, on the crank-shaft. A forked lever, 6, which has pins resting between the flanches on the circular brass slide, which is operated upon by the governor-balls in the usual manner, has its fulcrum on the shaft 7, to which it is attached; this shaft vibrates in bearings on two small columns 8, secured to the bottom flanch of the cylinder, and on the outside of one of these bearings it has a lever, 9, keyed to it, which is connected to the throttle-valve lever 10 by means of a light rod 11. The throttle-valve lever is furnished with an adjustable slide to which the end of the rod 11 is attached, so that the effect of the motion communicated by the governor to throttle-valve may be varied at pleasure. The governor itself varies but little in point of principle from many now in use; it may be remarked, however, that, by constructing the pendulum and raising-rods round instead of flat, a much more light elegant appearance is given to it, at the same time greater facility in point of construction is obtained.

The feed-pump S is attached to one of the crossbars of the foundation-plate, as seen on reference to Fig. 3, and is of ordinary construction. The plunger is worked by a rod having an ordinary stub end working on the pin L in the beam, and is forked near the plunger, to which it is connected by means of a taper-pin; the plunger has a continuation which passes through a guide fixed to the column. The column B is so inclosed at top and bottom as to become a steam-tight chamber, into which the waste steam is admitted; the latter is carried off through another pipe not shown in drawing, which passes through the foundation into the inside of the column, near the top of which it terminates. A supply of cold water, obtained from any convenient source, is maintained to the heater, whence it is withdrawn, at an increased temperature, through the pipe X^1 and valves X^2 into the pump, and then discharged towards the boiler through the pipe X^3.

The fly-wheel, connecting-rod, crosshead link, and other portions of the engine, not described, are of the ordinary construction, and require no further reference, as the plate itself will furnish any information required.

General Dimensions.

	Feet.	Inches.
Diameter of cylinder		16
Length of stroke	4	
Diameter of piston-rod		$2\frac{7}{8}$
Size of steam openings		$7\frac{1}{2}\times1\frac{1}{2}$
Size of exhaust openings		$7\frac{1}{2}\times2\frac{1}{2}$
Lap of valve		$\frac{3}{4}$
From outside edge to outside edge of steam-ports		$8\frac{1}{4}$
From centre of cylinder to centre of valve-spindle		$15\frac{1}{2}$

	Feet.	Inches.
Movement of valve		4
Length of crosshead link	3	$1\frac{1}{4}$
Diameter of crosshead at small . . .		3
Crosshead bearing, 4 inches in diameter, 5 broad.		
Bearing of link on beam, 3 inches in diameter, 5 broad.		
Length of connecting-rod, 10 inches in diameter, $9\frac{3}{4}$ broad.		
Bearing at beam, 3 inches in diameter, 5 broad.		
Bearing at crank-pin, $3\frac{7}{8}$ inches in diameter, 6 broad.		
Diameter of connecting-rod at small, 3 inches.		
Length of beam from link to connecting-rod centres	12	
Diameter of fly-wheel	16	
Diameter of crankshaft bearing - . . .		9
Breadth of do.		$14\frac{3}{4}$
Diameter of feed-pump		$3\frac{1}{2}$
Stroke of do.		$16\frac{1}{2}$

HORSE-POWER.

If the steam in the cylinder C, Fig. 4, have a mean or constant pressure of 40 lbs. to the square inch, and if 40 lbs. be placed on every square inch of the circular area of the piston, which is the same as the area of the circular section of the cylinder, then the elastic force of the steam would just be able to move the piston with its weights through the length of its stroke in opposition to the force of gravity. Hence, the work done by the steam on one square inch of the piston in one stroke, will be the pressure of the steam upon one inch multiplied by the number of feet in the stroke, and the work done by the steam on the whole piston will be the work upon one inch multiplied by the number of square inches in the circle of the piston. In the high-pressure engine, the pressure of the atmosphere is about 14.7 lbs. to the square inch, and is opposed to the pressure of the steam. There is also a considerable portion of the steam required to overcome the friction of the moving parts of the engine. From $\frac{3}{4}$ to $1\frac{1}{4}$ lbs. to the square inch is allowed for the friction due to the engine when unloaded; and from $\frac{1}{8}$th to $\frac{1}{10}$th the effective pressure for the resistance necessary to overcome the friction of the loaded engine. In the example before us, let 1 lb. to the square inch be allowed for the friction of the engine when unloaded, and $\frac{1}{7}$th the useful or effective pressure for the resistance necessary to overcome the friction of the engine when loaded; and let the number of strokes be 22 the minute; what is the effective horse-power?

10

```
      lbs.
From 40   given by the indicator,
Take  1   friction of the engine.
     ---
     39
     14.7 pressure of atmosphere.
     ----
     24.3
        7 — 1⅐th = ⅞th.
     ----
   8)170.1
     -----
     21.26 lbs. effective pressure of the
```

steam on the square inch.

Diameter of the cylinder being 16 inches, the area is 201.06 square inches.

```
201.06 × 21.26 = 4274.5356
Length of stroke           4 feet.
                 ----------------
                 17098.1424
Strokes a minute         22
                 ----------------
                  341962848
                 341962848
                 ----------------
                 376159.1328
```

$\frac{376159.1328}{33000} = 11.4$ effective horse-power of the engine, nearly. If 119.7 lbs. be the pressure given by the indicator, then 51 will be the horse-power, nearly.

A unit of work is equal to the labor required to raise 1 lb. through the height of one foot; hence, a unit of work is done if 1 lb. pressure is exerted in any direction through a space of 1 foot. And if 5 lbs. be raised 3 feet perpendicularly, 15 units of work are done. Kane Fitzgerrald estimated that a horse could perform 33,000 units of work in a minute, or raise 1000 lbs. 33 feet high in a minute; or, which is the same work, to raise 33,000 lbs. one foot high in the same time. It may be observed that, in the condensing engine, the pressure of the vapor in the condenser, must be taken instead of the atmospheric pressure. This pressure varies from 3 to 5 lbs. on the square inch. Let L be the load, then $L + \frac{1}{8} L + 1 + 4 =$ the total pressure of the steam in the cylinder, which may be ascertained by the indicator. In this formula, we have taken $\frac{1}{8}$th the effective pressure, or useful load, for the resistance necessary to overcome the friction of the loaded engine, 4 lbs. for the pressure of the vapor in the condenser, 1 lb. for the friction due to the engine. See page 76.

BOILER AND FOUNDATION

ARRANGED FOR A

HIGH-PRESSURE ENGINE WITH 16 INCH CYLINDER AND 48 INCH STROKE.

BY J. T. SUTTON & CO., FRANKLIN IRON WORKS, PHILADELPHIA.

PLATE XIII.

IN Plate XIII. are represented four views of Messrs. Sutton and Co.'s arrangement of high-pressure boilers, of a size requisite for the beam-engine shown in Plate VI.

Fig. 1, is a front elevation at the firing end.

Fig. 2, a longitudinal section through the middle boiler.

Fig. 3, a cross section through the line AB.

Fig. 4, a plan with the upper brickwork removed.

The boilers, which are 40 feet long, and 3 ft. 6 in. diameter, are supported in the middle and at the chimney end on the brick piers A and B. In order that they may expand or contract without injuring these piers or displacing the fire-front, cast-iron saddles, *a a*, are placed under the boilers, and between these saddles and a plate on the top of the piers, intervene small cast-iron rollers *b b*.

The front of the boilers rests on the framework, which forms the fire-front. This frame consists of two horizontal plates, C and D; on the top one, *e* C, are cast curved projections for the reception of the ends of the boilers, a groove being left in the curved-bearing surface, for the reception of the projecting rivets, as seen in Fig. 2. The plates C and D are connected together by the box-shaped castings E. On these are cast small lugs, to which are hung the fire-doors F, and the whole is supported on the three columns G, which rest on a cast-iron plate, H, laid on the foundation.

I I are two cast-iron plates built partially into the wall on each side of the fire-front, and to these are bolted the horizontal plates C and D, the foundation-plate H, and the cornice K. In order that the fire-front may have no tendency to lean outwards, two bars of iron L L, shown in dotted lines (Fig. 4), are connected to the frame by the same bolts which tie the plates C and D to the upright plates I I, the other ends of the bars being bent and built into the brickwork.

Two fluted pilasters M are secured to the side plates I, and on the top rests the cornice K. Both the pilasters and cornice have small flanges, to which are bolted a plate-iron casing which covers the space confined between the plate C and the cornice, and between the two pilasters, holes being left in the plate for the boiler-heads.

The fire-bars N, are supported at the back on a bar of iron built into the wall on each side of the boilers and resting on the bridge O, a similar bar supporting the front of the grate. Between the front of the fire-bars and the dead-plate P, which is likewise built into each side wall, a small space intervenes, so that the expansion of the bars may have no tendency to dislodge the brick bridge.

The boilers are furnished with safety-valve gage-cocks, feed and blow-off pipes, throttle-valve, damper, &c., in the usual manner.

Suppose the diameter of a cylinder-boiler is 42 inches, and that it is to be formed from iron of a tenacity that will bear 50,000 lbs. to the square inch direct strain, what ought to be the thickness of the metal, or boiler-plate, to sustain 400 lbs. pressure on the square inch. 400 lbs. is supposed to be the pressure of the steam.

$$\frac{42 \times 400}{2 \times 50{,}000} = 168; \text{ nearly } \tfrac{1}{6}\text{th of an inch.}$$

This rule is simple, and may be applied to other boiler and various kinds of metal.

ENGINES OF THE STEAM-SHIP BENJAMIN FRANKLIN.

PLATES XI. AND XII.

IN Plates XI. and XII. are represented several views of the above engines, which were manufactured by Messrs. I. P. Morris & Co., of the Port Richmond Iron Works, and designed by, and erected under the superintendence of W. A. Inglis, now of the People's Works, Kensington, Philadelphia, for the Philadelphia and Boston Steam-Ship Co.'s packet Benjamin Franklin.

The cylinders are placed immediately over, and in a line with the propeller-shaft, and supported on two inclined standards bolted to the base-plate.

One of these standards is cast hollow, and serves as an exhaust pipe, communicating at the top with a belt on the cylinder, which receives the waste steam from the valve, and at the bottom with the condenser.

The piston-rod has a crosshead forged into its lower end, which slides in guides fixed to each standard.

Motion is conveyed direct from the crosshead to the crank on the propeller-shaft by a connecting-rod twice the length of stroke.

The hotwell and a portion of the condenser are cast into the hollow standard, and within the former is the air-pump, furnished with gum-valves. The air-pump bucket receives its motion from two levers, which have their fulcrum on two pillow-blocks attached to the side of the hollow standard; these levers are connected at one end by means of links to the pin of the crosshead, and at the other by similar links to the air-pump crosshead.

Attached to the ends of the latter are the plungers of two bilge-pumps, which serve the purpose of slides in maintaining the parallelism of the air-pump rod.

Two feed-pumps are also attached to each hollow standard; these have hollow plungers, which are actuated by rods connected to the same levers which work the air and bilge pumps.

The valves form a distinctive feature of the engines, being so arranged as to cut off steam at any portion of the stroke, by merely changing the position of the link, and thereby altering the movement of the valve as hereafter more fully explained.

The remarkable small space which these engines occupy, the solidity and compactness of the several parts which are at the same time easy of access, and the general excellent effect obtained, ample evidence of which is afforded by the accompanying indicator diagrams, reflect great credit on both designer and builder.

Fig. 1. Plate XI. is a sectional elevation on the line AB, Plate XII. of the engine nearest the propeller.

Fig. 2. A side view of the two engines, one being shown in section on the line BC, Plate XII., the other in elevation looking towards the air-pump.

Fig. 3. Plate XII., a plan of the two engines, one being a section on the line CD, the other on the line DE, Plate XI.

Fig. 4. Is a section on EF (Fig. 2), showing the eccentric link motion, and starting and reversing apparatus.

Fig. 5. Is an enlarged view of a portion of the crosshead, showing the arrangement for taking up the slides when worn.

Fig. 6. A portion of the air-pump bucket, with its metallic packing, &c.

Fig. 7. Part of one of the holding-down bolts, showing the peculiar shape of thread used for screwing into the timbers of the vessel.

The same letters of reference allude to similar parts throughout.

The foundation consists of two cast-iron box-shaped base-plates A, connected together at the middle by a series of bolts, and further secured by wrought-iron hoops *a*, which are fitted into recesses formed in both the upper and lower surfaces of the plates, and, being driven into their places while hot, are allowed to shrink and thus draw the two plates together.

An oblong opening is left in each plate for the

accommodation of the cranks, and on each side of these openings are cast the pillow-blocks for the crank or propeller shaft.

The portion of the base-plate to which the inclined frame B is bolted, is for additional strength made cellular, and the part which reviews the hollow standard C, is so constructed as to form a portion of the condenser.

Immediately under the bearings of the propeller or crank shaft, where the plates necessarily become narrow, additional thickness of metal is given, as shown in Fig. 2.

Holding-down bolts *b*, are placed at suitable intervals, as shown in Fig. 3, on the left-hand side of the plate; on the opposite side are a similar number of bolts not shown in the engraving.

On the top of the inclined standards B and C are planed flanges, for the reception of similar flanges cast on the cylinder D, to which they are bolted. A belt or passage, *c*, passes round the cylinder immediately above the lower flange, and this passage communicates on both sides with the exhaust opening in the face of the cylinder, and with the hollow standard C, which forms the exhaust pipe.

The piston, shown in section at Figs. 2 and 3, is cast hollow with five webs or arms radiating from the centre hub to the rim; the latter receives on its top surface a series of screws, which secure the ring cover *d*, to the body of the piston. In the annular space, thus intervening between the cover and the lower flange of the piston, are two external and one internal ring, all of cast-iron, about half an inch thick, and cut through in one place to allow for expansion, the rings being so situated in regard to each other that the openings caused by the cuts in the rings do not coincide with each other. In order to keep these rings pressed against the inside of the cylinder, small studs are screwed into the edge of the rim, the heads of which are furnished with small projections which fit loosely into holes bored into the elliptical springs (there being a spring to each bolt), and their width is such as to allow them free action in the annular space between the packing rivets and the rim of the piston.

It will be easily seen that on the external rings being worn, the piston in consequence requiring retightening, all that is necessary is to remove the annular cover and turn the small screws so as to give greater rigidity to the springs, which thus press the packing-rings closer to the side of the cylinder.

The piston-rod, F, is secured to the piston by a nut, *g*, which, screwing to the end of the rod, draws its conical end tight into the hub of the piston.

To the end of the piston-rod is forged the crosshead G, this is furnished with brass steps similar to those of an ordinary pillow-block, the lower step being retained in its place by the cap H, through which, and the crosshead, pass the two bolts *h*.

The pin *i* is keyed to the forked end of the connecting-rod I, and is allowed to work loosely between the steps of the crosshead, projecting on each side of the forked crossheads and forged into the pin are bearings for the reception of the links J, connected to the air-pump lever O.

The crosshead is furnished with two brass slides *k*, which have flanges on each side grasping the crosshead; these flanges have oblong holes for the reception of studs, which screw into the side of the crosshead and serve to prevent the slides from any vertical movement; the oval holes, however, allowing them to move outwards towards the slides.

The latter movement is obtained by an arrangement of wedges and screws, which will be best understood on reference to Fig. 5. A wedge *j*, of the same width as the crosshead, intervenes between the latter and the brass slides *k*, a screw *l*, whose thread acts on the top of the crosshead only, passes through the thick end of the wedge, and is retained therein by a collar working inside the wedge and the head of the screw outside; on turning this head in either direction, it is evident that the wedge will be acted upon in such a manner as to either tighten or slacken the slides *k;* the screw is furnished with a tightening nut, on the top, which prevents it from turning, and thereby retains the wedge in its place after the slides have been adjusted.

Cast-iron guides KK, are secured to the inside of the standards B and C, and have projecting flanges, against which work the sides of the crosshead slides *k*.

The lower end of the connecting-rod I, is furnished with an ordinary stub end, having brass steps, gib and cotter, &c., in the usual manner.

The cranks L are cast-iron disks, with flanges raised on their outer edges, on which are shrunk wrought-iron bands; in the centre are the hubs, which fit on to the crank or propeller shafts, and at a suitable distance from the centre are smaller hubs for the crank-pins.

It will be observed on reference to the vertical

section (Fig. 2), that in the crank nearest the propeller, the hub for the reception of the crank-pin has its hole oblong, having two flat surfaces on opposite sides; the crank-pin *n*, where it passes through this hole, has likewise two corresponding planed surfaces, one opposite the other; between these and the plates inside the hub intervene two adjustable wedges *m*, the ends of which are turned up in such a manner that a screw may pass through them into the hub of the crank-pin; by turning these screws, the keys are adjusted as circumstances may require, and retained permanently after adjustment by means of tightening nuts.

The crank on the intermediate shaft M, has the pin *n* secured to it by means of two cone-bearing surfaces, drawn tight into the hub by a nut on the back of the crank.

The crank-pin of the engine furthest from the propeller, is secured to the crank by cones and nuts in a similar manner to the above.

The bearings of the propeller-shaft N, and intermediate shaft M, consists of brass steps, which are let into pillow-blocks cast on to the base-plate, and confined by strong caps, through which pass the bolts *r*; the latter are secured to the base-plate by means of keys, as shown in drawing, and in addition have two nuts beneath the plate.

The air-pump levers O, are of cast-iron, with strong wrought-iron bands shrunk around the outer edge, and are keyed to the rock-shaft P, which has its bearings in two pillow-blocks *p*, situated between the levers O, and bolted to the hollow standard C. The levers are connected at one end to the pin of the piston crosshead *i*, by means of the links J, and at the other end by similar links *o*, to the air-pump crosshead Q, the pins for these links being secured to the levers by means of cone-ends and nuts, in a manner similar to that explained in reference to the crank-pins.

The air-pump rod R, is attached to the crosshead Q, in a similar manner, and after passing through a stuffing-box in the cover of the hotwell S, and through the discharge valve T, is attached to the bucket U, by a cone-end and nut, in the usual manner.

The air-pump V, which is composed entirely of brass, is let into the condenser and bolted to the bottom of the hotwell S; and to the top flange of the air-pump is bolted the seat of the discharge-valve T, which has a flange projecting from its under side, and fitting close to the inside of the pump; this seat is composed of a series of radiating ribs, and a central ring leaving orifices for the passage of the waste water as best seen on reference to the plan, Fig. 3; on the top of the grating thus formed rests, when the bucket descends, the valve *t*, which is a disk of prepared gum-elastic with a hole in the centre sufficiently large to admit, with ease, the hub of the grated guard T, which limits the valve to the required height of perpendicular movement on the ascent of the bucket.

It will be observed that the hub of the greater guard is carried upwards, surrounding the rod R, until it enters the bottom of the stuffing-box in the hotwell cover, thus forming a support for the packing, the pressure given to which by the guide, serves to keep down the hub of the guard in the annular space left for its reception in the centre of the valve-seat. The air-pump bucket U, a portion of which is shown on an enlarged scale, at Fig. 6, is secured to the conical end of the rod R, by the screwed hub of a grated guard, similar to that of the discharge-valve, and a tightening nut on the top.

The upper portion of the bucket has likewise a grating, which forms the seat of a gum-valve.

In the annular space between the bucket and the inside surface of the air-pump, are brass packing rings, each of which are bevelled on their top and bottom edges in such a manner that the outside of the two upper and two lower rings will have a tendency to bear against the internal surface of the air-pump, while the inside of the two middle rings will be pressed against the bucket. It will of course be understood, that these rings are cut through in such a manner that they may expand or contract, as may be required, care being taken that the openings in the rings do not coincide, as remarked in reference to the piston-rings.

It may be here remarked that the above-described system of packing is carried out in the whole of the stuffing-boxes throughout the two engines. The foot-valve W, is similar in principle to the valves already described, and will be easily understood on reference to the drawing.

Note.—It will be remarked, that the area of the grated openings in the foot-valve is less than those in the bucket-valve, and this, again, has less area than the discharge-valve. This arrangement the designer has found, from experience, to work with much less noise and jarring effect to the valves.

The waste water is discharged through the pipe *s*, which communicates immediately with the delivery valve on the side of the vessel.

Cast to each side of the hotwell S, are the two bilge pumps X, the solid plungers of which are connected to the ends of the air-pump crosshead Q. These pumps are furnished with ordinary clack suction-valves contained in boxes x, secured near the bottom of the hotwell, and have discharge-valves of a similar construction bolted to the inside of the hotwell.

YY are the feed-pumps, two being attached to each engine, one on each side of the hollow standard C. These pumps have hollow plungers, with a joint at the bottom, to which is connected the lower end of a rod shown in dotted lines, Fig. 1, the other ends of the rod having an ordinary stub end working on to pins projecting from the outside of the levers O, and secured thereto in a similar manner to that described in reference to the link-pins.

The suction and discharge valves of these pumps are similar to those attached to the feed-pump, the box containing the suction-valve has a branch communicating direct with the hotwell. The heated water is forced down the vertical pipe y, thence through a force-valve into the pipes $y2$, which communicate with the general receiving-pipe Z; the latter is furnished with two plate-iron air-vessels, one opposite each engine; and in the centre, between the engines, with a weighted lever safety-valve of the ordinary construction; the pipe Z, passing round the base-plate of the engine, communicates with the check-valves on the boiler.

The valves, which form a peculiar feature in these engines, are so arranged that one pair of eccentrics to each is not only sufficient to give them the ordinary movement, but have likewise the capability, by suitable alterations in their position, of imparting such an amount of motive power to the valves, as to cut off steam at any stated portion of stroke.

It will be observed on reference to Fig. 2, that the steam and exhaust ports are, although of similar form, considerably larger than those of an ordinary engine of the same power.

The valve 2 has, on the face which works against the cylinder, two small openings near its upper and lower extremities, besides the usual passage in the middle; at the back it has four openings, which communicate with the two openings in front and at the back with ports in the wedge-shaped block 3. The ports in the block, and those in the back of the valve, coincide, at different times, and with different extents of opening, according to the amount of stroke given to the valves.

It will be perceived, on referring to Fig. 3, that the block 3 bears against the bevelled back of the valves, the amount of bearing being regulated by a rod which passes through a stuffing-box in the side of the steam-chest, and furnished outside with a guide and handwheel; the end of the rod screws into a hub, forged in the centre of an elliptical spring 4, which has its ends secured to the top and bottom of the block 3. This spring serves to restrict the wedge-shaped block from any propensity it may have to bind the valves too hard against the faces of the cylinder.

Two guides project, one from the upper and one from the lower cover of the steam-chest, which prevents the block from any vertical, at the same time allowing it the required lateral movement.

When the engines are going, steam is at all times admitted to the interior of the block, as well as the steam-chest, and passes through the three orifices on each face of the block to the ports on the back of the valve, and thence to the cylinder ports at the particular part of the stroke, and to the amount of opening regulated by the extent of movement given to the valves.

The valves themselves are actuated each by two eccentrics working in conjunction with the well-known reversing link, in a manner easily understood, on reference to the detached view, Fig. 4. The eccentrics 5, which have nothing peculiar in their construction from those of ordinary engines, have their rods connected to the ends of the wrought-iron links 6, by forked joints and pins, the valve-spindle, 7, having likewise forked joints, which grasp the link; inside the latter works a steel sliding-block, through which and the forked end of the valve-spindles passes a pin, the whole being so arranged that the link may be moved with ease on the sliding-block. This movement is imparted to the link, and consequently to the eccentrics and their rods, by the two rods 8, which are connected at one end to projections on each side of the links, and at the other end to the short arm of the toothed lever, 9. This lever has its fulcrum on a stay, which serves to bind together the two frames 10, the latter being bolted to the outside of the steam-chest, as shown in Fig. 3. Geering into the teeth of the lever 9, is the pinion 11, which is allowed to run loosely on the shaft 12, the hub of the pinion passing through and having its bearing in the frames 10, on the outside of which, and to the hub of the pinions, are the hand-wheels 13.

In order to retain the links in the position required, small catches 14, fit into the teeth of the lever and slide on a wrought-iron stay 15, which likewise ties together the two frames 10. The centre of the stay is swelled out in order to receive the hub of a hand-wheel 16, which is allowed to turn freely in its bearing.

Two opposite arms of the hand-wheel are connected to the sliding-catches 14, by two small rods, so that, on turning the wheel in either direction, the sliding-catches are admitted to or withdrawn from the teeth of the lever. Passing through and acting independently of the hub of the wheel 16, and the stay 15, is a vertical shaft 17, which is likewise furnished at the top with a hand-wheel situated above the wheel 16, as seen in Fig. 1; this shaft is connected at the bottom by levers and rods somewhat similar to those which actuate the sliding-catches to the two injection-cocks (the internal pipe from which is shown at 18, Fig. 1), so that, on turning the shaft 17, the injection is cut off from or admitted to the condenser of both engines simultaneously.

General Dimensions.

	Inches.
Diameter of cylinders	40
Length of stroke	34
Diameter of piston-rod	5
Diameter of crosshead-pin	5½
Breadth of bearing on crosshead-pin	7
Length of connecting-rod	68
Diameter of crank-pin in engine nearest the propeller	8½
Breadth of bearing on do. do. do.	7
Diameter of crank-pin of forward engine	5½
Breadth of bearing in do. do.	7
Diameter of bearing for crank and intermediate shafts	10
Breadth of do. do. do.	13
Length of links from crosshead to air-pump levers	9½
Diameters of bearing for do. do. do.	2⅝
Breadth of do. do. do. do. do.	3½
Length of links from air-pump lever to air-pump crosshead	12
Diameter of bearing on lever-pin	3¼
Breadth of do. do.	3¾
Diameter of bearing on air-pump crosshead	3¾
Breadth of do. do. do.	3¾
Diameter of air-pump	22
Stroke of do.	17
Diameter of air-pump rod	3½
Diameter of bilge-pumps	5
Stroke of do.	17
Diameter of feed-pump	9
Stroke of do.	7
Diameter of injection-pipes	3½

BOILERS.

The boilers shown in the accompanying woodcut were designed for the engines of the Benjamin Franklin; others, on the well-known Montgomery principle were, however, used in preference.

Fig. 151 is a view of the proposed boilers, showing the fire-pan, and partly in section through the fireplaces.

Fig. 151.

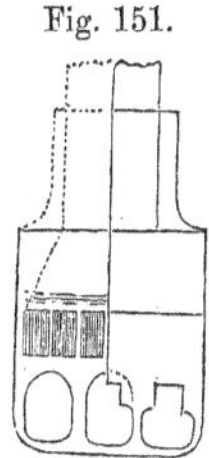

Fig. 152, a view showing the method of firing athwart ship.

Fig. 152.

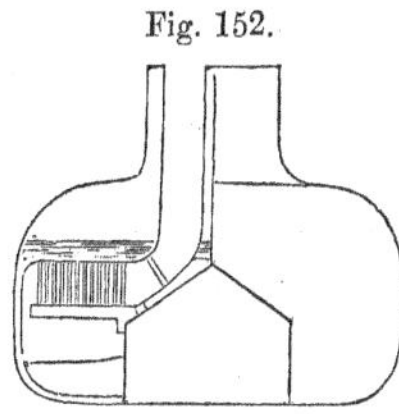

The object of this arrangement of boilers is to gain space, and to obtain a free ventilation fore and aft the ships.

INDICATOR DIAGRAMS OF THE ENGINES OF THE STEAM-SHIP BENJAMIN FRANKLIN.

Fig. 153.

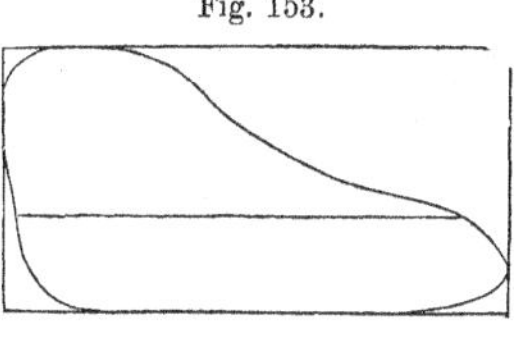

Fig. 154.

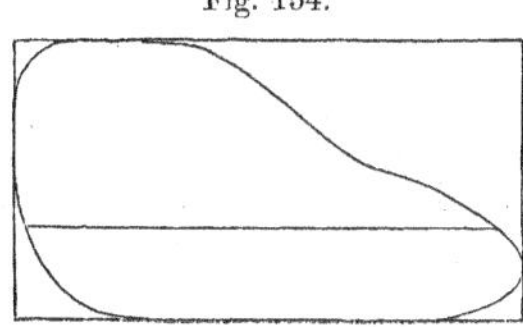

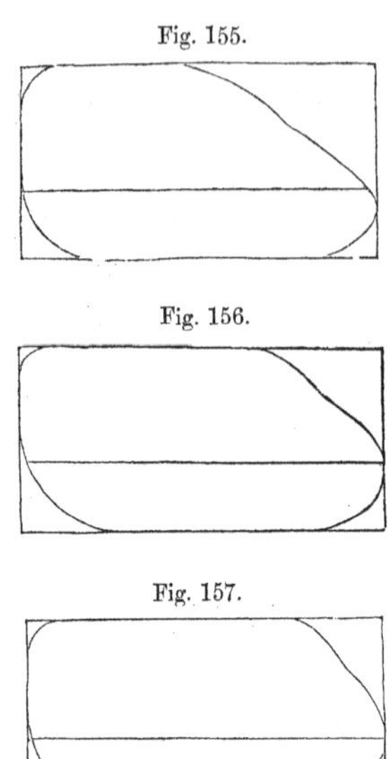

Fig. 155.

Fig. 156.

Fig. 157.

Fig.				
Fig. 153.	Diagram	taken at	$\frac{1}{4}$	the stroke.
154.	do.	do.	$\frac{3}{8}$	do
155.	do.	do.	$\frac{1}{2}$	do.
156.	do.	do.	$\frac{5}{8}$	do.
157.	do.	do.	$\frac{3}{4}$	do.

From the diagram Fig. 153, let the mean pressure of the steam be 46.38 lbs. to the square inch, and 30 the number of strokes the minute, the effective horse-power is required; supposing the pressure of the vapor in the condenser to be 3 lbs. to the square inch of the piston, 1.35 lbs. to be allowed for the friction of the engine when loaded, and $\frac{1}{8}$th the effective pressure or useful load, the allowance for the resistance necessary to overcome the friction of the engine when loaded.

46.38 lbs. given by
1.35 indicator.

45.03
3.00

42.03
$8 — 1\frac{1}{8} = \frac{9}{8}$

9)336.24

37.36

The diameter of the cylinder being 40 inches, its area is 1256.6 square inches.

$\therefore 1256.6 \times 37.36 = 46946.576$

46946.576
$2\frac{10}{12}$ feet, length of stroke.

93893.152
39122.146

133015.298
30 strokes the minute

3990458.940

$$\frac{3990458.94}{33000} = 120.9 \text{ effective horse-power, nearly.}$$

In another place, we show how the indicator is applied; our object in this place is merely to show how the effective power is estimated when the mean effective pressure on the square inch is ascertained. It is well known that the pressure of the steam and the state of the vacuum, on diagrams like Figs. 153, 154, 155, 156, 157, do not correspond with the boiler pressure and condenser vacuum. The truth is, the result will always be less. The difference will depend on the size of the posts, and the work the engine has to do; the distance the steam has to travel, the impediments it meets with in its passage from the boiler to the cylinder, and from the cylinder to the condenser. It is evident that the diagram taken from the top of the cylinder shows only the pressure of the vacuum on the upper surface of the piston, and, therefore, cannot indicate what is going on below the piston. If our object be merely to calculate the *horse-power* of the engine, and it be in good working condition, it is not of much consequence whether the diagram be taken from above or below the piston; but, if the actual state of the engine be required, it is necessary to examine into what is passing both above and below the piston, because the errors in one part may have no connection with the errors in another. This will be the case if the slide is too long or too short, so that the upper part may be properly covered, and the lower one disarranged, or the upper slide may be steam-tight, and the lower one leaky; and if the indicator be applied to the top and bottom, it will detect all these inaccuracies, and prevent our attempting to improve the working of one side to the detriment of the other.

In unbalanced engines, the diagram from one side of the piston is generally superior to that from the other; because, since the steam has more work to accomplish, the piston does not run away from the steam so readily, and, in consequence, the steam pressure is better maintained; and there generally is a little *more* lead to the slide, to allow a freer ingress to the steam. Consequently, if great accuracy be required, the mean pressure obtained from the top and bottom diagrams should be taken, in calculating the effective horse-power. Experiment tells us that, whatever may be the pressure at which steam is formed, the weight of fuel necessary to evaporate a given volume of water is nearly always the same; and, consequently, it is more advantageous to employ steam of a high pressure. It is easily deduced from the formula of M. V. Regnault, that

$$V = \frac{20578}{P^{\frac{40}{43}}} + 13.$$

In which V is the volume of a cubic foot of water, in the form of steam at P lbs. pressure. Suppose the pressure of the steam to be that of the atmosphere, or 14.7 lbs. to the square inch nearly, then the volume V will be $=$ 1701.6 times, which is thus calculated—

$$\begin{array}{lr} Log. - 14.7 = & 1.1673173 \\ & 40 \\ \hline & 43)46.6926920 \\ \hline & 1.0858764 \\ Log.\ 20578 = & 4.3134032 \\ \text{take} & 1.0858764 \\ \hline Log.\ \text{of } 1688.6 = & 3.2275268 \\ \hline \end{array}$$

$1688.6 + 13 = 1701.6$ the volume;

so that a cubic inch of water will nearly form a cubic foot of steam, when the pressure of the steam is nearly equal to that of the atmosphere.

We obtain from the same formula a volume of steam 888 times the bulk of the water from which it is produced, when the pressure on the square inch is 30 lbs. The volume will be 680 when the pressure is 40 lbs., and 555 when the pressure is 50 lbs.; so that the relation between the volume of water and the volume of steam consumed, is readily found when the pressure is known. The young engineer must remember that steam is worked in three different ways: expansively, on the high-pressure principle, and by mere condensation, as in the atmospheric engine. If steam at 212° temperature be allowed to enter the lower part of the cylinder, its pressure will just counterpoise that of the air upon the piston; then, with very little more force, the piston will rise. Then, if the steam be condensed by jets of water, the piston will be pressed down with the whole force of the atmosphere, which is about 15 lbs. to the square inch. But, since water gives off steam at all temperatures, a perfect vacuum cannot be formed in this way. On account of the pressure in the condenser, we cannot obtain more than from 10 to 11 lbs. upon the square inch of the piston in the atmospheric engine. Let it be required to find the units of work that may be done by condensing a cubic foot of water raised into steam of 1700 times the volume, which is about able to overcome the pressure of the atmosphere. The heat of this steam is about 213° Fah.

14.7 lbs. atmospheric pressure.
 3.7 supposed to be the elasticity of the vapor in the condenser.
——
11.0

Hence, 11 lbs. is the effective pressure on the piston. For a moment, we may suppose the area of the piston to be one square foot, then the length of stroke will be 1700 feet. And, since 144 square inches $=$ 1 square foot,

$1700 \times 144 \times 11 = 2692800$ units of work;

and, if these be done in a minute, the horse-power will be

$$\frac{2692800}{33000} = 81.6.$$

Let it be required to find the evaporation of the boiler of an atmospheric-engine, 200 being the horse-power, 4.7 lbs. being allowed for the elasticity of the vapor in the condenser.

$$33000 \times 200 = 6600000$$

the units of work done by the engine a minute. In this case, the work developed by condensing a cubic foot of water is

$$144 \times (14.7 - 4.7) \times 1700 =$$
$$144 \times 10 \times 1700 = 244800$$

$$\therefore \frac{6600000}{2448000} = 2\tfrac{71}{102} \text{ cubic feet of water evaporated}$$

in a minute. It has been found by experiment that from 8 to 10 lbs. of water may be evaporated from a temperature of 212° F. by a pound of Virginia, Maryland, or Pennsylvania coal; so that there exists a fixed relation between the quantities of fuel, steam, and water.

STEAM-PUMPING ENGINE,

ARRANGED FOR

SUPPLYING RAILWAY TANKS WITH WATER,

BY MR. W. A. INGLIS, OF THE PEOPLE'S WORKS, PHILADELPHIA.

The necessity of supplying locomotive tenders with water at stated intervals on a long line of railway, has caused engineers to resort to a variety of means in order that the demand may be at hand and furnished with the least possible delay. The principal, and, in fact, indispensable requisite for this purpose, is a reservoir, or tank, at every watering station; this is generally constructed of iron, and is situated sufficiently high, that the required head of water may be obtained.

The means of keeping a regular supply of water in these tanks, must, of course, vary according to circumstances. Should there be a natural head of water in the neighborhood of, or even at a considerable distance from a watering station, an economical source of filling the tank at once presents itself, or should there be in the vicinity any workshops where power is used, a pump might be worked at comparatively little cost. On nearly all long lines of railway, however, there are situations where it is necessary to locate watering stations, and where neither of the above accommodations are at hand, in which case it becomes necessary to draw the water from a well or other source, and to force it to the required height by steam, or other power, arranged especially for the purpose.

Mr. Inglis's steam-pumping apparatus, shown in Plate VIII., combines, in its general arrangement, as well as in its detailed parts, the qualities of simplicity and neatness; and it is scarcely necessary to add that it is admirably adapted to other, than railway purposes.

Fig. 1, Plate VIII. is a side elevation, showing the frames in section.

Fig. 2, a sectional elevation on the line A B, looking towards the cylinder.

Fig. 3, a plan looking on the top of the pumps with the foundation removed.

Fig. 4, a face-view of the eccentric.

The same letters refer to the same parts throughout the four views.

The foundation consists of two cast-iron beams A A, placed at a suitable distance apart, and connected together at each end by cross-beams, as shown in dotted lines, Fig. 1. These beams are laid across the well B, and built into the sides in such a manner that the tops of the beams and the floor are on the same level. The sole plate C rests on and is secured to the top flanges of the girders A A, and to this plate are bolted the two standards D D, the feet of which are held by keys and lugs cast on the plate. As a further security, the standards D are tied together at the top by means of the stay-bolts *a a*. The cylinder E (the upper flange of which rests on the sole-plate), is of the form usually adopted in high-pressure engines, the piston slide-valve and passages being of the common construction.

The piston-rod F has the crosshead G attached to it, and on this crosshead are forged two pins for the reception of the stub-ends of the forked connecting-rod H. The parallelism of the piston-rod is maintained by the guide I, secured to the standard D; this guide is furnished with a brass bush, through which passes the continuation J, of the piston-rod F. The upper end of the connecting-rod has the usual stub-end which works on the pin of the crank K. Immediately behind the crank is the eccentric L, which, by a neat arrangement, actuates the eccentric-rod in such a manner that its movement is parallel. This will be best understood on referring to Fig. 4. The eccentric has a groove cut into its edge sufficiently wide to admit the two bolts *s*; the bottom of the groove is concentric with the crank-shaft, and is curved so as to fit the bolts, which must, consequently, serve

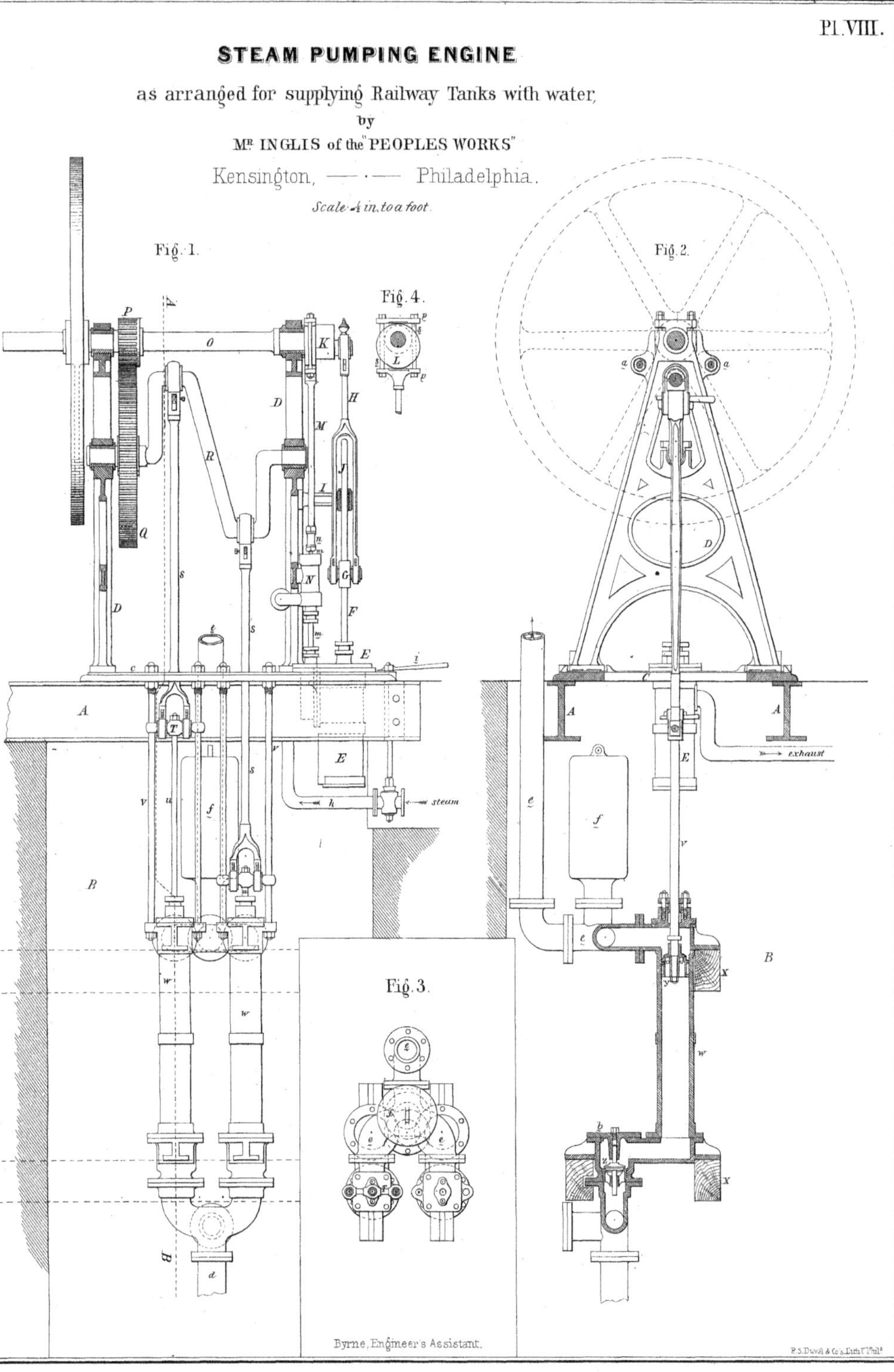
Pl. VIII.
STEAM PUMPING ENGINE
as arranged for supplying Railway Tanks with water,
by
Mr. INGLIS of the "PEOPLES WORKS"
Kensington, — · — Philadelphia.
Scale ¼ in. to a foot.
Fig. 1.
Fig. 2.
Fig. 3.
Fig. 4.
steam
exhaust
Byrne, Engineer's Assistant.
P. S. Duval & Co's. Lith. Phila.

as guides as well as a means of causing the top and bottom plates *p p*, to bear against the eccentric. To the lower of the two plates is attached the eccentric-rod M, which is connected to another rod *m*, by means of a brass-coupling *n*, one rod being screwed into the latter with a left, the other with a right-handed thread, so that, on turning the coupling in either direction, the rod *m* may be adjusted to the greatest nicety. N is the feed-pump secured to the standard D; it is furnished with suction-pipe and valve, and discharge-pipe and valve, in the usual manner.

The pump is open at the top, and has a stuffing-box at the bottom; the rod *m*, to which the plunger is attached, passes through this stuffing-box, and, as will easily be perceived, acts as the valve-spindle.

On the crank-shaft O (which revolves in brass-bearings, let into the frame, and confined by a cap in the usual manner), is keyed the pinion P, geering into the spur-wheel Q, on the double-cranked shaft R (which, likewise, revolves in brass-bearings, attached to the standard D), and actuates the two connecting-rods S.

These rods, which pass through oblong holes in the sole-plate C, are supplied at the top with stub-ends, similar to that on the rod H; the lower ends are forked, and work on the crossheads T, to which are secured the pump-rods *u*. The crossheads slide on the rods V, which are bolted at the top to the sole-plate C, and at the bottom to lugs cast on the pump-barrels, thus answering the double purpose of guiding the pump-rods and of receiving the strain exerted on the pump-barrels on the downward stroke of the plunger. It may be here observed that, in the drawing, the pumps are shown near the top of the well; in some cases, however, they require to be placed some distance down, under which circumstances all that is necessary is to have the guide-rods V, and pump-rods U, made of a length corresponding to the distance between the sole-plate and the pump. The pumps are further supported by beams X, laid across and built into the sides of the well. The plunger, or bucket Y, consists of a brass piston, with common hemp-packing, the top of the piston forming the seat for a conical valve, which is guided by the pump-rod *u*, and confined in its upward movement by a collar forged on the latter. The lower, or suction-valve Z, is likewise of brass, and is guided by the seat, as well as by a projection underneath the cover *b*, a small stud being screwed into the top of the cover for the valve to strike against, so that the rise may be regulated at pleasure. The water is raised through the pipe *d*, which has a branch leading to each pump-barrel, thence on the downward stroke of the bucket it passes through its valve, and on the upward stroke is forced into the pipe *e*, to the height required. Where the two branches of the force-pipe meet, an air-vessel *f*, is situated (see Fig. 3), which serves to regulate the flow of water projected from both pumps.

Steam is admitted to the cylinder through the pipe *h*, which is furnished with a cock, the plug of which is acted upon by a handle *i*, conveniently placed above the sole-plate.

Principal Dimensions.

Diameter of cylinder, 7 in.	Diameter of each pump, 5 in.
Length of stroke, 18 in.	Lift of " 30 in.

STRENGTH OF MATERIALS.

Tenacity of various Materials.

S represents the weight required to break a rod whose cross section a, is one square inch, when pulled in the direction of its length; for rods of other dimensions, the breaking weight $W = S\,a$; the weight of the rod being neglected.

METALS.		*Value of S.*
Cast-steel		134,000 lbs.
Bar-iron	Swedish	72,000
	Salisbury, Conn.	66,000
	Bellefonte, Pa.	58,500
	English	56,000
	Pittsfield, Mass.	57,000
Cast-iron	Pig metal	15,000
	Good, common castings	20,000
	Specimens from gun-heads	24,000 / 39,500
Cast-steel		128,000
Bronze—gun-metal		30,000 / 42,000
Copper, cast (Lake Superior)		24,138
Brass		18,000
Copper	Wrought	34,000
	Cast	19,000
Tin, cast		4,800
Zinc		3,500
Platinum		56,000
Silver		40,000
Gold		30,000
Lead		1,800

WOODS.	*Value of S.*
Ash	15,800
Mahogany	11,500
Oak	11,600
White pine	11,800
Walnut	7,700

In general, the tenacity of metals is increased by hammering and wiredrawing.

The strength of Pittsfield bar-iron, given in the above table, is the mean of four trials, with cylinders 1 in. long and 0.9 in. diameter. They were extended in length, before fracture, to 1.4 in., and they were reduced in diameter to 0.6 in. in the middle.

A bar of wrought-iron is extended about one-hundredth part of its length for every ton of strain on a square inch.

Transverse Strength.

$S=$ the weight in pounds required to break a beam 1 in. square and 1 in. long, fixed at one end and loaded at the other; b the breadth, d the depth, and l the length, in inches, of any other beam of the same material, and W the weight which will cause it to break, neglecting the weight of the beam itself.

1. *If the beam is supported at one end and loaded at the other:*

$$W = S\frac{b\,d^2}{l}$$

2. *If the beam is supported at one end and the load distributed over its whole length:*

$$W = 2\,S\frac{b\,d^2}{l}$$

3. *If the beam is supported at both ends and loaded in the middle:*

$$W = 4\,S\frac{b\,d^2}{l}$$

4. *If the beam is supported at both ends and loaded uniformly over its whole length:*

$$W = 8\,S\frac{b\,d^2}{l}$$

5. *If the beam is supported at both ends and loaded at the distance m from one end:*

$$W = S\frac{l\,b\,d^2}{m\,(l-m)}$$

Values of the coefficient S.

Good English bar-iron . . .	6,150
Cast-iron	7,644
English oak	1,200
Ash	2,025
Pitch pine	1,632
Riga fir	1,128

In practice, about one-half or one-third of these values should be used, in computing the strain to which a beam should be subjected.

Resistance to longitudinal Compression.

$S=$ the weight required to crush a bar 1 inch square, in the direction of its length. The area of the cross section of any other bar being denoted by a, the weight required to crush it is $W = S\,a$; the length of the bar being not more than three times, nor less than once and a half, its breadth.

Practical Formulæ for computing the Weight which a Column will sustain.

b, the side of a square column, in inches;
d, the diameter of a cylindrical column, in inches;
l, the length of the column, in feet;
W, the weight it will sustain, in pounds.

MATERIAL.	SOLID SQUARE COLUMN.	SOLID CYLINDRICAL COLUMN.
Cast-iron . .	$W=\frac{15300\,b^4}{4\,b^2+.18\,l^2}$	$W=\frac{9562\,d^4}{4\,d^2+.18\,l^2}$
Wrought-iron .	$W=\frac{17800\,b^4}{4\,b^2+.16\,l^2}$	$W=\frac{11125\,d^4}{4\,d^2+.16\,l^2}$
Oak	$W=\frac{3960\,b^4}{4\,b^2+.5\,l^2}$	$W=\frac{2470\,d^4}{4\,d^2+.5\,l^2}$

Resistance to Torsion.

$S=$ the weight in pounds required to break, by twisting, a solid cylinder, 1 inch diameter; the weight acting at the distance of 1 in. from the axis of the cylinder; d, the diameter in inches of any other cylinder of the same material; r, the distance from its axis to the point where the breaking weight W is applied, then:—

$$W = S\frac{d^3}{r}.$$

Torsional Strength of Hollow Cylinders.

D the exterior, and d the interior diameter of the cylinder in inches; S, W, and r, as before.

$$W = S\frac{D^4 - d^4}{D\,r}.$$

Relative torsional strength of cast-iron shafts, of different forms, having equal areas of cross sections.

From experiments on shafts whose cross sections were 1, 2, and 3 square inches.

SOLID CYLINDER.	SOLID SQUARE.	Hollow cylinders, whose interior and exterior diameters are in the proportion of				
		4 to 10	5 to 10	6 to 10	7 to 10	8 to 10
1.0000	0.8750	1.2656	1.4433	1.7000	2.0864	2.7377

Values of the Coefficients S for the Strength of certain Metals.

Kind of metal.	Values of S. Tenacity.	Transverse strength.	Compression.	Torsion.	Specific gravity.
	Lbs.	Lbs.	Lbs.	Lbs.	
Cast-iron. Mean results. Common pig-iron	15,000	6,000	—	—	7.000
Cast-iron. Mean results. Good, common casting	20,000	7,500	—	7,000	7.180
Cast-iron. Mean results. Gun-iron, from gun-heads (Boston, and West Point, 1848 and 1849.)	32,000	—	105,000	—	7.280
Cast-iron. Mean results. Gun-iron, cast in small bars	34,000	9,500	130,000	9,000	7.320
Cast-iron. Extremes. Least	9,000	5,000	—	—	6.900
Cast-iron. Extremes. Greatest	39,500	11,500	—	10,000	7.724
Cast-steel	128,000	23,000	—	—	7.846
Wrought-iron. Begins to yield, taking a permanent set	31,000	6,500	40,000	3,600	7.855
Wrought-iron. Ultimate strength	57,000	—	—	—	
Wrought-iron. Bends and endures without breaking	—	—	116,000	7,700	
Bronze. Begins to yield, taking a permanent set	19,000	—	—	2,300	8.710
Bronze. Ultimate strength	42,000	—	—	—	
Bronze. Bends and endures without breaking	—	—	—	5,500	
Cast-copper (Lake Superior), ultimate strength	24,138	—	—	—	8.712

The torsional strains, which the wrought-iron and bronze endured without breaking, twisted the cylinders about 100°.

Weight and Strength of Iron Chains.

The proof weights are computed at the rate of 420 lbs. to one eighth of an inch diameter of the iron for the links.

Diam. of iron for the links.	Weight of 1 foot of chain.	Breaking weight.	Proof weight.
In.	Lbs.	Lbs.	Lbs.
0.1875	0.325	2,240	948
0.25	0.65	4,256	1,680
0.3125	0.967	6,720	2,464
0.375	1.383	9,634	3,584
0.4375	1.767	13,216	5,152
0.5	2.633	17,248	6,720
0.5625	3.333	21,728	8,512
0.625	4.217	26,880	10,304
0.6875	4.833	32,704	12,544
0.75	5.75	38,752	15,232
0.8125	6.667	45,696	17,696
0.875	7.5	51,744	20,384
0.9375	9.333	58,464	23,520
1.	10.817	65,632	26,880

Weight and Strength of Hemp and Iron Wire Ropes.

Hemp rope. Circumference	Hawser-laid 3 strands. Weight of 1 foot.	Hawser-laid 3 strands. Breaking weight.	Cable-laid. Weight of 1 foot.	Cable-laid. Breaking weight.	Iron wire rope. Circumference.	Weight of 1 foot.	Breaking weight.
In.	Lbs.	Lbs.	Lbs.	Lbs.	In.	Lbs.	Lbs.
0.75	0.028	291	....	.....	0.75	0.070	2,240
1.	0.038	560	....	.....	1.	0.125	3,360
1.5	0.087	1,120	....	.....	1.5	0.280	6,160
2.	0.153	2,016	....	.....	2.375	0.680	15,680
2.5	0.238	3,136	....	.....	2.625	0.860	16,800
3.	0.343	4,256	0.301	3,674	3.125	1.230	24,520
3.5	0.467	5,824	0.422	4,480	3.75	1.770	30,244
4.	0.612	7,616	0.552	6,440	4.125	2.140	44,800
4.5	0.773	9,428	0.697	8,154			
5.	0.955	11,872	0.862	10,060			
5.5	1.155	14,336	1.042	12,183			
6.	1.375	17,044	1.240	14,515			
6.5	1.613	19,936	1.455	17,024			
7.	1.872	23,072	1.687	19,712			
7.5	2.148	26,432	1.928	22,400			
8.	2.445	30,016	2.138	25,805			
8.5	2.760	34,048	2.613	29,120			
9.	3.095	38,080	2.850	32,660			
9.5	3.533	42,336	3.088	36,378			
10.	3.822	44,800	3.327	40,320			

THE INDICATOR.

The inventor of this useful instrument is not made known. It is simply a small cylinder, truly bored, into which a piston is inserted and loaded by a spring of suitable elasticity. Fig. 158 is an ele-

Fig. 158. Fig. 159.

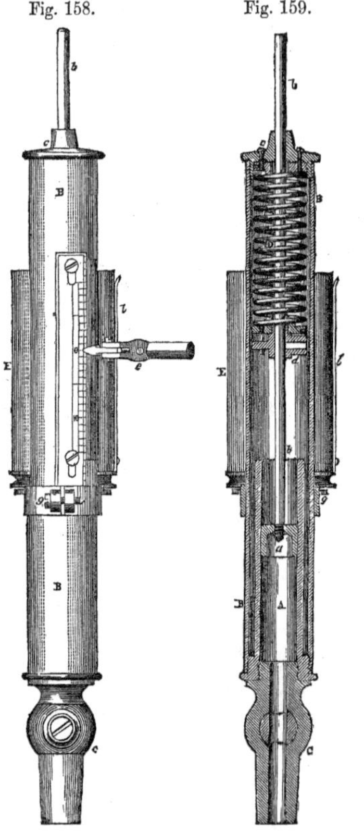

vation, Fig. 159 a longitudinal section, and Fig. 160 cross sections of the instrument.

The zero-point is that at which the index stands when the cock C is shut and the piston *a* remains undisturbed, and therefore, when the instrument is in action, it denotes that point in the stroke at which the pressures above and below the piston are balanced.

Fig. 160.

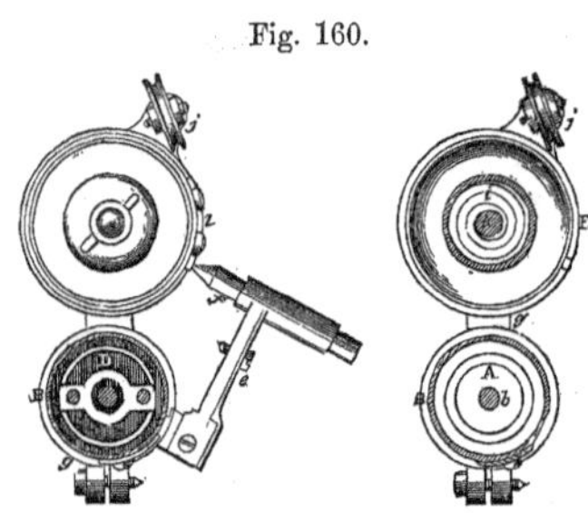

From these explanations it will be obvious that, by attaching the instrument to the cylinder of a steam-engine, and observing the motion of the index upon the scale, the maximum steam pressure and vacuum may be at once ascertained. But this is not the only, nor even the most important function of the indicator. It was desirable to find out the exact periods and modes in which these two elements of power come into operation, and especially the *mean* effective values of each; the rapidity of the motion through so short a space precluding the possibility of taking these observations with any degree of accuracy. These important objects are fully attained by the help of a simple and beautiful contrivance, by which the instrument is made to register its own performances.

An arm or bracket *g*, is firmly attached to the indicator by being clamped to the external casing B, on which it may be set to any convenient elevation, and there secured by a screw. To this bracket is riveted an upright axis *h*, Fig. 160, on which, by a long socket, to insure steadiness of motion, is accurately fitted a cylindrical piece F, formed into a pulley at its lower end. The other extremity of the socket carries a small cylindrical box, containing a spiral spring *i*, similar to the main-spring of a watch, and attached at one end to the fixed axis *h*, and at the other to the internal surface of the box in which it is inclosed. The bracket g, carries also a small friction-pulley j, for the purpose of guiding a cord wrapped round and attached to the pulley F, to any convenient moving part of the engine; a small catch k, screwed into the latter, serving to circumscribe its motion to a single revolution. An external cylinder or drum E, which may be withdrawn from the instrument at pleasure, is fitted over the revolving cylindrical piece F, so as to partake of its motion, and upon it is fixed a slip of brass formed into a double spring l, l, for the purpose of securing the slip of paper on which the instrument is to register its performance. This is effected by means of a pencil f, placed in a holder e, jointed to the piece of steel on which the index or pointer is formed, and fitted with a small spring, so as to press the point of the pencil gently against the paper cylinder, or admit of its being withdrawn from contact with it at pleasure. From these arrangements it will be seen that, if the piston a be moved up and down while the pencil is in contact with the cylinder E, a straight line will be traced upon it in the direction of its length, and if, on the other hand, the cylinder be made to turn upon its axis by pulling the cord, while the piston remains at rest, a straight line will be traced round it at right angles to the former. By the combination of these two motions when the instrument is in operation, a diagram is produced, which represents the performance of the engine at all parts of its stroke.

Action of the Instrument.—The mode of applying the indicator to the cylinder of an engine: The cock C is inserted into the corresponding socket prepared for its reception, and the cord which passes under the pulley j, is attached to the radius bar or other moving part of the engine, so as to cause the cylinder E to make one revolution on its axis, coincident with and representing the stroke of the engine; on the relaxation of the cord at the termination of the up stroke, it is taken up again by the action of the spring i, and the cylinder E resumes its original position. The slip of paper is then to be wrapped tightly round the cylinder, its ends being secured by the pressure of the two springs l, l. These arrangements having been made, the pencil f is turned down into contact with the paper, and the engine is allowed to make a stroke or two with the cock C shut, so as to form an *atmospheric line* A B. A communication is then opened with the interior of the cylinder of the engine by turning the cock C, and a figure or diagram is traced upon the slip of paper, exactly representing the successive pressures of the steam above, and corresponding degrees of exhaustion below the atmospheric line at every part of the stroke. To find the mean effective values of each of these pressures respectively, the figure is to be divided, in the direction of its length, into any number of equal parts, the perpendicular distances of the outline of the diagram above and below the atmospheric line at each of these points, to be carefully measured upon the scale of the instrument, and the sum of these to be divided by the number of points taken. Hence the actual power of the engine is easily calculated.

As an exemplification of these processes, we refer to the annexed wood-cuts. Fig. 161 is a fac-simile

Fig. 161.

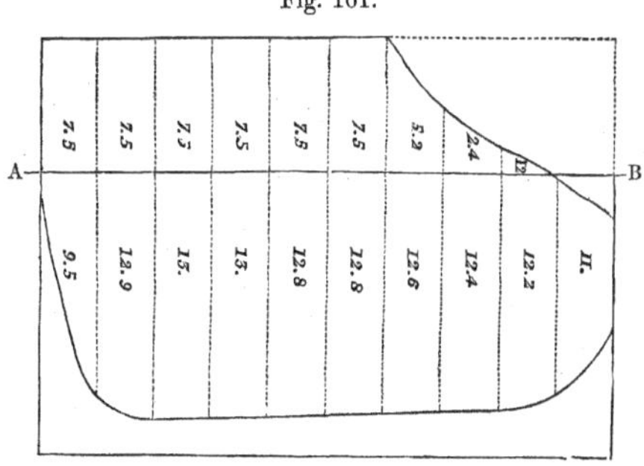

of a diagram taken from a condensing marine-engine, in excellent working order; working expansively, and showing a very large amount of gross effective pressure on the piston in proportion to the consumption of steam.

It is evident that the most accurate method to ascertain the power of an engine is by means of an indicator, because the diagram gives the pressure on the piston; and hence, knowing the number of revolutions of the crank or paddle-wheel, and the length of stroke, the laboring force can be ascertained.

The diagram traced by the pencil being divided by a series of equidistant vertical lines, the closer the better, and taking the atmospheric line A B marked 0, as the origin; observe in the middle of each space the number of pounds and tenths between the steam and vacuum-lines; this is best done by taking the distances with a pair of compasses, and setting them off on the scale of pounds attached to the instrument. Write these in their proper columns as in the figure along the diagram, and add them together. Then divide the gross result by the number of columns, and we obtain the gross average pressure on one side of the piston during the up and down stroke.

Taken from the Diagram.

	Steam-Pressure.	Vacuum-Pressure.
	1.2 pounds.	11.0 pounds.
	2.4 "	12.2 "
	5.2 "	12.4 "
	7.5 "	12.6 "
	7.5 "	12.8 "
	7.5 "	12.8 "
	7.5 "	13.0 "
Number of	7.5 "	13.0 "
spaces in this	7.5 "	12.9 "
example or	——	9.5 "
diagram =10)	53.8	——
	——	10)122.2
	5.38	——
		12.22

5.38+12.22=17.60 lbs. the gross average pressure on each square inch on one side of the piston during the up and down stroke. In other cases, where we calculated the horse-power from the pressure of the steam only, we had to allow for the pressure in the condenser; but in this case that allowance is made. This is obvious from the pressures taken below the atmospheric line. Allowing 14.7 lbs. to be the average pressure of the atmosphere, the average pressure of the vapor in the condenser is thus obtained:—

14.7—11.0=3.7
14.7—12.2=2.5
14.7—12.4=2.3
14.7—12.6=2.1
14.7—12.8=1.9
14.7—12.8=1.8
14.7—13.0=1.7
14.7—13.0=1.7
14.7—12.9=1.8
14.7— 9.5=5.2
——
10)25.7
——
2.57 pounds.

In other cases, we allowed from 3 to 5 lbs. for the pressure of the vapor in the condenser; in this example, we make it but $2\frac{1}{2}$ lbs. nearly. The total pressure of the steam on an average on the square inch might be found by adding 14.7 to the other numbers on the diagram taken above the atmospheric line A B. Let us suppose this diagram to be taken from the Steamship "ARCTIC," of which the late John Faron, Esq., was Chief Engineer. The cylinder is 95 inches diameter, and 10 feet stroke. Average number of revolutions $13\frac{3}{4}$ the minute, or $13\frac{3}{4}$ up and down stroke a minute.

The square of the diameter in inches, multiplied by .7854, gives the number of square inches on the surface of the piston, when a table is not convenient.

$\therefore 95 \times 95 \times .7854 = 7088.235$ square inches.

From 17.6 lbs. take one pound for the friction of the engine unloaded, then we have 16.6 lbs. And let us suppose that one-fifth the effective pressure or useful load be allowed for the resistance necessary to overcome the loaded engine.

16.6
5 $\qquad 1\frac{1}{5}=\frac{6}{5}$.
——
6)83.0
——

$13\frac{5}{6}$ lbs. the useful pressure of the piston for each square inch.

$7088.235 \times 13\frac{5}{6} = 98053.9175$ lbs. the useful pressure of the whole piston.

$13\frac{3}{4} \times 20 = 275$ feet the velocity of the piston a minute.

$$\frac{98053.9175 \times 275}{33{,}000} = 817 \text{ horse-power nearly.}$$

The allowances here made, to find the available horse-power of the engine, are varied according to the circumstances and nature of the case. The nominal horse-power of an engine must not be confounded with the actual horse-power; the nominal horse-power is estimated differently by different engineers, and in different countries; some engineers measure the size of their engines by nominal horse-power, but the indicated horse-power and the nominal horse-power cannot be compared; they are totally different. The ratio between the nominal and actual power of an engine is very variable, and indeed not constant in the same engine at different times; for the nominal power remains the same, whether the engine is working effectively or not, while the actual power obtained from the indicator is an expression of efficiency with which the engine works. Of nominal horse-power, we will say more hereafter. From the indicated power, the available power is calculated in different ways; almost every engineer has a method of his own, which to him is the best. Some would calculate the horse-power of this engine thus:—

17.6 lbs. pressure by the indicator.
1.5 deduction for friction.

16.1 effective pressure to the inch.
7088.235 square inch on surface of piston.

7088235
42529410
7088235

114120.5835 pressure in lbs. on piston.
275=13¾×20 vel. of piston a minute,

which, when multiplied together and divided by 33,000, gives 951 for the effective horse-power; by the last method we obtained 817 for the horse-power.

Some engineers deduct as much as 2.5 lbs. from the indicated pressure to obtain the available force on the square inch. To exemplify this, suppose the indicated average pressure taken from the indicated diagram to be 18.48 lbs. the square inch, the diameter of the cylinder 32 inches, and the velocity of the piston 226 feet a minute.

18.48—2.5=15.98 lbs. available force to each square inch.

Then $\frac{32^2 \times .7854 \times 15.98 \times 226}{33000}=88$ horse-power.

Fig. 162 is from a good high-pressure engine, receiving steam to the end of the stroke, and with a pressure of 40 lbs. in the boilers, the diagram show-

Fig. 162.

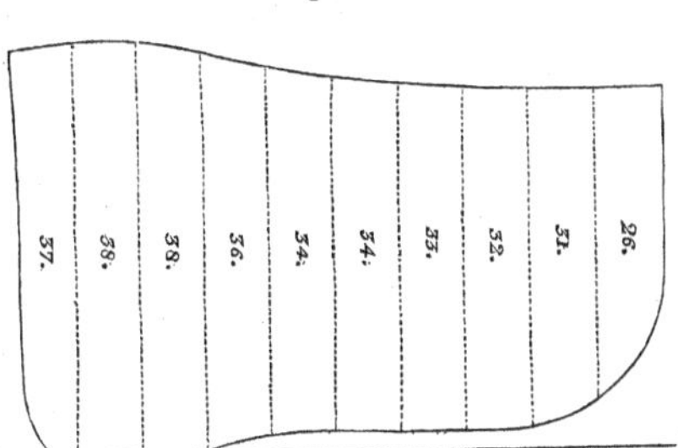

ing a difference between the average pressure in the cylinder and that in the boiler, to the amount of nearly 6 lbs. In such engines, it is almost unnecessary to remark, the diagram is situated entirely above the atmospheric line A B.

26+31+32+33+34+34+36+38+38+37=339,

and $\frac{339}{10}$=33.9 lbs. average pressure above that of the atmosphere. In other examples we took the whole pressure of the steam, and deducted 15 lbs. for the pressure of the atmosphere in high-pressure engines. The average pressure of the steam in this cylinder is 33.9+15, or, more properly,

33.9+14.7=48.6 lbs.

And the pressure of the steam in the boiler in this case will be

40+14.7=54.7 lbs.

To apply this to some useful purpose, let us suppose the area of the piston of the high-pressure engine, from which this indicator diagram was taken, to be 900 square inches, the length of stroke 7 feet, the number of strokes a minute 22; what is the number of cubic feet of water that the engine will pump a minute from a mine 500 feet deep, allowing .9 lbs. to the square inch to overcome the friction of the parts of the engine, and $\frac{1}{9}$th of the effective pressure or useful load, for the resistance necessary to overcome the friction of the loaded engine. And further, let us allow the working of the pump to consume ⅓d of this available force.

33.9 lbs. given by the indicator.
.9 for friction of the engine.

$\frac{8}{9}$ load 33. lbs.
8

9)264

29⅓ lbs. to the square inch that the engine would lift but for the intervention of the pump which destroys ⅓d of this useful load.

3)29⅓
$9\frac{5}{9}$

$19\frac{7}{9}$ lbs. useful work of each square inch of the piston the minute.

$19\frac{7}{9} \times 900 \times 7 \times 22=2741200$

units of useful work of the engine a minute while employed pumping with this pressure of steam

$\frac{2741200}{33000}=83$ useful or available horse-power nearly.

A cubic foot of water weighs 62.5 lbs., then the units of work developed in pumping one cubic foot of water, 500 feet will be

62.5×500=31250.0

$\therefore \frac{2741200}{31250}=87.7184$ cubic feet of water, that the engine will raise in a minute.

Morin's Indicator.—That eminent French mechanician, M. Arthur Morin, conceiving with reason that considerable inaccuracy was likely to result from the difficulty of constructing the spiral springs in the common indicator, so as at all parts of the stroke to denote equal pressures by equal divisions, and, moreover, considering it desirable to ascertain with greater precision the mean pressures and consequent actual power of engines by taking indications throughout several consecutive strokes, has invented a machine by which the former difficulty is obviated and the latter object is attained. This instrument we have represented in the following figures :—

Fig. 163 is a side elevation, Fig. 164 an end elevation, and Fig. 165 a plan of the machine. Fig. 166 represents a vertical section of the working cylinder and its appendages.

Fig. 163.

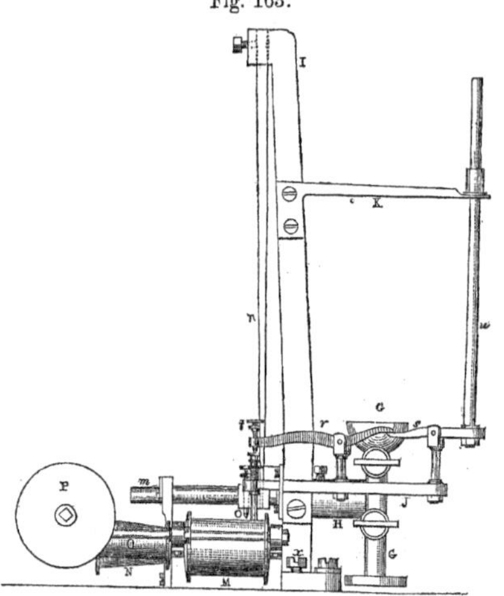

Fig. 164.

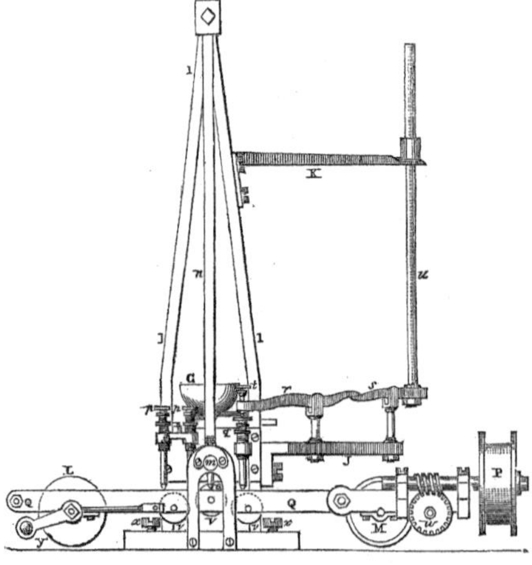

Fig. 165.

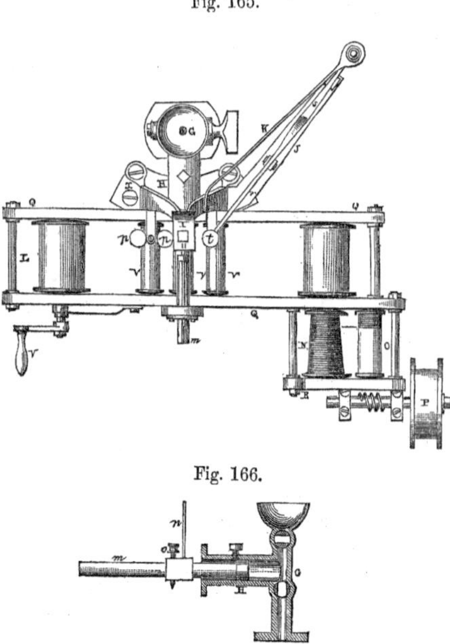

Fig. 166.

This indicator, like that we have already described, is adapted for being fitted to the cylinder cover of the engine; it carries a stop-cock pipe G, furnished with two keys; between these is situated a small horizontal cylinder H, in which a solid piston is accurately fitted to work steam-tight. Towards the middle of the piston-rod *m*, which is properly guided to a rectilinear course, is a square part in which is inserted the lower end of a long parabolic spring *n*, the other extremity of which is fixed to the summit of a standard I, forming part of the framework of the machine, the spring being so fitted as to admit of a certain amount of travel in the piston in both directions. The square boss of the piston-rod carries also a small pencil *o*, for the purpose of tracing the different degrees of tension of the steam on the opening of the lower cock G.

Two pencils *p p*, are placed in holders fixed to the framing exactly opposite to the point at which the pencil *o* stands when the stop-cock G is shut, and, being thus immovable, serve to mark a continuous atmosphere line. A third pencil *q*, which is susceptible of a slight degree of vertical motion in its socket, and is destined to mark the termination of each stroke, is brought into contact with the paper by placing the instrument so that the working-beam, crosshead, or any other rigid part of the engine may touch lightly at the end of the stroke, the top of an upright rod *u*, which is connected by a system of levers *r*, *s*, *t*, with the top of the pencil *q*.

A continuous band or roll of paper may be subjected to the action of this machine for an indefinite period, so as to produce diagrams representing the action of the engine during several successive strokes. The manner in which this is accomplished is as follows: the roll of paper is first wound upon the cylinder L, by means of the handle *y*; it is then passed over the three small rollers *v*, *v*, *v*, placed to oppose the pressure of the pencils, and is received upon the cylinder M, situated at the opposite end of the framing Q, Q. The axis of this latter cylinder is produced on one side so as to form also the axis of a conical pulley or fusee N, opposite to which is situated a cylindrical drum O, which receives a uniform motion from any rotating part of the engine to be operated on, by means of a worm-wheel *w*, on its axis, geering with an endless screw on the axis of the strap-pulley P. The cylindrical roller O, communicates motion to the conical roller N, by a cord wrapped round both and fastened at opposite extremities of each. The object of this arrangement is to compensate for the increased surface velocity due to the increased diameter of the cylinder M, as the paper is wound on to it, by imparting to it a proportionally retarded motion.

Although, as before observed, there is no ratio existing between what engineers term nominal horse-power, and the actual available power of an engine; yet, when greater accuracy is not required, the succeeding rules will be found convenient. Multiply the square of the diameter of the cylinder in inches by the velocity of the piston in feet a minute, and divide the product by 6,000, the quotient is what the English term nominal horse-power. In using this rule, it is necessary to adopt the speed of piston, which varies with the length of stroke. The speed of piston with two feet stroke is, according to this system, 160 a minute; 2.5 feet stroke, 170; 3 feet, 180; 3.5 feet, 189; 4 feet, 200; 5 feet, 215; 6 feet, 228; 7 feet, 245; 8 feet, 256 feet. By finding the ratio in which the velocity of the piston is supposed to increase with the length of stroke, English writers omit or cast out the element of velocity altogether, and give the following rule: Multiply the square of the diameter of the cylinder in inches, by the cube root of the stroke in feet, and divide the product by 47, the quotient is termed the nominal horse-power of the engine. This rule, further supposes a uniform effective pressure of 7 lbs. to the square inch. Such empirical rules and assumptions are of little value. However, we are furnished with very long tables of nominal horse-power of engines. The nominal horse-power of an engine of 6 feet stroke, the cylinder 50 inches in diameter, according to this system, will be thus calculated:—

The cube root of 6=1.817.

$$\frac{1.817 \times 50^2}{47} = 96.65,$$ the nominal horse-power. Such silly calculations are of very little real value, although they were laid down by that great Scottish Celt, James Watt, who was taught by an Irish Celt, Dr. Black. The nominal horse-power of a high-pressure engine has never been defined, but the following rule is given by some writers: Multiply the square of the diameter of the cylinder in inches by the pressure on the piston in pounds, the square inch and the cube root of the stroke in feet; divide the product by 940, the quotient is the nominal horse-power of the engine. In this rule, the speed is supposed to be 128 times the cube root of the stroke, the reason of which is very badly defined. The nominal horse-power of a high-pressure engine of 3 feet stroke, with a pressure of 60 lbs. on the square inch, which is the pressure usually allowed, and a cylinder 30 inches diameter. According to this empirical rule, the horse-power of the engine may be thus found:—

The cube root of 3=1.442.

$$\frac{1.442 \times 30^2 \times 60}{940} = 82.84$$ nominal horse-power.

For the convenience of persons not much acquainted with the action of steam, a very simple and easily remembered rule for calculating the power of engines with steam at full pressure, and the slide-valves opening by the eccentric motion, is to multiply the diameter of the piston squared by decimal .7854, and then multiply the product or the square inches in the area of the piston, by ⅘th of the pressure of the steam in the boiler in pounds, ⅕th being deducted for friction. Then multiply this product by the number of strokes per minute and length of the stroke; or, in other words, the number of feet the piston travels in a minute;

divide this sum by 33,000, allow $\frac{4}{10}$th for friction, and the remainder is the horse-power. Some prefer dividing by 44,000, in which case they do not allow for friction; but the general rule is 33,000, with allowance for friction; and by some less, and by others more friction is allowed. The following examples will serve to illustrate the mode of calculating the power of steam-engines, according to the preceding rule:—

Required to find the power of a high-pressure reciprocating engine, whose cylinder is 12 inches in diameter and 2½ feet in height, the mean pressure in the boiler being fully 33 lbs. on the square inch, and the engine making 40 strokes per minute.

The area of the piston, as ascertained by calculation, or by a table of the areas of circles, is

$$12^2 \times .7854 = 113.0976 \text{ square inches.}$$

Deducting ¼th of the pressure of steam in the boiler for the effect of cooling, friction, &c., we have 33×¼—8¼=25 lbs. per square inch, effective pressure; and the length of the cylinder being 2½ feet, the stroke will be 5 feet. Hence, applying the rule, we have

$$113.0976 \times 25 \times 40 \times 5 = \frac{565488.0000}{33,000} = 17.1360,$$

the nominal horse-power; and deducting $\frac{4}{10}$th for friction,

17.1360—6.8544=10.2816, or fully 10 horse-power, for the actual power of the engine.

Again, suppose an engine, with a cylinder 10¼ inches diameter and 2 feet in length, or with a stroke of 4 feet, making 50 strokes per minute, mean pressure about 35 lbs., and with an effective pressure of 26 lbs. on the square inch, after deducting ¼th for friction. What is the power?

The area being, 82.5160, we have here

$$82.5160 \times 26 \times 50 \times 4 = \frac{429013.2000}{33,000} = 13.0025,$$

nominal horse-power; and subtracting $\frac{4}{10}$th we have

13.0028—5.2008=7.817, or nearly 8 horse-power, for the actual power.

Supposing the diameter of the cylinder of the engine to be 10 inches—the mean pressure 36 lbs., and the effective pressure 27 lbs., instead of 26 lbs.; the result would be nearly the same, thus:—

$$10^2 \times .7854 = 78.5400 \text{ square inches, and}$$

$$78.5400 \times 27 \times 50 \times 4 = \frac{424116.0000}{33,000} = 12.8520,$$

nominal horse-power, and deducting $\frac{4}{10}$th for friction, there is, 12.850—5.1408=7.7112, as the actual horse-power. But supposing that the cylinder be taken at 10¼ inches diameter, and that the effective pressure be increased to 30 lbs., the result would be very different, thus: 82.5160×30×4×50= 15.0029, nominal horse-power, and deducting $\frac{4}{10}$th for friction, there is 15.0022—6.0008=9.0012; or 9 horses as the apparent power of the engine.

From the preceding simple rule, and by these calculations, it will be perceived that the result, brought out as the nominal horse-power, is materially affected by the amount deducted for friction, as also by the number of strokes and pressure of the steam; which facts prove the necessity of careful consideration when estimating the horse-power of a steam-engine, to prevent erroneous deductions.

M. V. Regnault has proved, by experiment, that the laws of Boyle and Gay-Lussac do not hold for steam air and other gases to any great extent; consequently, the rules depending upon these laws must be erroneous. The basis of all calculations respecting the mechanical action of aeriform fluids generally has been made to depend upon Boyle's law, which is this: *The elastic force or pressure exerted by the fluid upon a given unit of the surface of the vessel that contains it, varies directly as the density varies, the temperature being constant.* The law of Gay-Lussac lays down that all aeriform fluids, submitted to the same constant pressure, receive equal increments of volume for equal increments of temperature, provided the pressure to which they are submitted be the same, and constant. For a limited range or duration, these laws are not much in error; but when we take into account the results obtained from the actions of the three sorts of heat termed *latent, specific,* and *sensible,* we are obliged, from a careful examination, to conclude that the economical working of Ericsson's air-engine is not possible.

PUMPING ENGINE.

UNITED STATES DRY DOCK, BROOKLYN, NEW YORK.

PLATE XIV.

THIS engine and its pumps were designed by W. J. McAlpine, and constructed by Messrs. Kemble, at the West Point Foundry. As the tides rise but about five feet, this renders it necessary to provide the means of pumping out the chamber of the dock. For this purpose the steam-engine has been constructed of great power, with pumps of great capacity. The engine has to remove upwards of 600,000 cubic feet of water in from two to three hours, as follows:—

110,000 cubic feet	to be	raised	an	average	height of	2½ feet.
125,000 "	"	"	"	"	" 7½	"
115,000 "	"	"	"	"	" 12½	"
110,000 "	"	"	"	"	" 17½	"
110,000 "	"	"	"	"	" 22½	"
40,000 "	"	"	"	"	" 26	"

The engine is a condensing vertical beam-engine, with a cylinder B of fifty inches diameter, and the stroke of the piston A, twelve feet. The piston-rod A, of the cylinder B, is attached to one end of the beam C, and from the opposite end E, the connecting rod DD is attached, and extended to the crank EE. The beam *e*CC*e* is of cast-iron, thirty-two feet long, with suitable bearings FFH, provided for attaching the draining and air-pumps GGK. The crank shaft E, upon which the fly-wheel JJ is fixed, is of wrought-iron finished up. The fly-wheel JJJ is twenty-four feet diameter with a cross section of eighty square inches. The condenser H is fifty-two inches diameter and five feet high.

The connecting-rod DDD is of wrought-iron. It is stiffened by a double truss brace of round iron *hhh*, which is secured by bolts to the rod near each end, and passes over a strut *ii* at the centre. This strut is screwed and furnished with nuts, by which the brace is tightened. The connecting-rod DD, and its appurtenances, are finished bright, in the same style as the front links *g*, *g*, *g*.

The air-pump K, is made of cast-iron and lined with a staving of M. Babbett's composition metal; it is forty-four inches diameter, and forty-two inches length of stroke, and is fitted with a floating top. The air-pump, bucket, foot-valve, seat, and rod L, are of composition metal. The cylinder B has double balance valves MM, made of composition metal, with valve-stem of cast-steel. The side pipes are of cast-iron, turned and polished, and provided with an expansion-piece. The cut-off motion is self-adjusting, so as to admit an increased quantity of steam to the cylinder, as the work of the engine increases, by lifting the water to a greater height. All the connections of the engine are of wrought-iron, and those above the bed-plate O O, are finished and polished.

The piston of the steam-cylinder B, has metallic packings moved by steel springs. All the boxes of the journals are of composition, and lined with M. Babbett's metal. Automaton oil-cups are fitted to the principal journals. The engine is fitted up with a register, a steam and vacuum gage, and an indicator. The engine-frame NNN, PPP, is of cast-iron, with a bed-plate OOO, set upon a granite foundation, raised 18 inches above the floor of the engine-room. Upon the bed-plate are five Gothic columns, PPPPP, and two pilasters on each side. The columns sustain Gothic arches of 10 feet span, and an entablature NN, of cast-iron. The engine-frame is surrounded by an iron railing. All the work which is not finished or polished, is painted and bronzed. The space for three feet, entirely around the engine, is covered with cast-iron flooring, figured in relief.

In the boiler-room are placed three marine boilers, made of the best Pennsylvania piled boiler-plate, 78 inches diameter, and 32 feet long, with 650 square feet of fire surface in each. The boilers are so arranged that one or all may be used, as occasion may require. Each has a steam drum, and cast-iron doors to the furnace and ash-pit. One of Worthington's feed-pumps is attached to each boiler. The boilers are warranted safe, to be used with a pressure of 50 pounds to the square inch. All the steam, feed, connecting, and injecting-pipes, are of copper. All the cocks and valves are of composition metal. All joints are faced metal and metal. Steam and water gages, and safety, feed, and blow valves, are put on each boiler. The steam-drums, pipes, and steam-cylinders, are covered with hair felting; that on the cylinder is cased with mahogany staving, reeded and banded with brass bands. The felting on the drums and pipes is covered with hemp-canvas, and painted. All the wrought-iron is hammered charcoal iron, and the cast-iron, cold-blast of the best quality. There are two draining-pumps, GG, each 63 inches diameter, and 8 feet length of stroke, so placed that one pump is driven by each arm of the beam; the rods are made fast at F and F. Each pump is provided with a suction-pipe and valve-chamber, and valve and floating top. The two suction-pipes are connected by a pipe to an air-vessel, which is common to each. The draining-pumps GG, air-pump K, and condenser H, are placed on a bed-plate RR, 11 feet below the bed-plate OO, of the engine. Between the bed-plates is a cast-iron reservoir, with hinge-valves, to exclude the tide water, but which will open at every stroke of the pumps. The chamber of the pumps is lined with a staving of composition; the bucket, rod, and valve, and valve-seats are of composition; the valves are covered with vulcanized India rubber. All the joints of the pumps, pipes, and bonnets are faced-metal and metal; all the connections which extend above the bed-plate of the engine are finished and polished. The piston-rod A is guided in its path by the parallel motion-rods *gggg*. In the construction of the United States Dry Dock, Brooklyn, several engineers were engaged. Col. Baldwin expended the sum of $5,000 in 1835. From August, 1841, to August, 1842, Mr. Courtenay expended $35,264. From August, 1844, to March, 1845, Gen. McNeil expended $114,675. From March, 1845, to February, 1846, Mr. Tanger expended $115,951. From February, 1846, to October, 1849, Mr. McAlpine expended $1,147,310. Mr. McAlpine was succeeded by Gen. C. B. Stuart, in October, 1849, and completed the work in August, 1851; he expended $732,974. So that the dock cost over two million dollars. One of the chief promoters of this great national work was the Hon. Henry C. Murphy, a member of Congress, from King's County, N. Y. For further particulars respecting the history of this matter, the reader is referred to Byrne's *Dictionary of Machines, Mechanics, Engine-work, and Engineering*, the last edition of which is published under a false title, by the Appletons, of New York.

$$
\begin{aligned}
110000 \times 2\tfrac{1}{2} &= 275000 \\
125000 \times 7\tfrac{1}{2} &= 937500 \\
115000 \times 12\tfrac{1}{2} &= 1437500 \\
110000 \times 17\tfrac{1}{2} &= 1925000 \\
110000 \times 22\tfrac{1}{2} &= 2475000 \\
40000 \times 26 &= 1040000 \\
\hline
&\ 8090000
\end{aligned}
$$

$\frac{8090000}{3 \times 60 \times 528} = 85$, nearly the available horse-power of the engine, when doing this work in 3 hours, or in 3×60 minutes. To raise 528 cubic feet of water a foot high in a minute, is a horse-power. The area of the piston, is 1963.5 square inches, and suppose the piston to make 13 up and down strokes in a minute, the speed of the piston will be $13 \times 24 = 312$ feet the minute. If A be the mean useful or effective pressure in lbs. on each square inch of the piston doing the above work, then the horse-power will be expressed by

$$\frac{A \times 1963.5 \times 312}{33000} = 85.$$

$$\therefore A = \frac{85 \times 33000}{1963.5 \times 312} = 4.6 \text{ lbs. effective pressure.}$$

Allowing $\frac{1}{7}$ of this for the amount of power necessary to overcome the friction of the load, $1\frac{1}{2}$ lbs. for the friction of the parts, and the pump to destroy $\frac{1}{3}$ of the effective pressure on the piston.

$$4.6 + \frac{4.6}{2} = 6.9 \text{ lbs.}$$

$$6.9 + \tfrac{1}{7} \times 6.9 = 7.88 \text{ lbs.}$$

$7.88 + 1.5 = 9.38$ lbs. under such circumstances that should be given by the indicated diagram.

PARALLEL MOTIONS.

Figs. 167 to 178, exhibit a variety of forms of parallel motions, such as are employed to maintain the rectilineal direction of the piston-rod of a steam-engine, under the constantly varying angular direction of the beam. Contrivances of this kind are required in other circumstances of the conversion of rotary and alternating angular motion into rectilineal motion, and the converse; but the absolute necessity there is of guiding the path of the piston in the steam-engine, has called forth more attention to the principles and mechanism of parallel motions than would otherwise, in all probability, have been awarded to the subject for other purposes. In the first place, the principle may be briefly indicated.

Fig. 167. Given ABD a right angle, it can be demonstrated that if the end A, of the right line

Fig. 167.

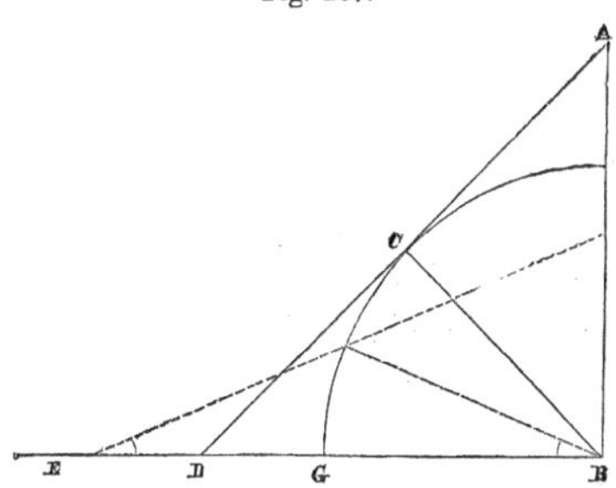

AD, descend from A to B along the line AB, while the end D moves along the line BE, a point C, in the middle of the line, will describe the circle CG. Hence, if a beam AD has one end sliding in a groove at D, and is connected or jointed at the middle C, in a guide BC, of half its length, this guide also moving on a joint at B, then, in every position of the beam, the point C will describe the circle CG, and the point A of the beam will move in a straight line.

Fig. 168. In practice, it may be more convenient to have the end D, of the beam, fixed to the end of a movable bar, as DN, of some feet in length, than to slide in a groove; for, though the arc described by the end D, will deviate a little from a straight line, yet the error produced thereby

Fig. 168.

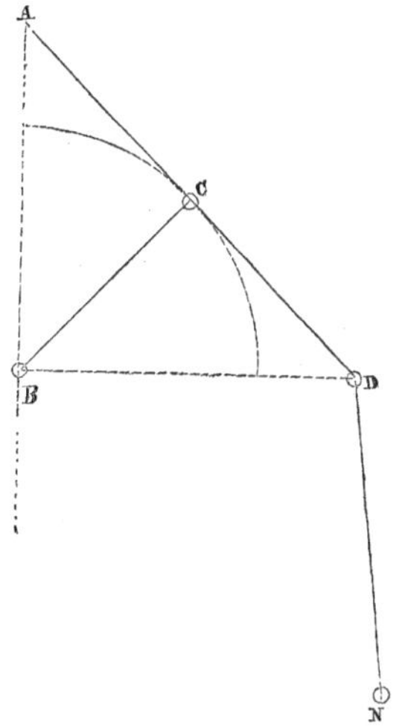

will be so very small, that it can have no bad effect, or even be discovered in practice.

In the steam-engine, there are various modes adopted by means of jointed-rods, &c., different from that described above, for causing the piston-rod, attached to the end of the beam, to move in a straight line, which, although not mathematically correct, are still so very near the truth as to answer the purpose wanted exceedingly well; such a system of jointed-rods is generally termed by engineers a *parallel motion*.

Fig. 169. In the beam *a*F, which is shown in its three positions, viz., at the middle and the two extremities of the stroke, the versed sine *ab* of the arc formed by the extremity of the beam is termed the vibration, and a piston-rod attached to the beam is made to move in a line bisecting this vibration: thus, if a piston-rod were attached to the beam *a*F, *cd* is the line in which the rod ought to move.

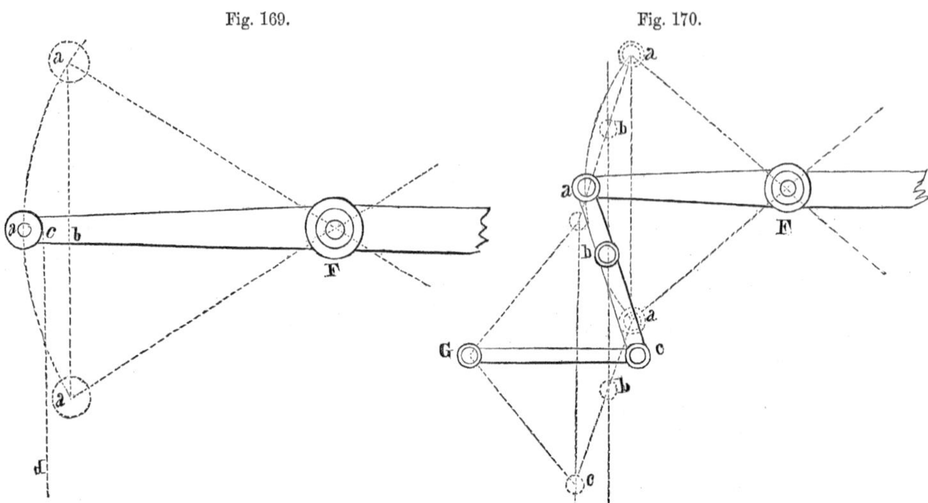

Fig. 169. Fig. 170.

Fig. 170 is a general mode of finding the length of the radius-rod G*c*, and shows the principle upon which parallel motions formed by jointed-rods are founded; *a*F is the beam, *ac* a strap, one end of which is attached to the beam, and the piston-rod is attached somewhere about the middle, as at *b*; the beam is then put in its three positions, and while the point *b*, to which the piston-rod is fixed, is kept in the straight line, bisecting the vibration, the positions of the lower end *c* of the strap are carefully marked, as at *c*, *c*, *c*; then the centre G of the circle, passing through these points, will be the point to which the radius-rod G*c*, connected to the strap at *c*, should be fixed, and the radius of the circle will be the length of the rod. If the point *b* be taken exactly in the middle of the strap, the length of the radius-rod G*c* will be equal to the portion of the beam *a*F.

Fig. 171 is another plan of a parallel motion sometimes used: the method of finding the length

Fig. 171.

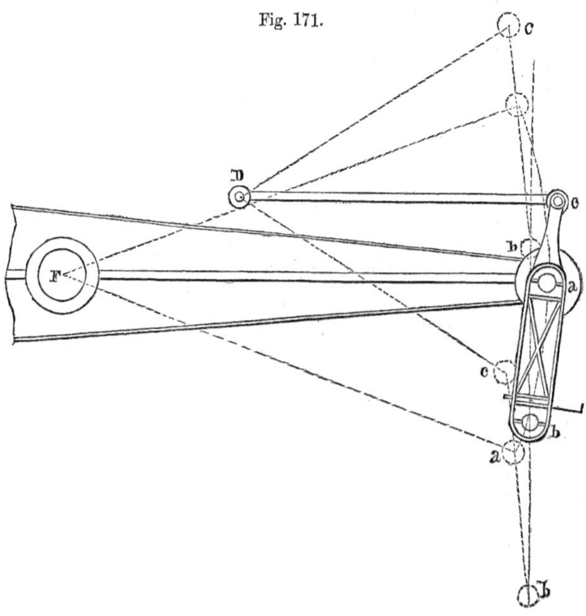

of the rod D*c*, and position of the point D, is the very same as that described in Fig. 170, viz., by putting the beam in its three positions, and marking the places of the points *c*, *c*, *c* of the strap, while the point *b*, to which the piston-rod is fixed, is kept in the same straight line: the radius D*c* of the circle passing through the points *c*, *c*, *c*, will be the length of the radius-rod, and the centre of same circle, the point to which it should be fixed.

Fig. 172 is a method of causing the piston-rod to describe a straight line, often adopted in forcing-pumps: the lever F has the centre of motion at O, in the upstandard S, fixed upon the cover of the pump. D is a cylindrical-rod, also fixed to the top of the pump, and set quite parallel to the pump-rod R; *g* is a crosshead attached to the top of the pump-rod, having a projecting arm *h*, terminating in a socket *f*, which moves on the rod D; the lever F is connected to the crosshead *g* by two straps, one of which is shown at *c*; upon moving the lever F, it will be quite clear that the piston-rod R must move parallel to D.

Fig. 172.

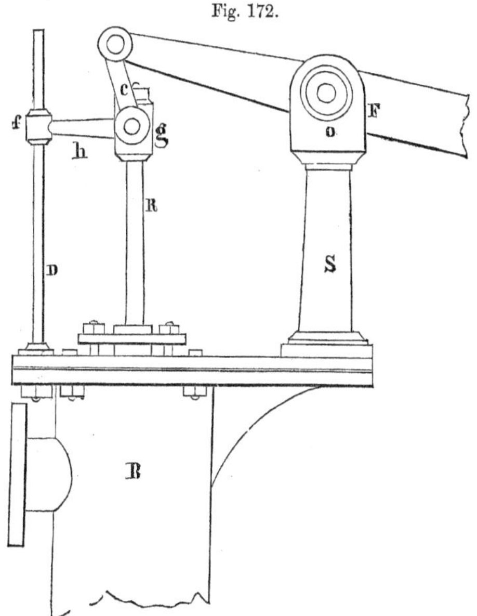

Fig. 173.

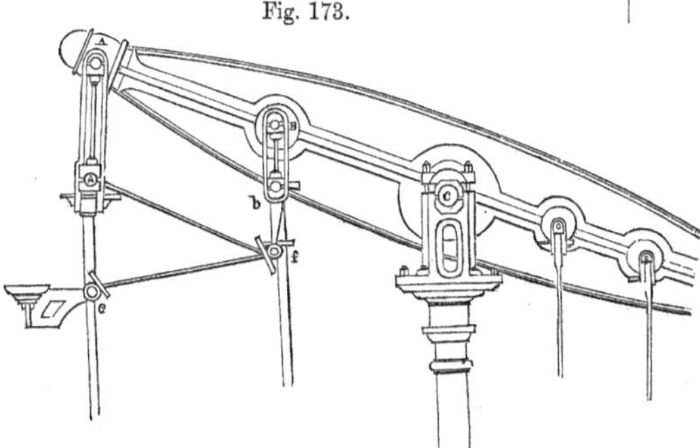

Fig. 173 is a drawing of a walking-beam for a twelve-horse engine, with parallel motion attached. The point B, to which the inner strap is fixed, is very often taken exactly in the centre, betwixt A and *c*; and when that is the case, the length of the radius-rods is equal to the same distance, or, in other words, equal to the fourth part of the whole length of beam.

When the inner strap is suspended from any other point than in the middle of the distance A*c*, the position of the centre and length of the rod *ef* would be found as described in Fig. 170. Keeping the point A, to which the piston-rod is attached, always in the same straight line in which it ought to move, and carefully marking the points assumed by the lower end of the strap *f*.

The point *b*, to which the air pump-rod is fixed, should be exactly in the middle of the strap, when the beam is divided into four equal parts, which will also insure a parallel motion for the bucket of the air-pump.

Fig. 174 is a mode of causing the piston-rod to describe a straight line by the use of the two friction-wheels WW, confined betwixt the guides GG;

Fig. 174.

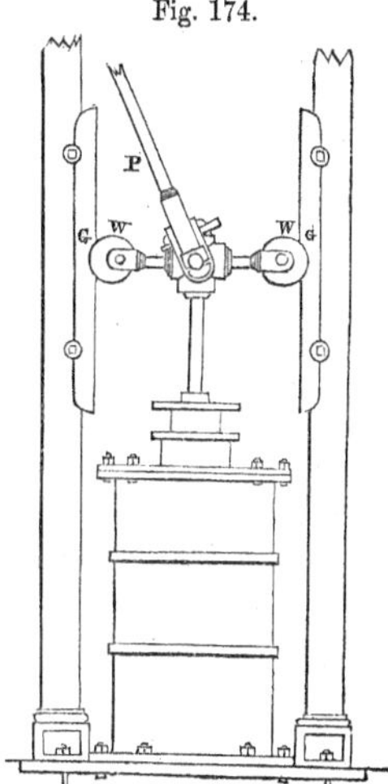

this plan is often used in small engines, when the crank to which the connecting-rod P is attached is immediately above the cylinder.

Fig. 175 is a plan of parallel motion usually employed in marine engines: the manner of finding the length and position of the radius-rod *gf* is precisely the same as in Fig. 170; this motion is, in fact, the common parallel motion modified to suit the circumstances in which it is placed. The length of the radius-bar *ef* is easily found in practice, by supposing the piston-rod to move in a right line, and finding three points through which a point in the side-rod A, assumed at pleasure, would pass in the highest, middle, and lowest positions of the piston-rod; then a circular arc passing through these points will give the radius and centre sought; and the point *e* assumed in the side-rod will be the point of connection of the radius-bar.

Fig. 175.

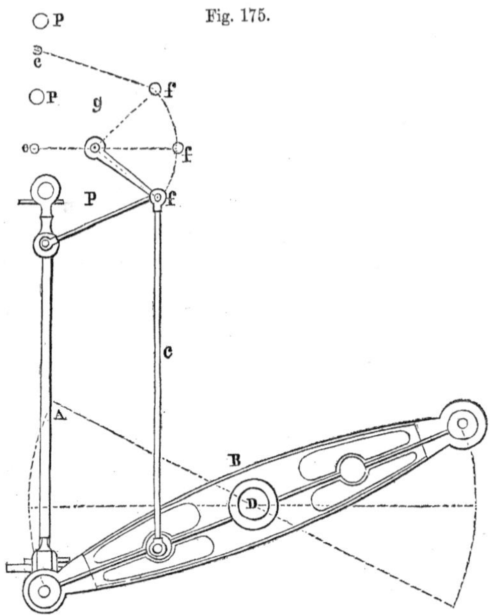

Now, in order that the point P of connection of the side-rod and piston-rod may describe a right line, the point *f* must describe an arc of curvature sufficient to neutralize the curvature which would be transmitted to it by the travel of the side-lever: to determine this arc *fff*, it is only necessary to describe from the middle point of the stroke, taken in the straight line *eee*, a right line *egf* equal in length to the length of the radius-bar, and perpendicular to it; also the highest position of the radius-bar forming the same angle with *egf* that the radius-bar forms with that line in its lowest position; then the three points *fff* being thus found, a circular arc drawn through them will determine the fixed centre *g*, and the length of the parallel bar *gf*.

The length of the side-bar *c*, from *f* to its connection with the side-lever, must of course be equal in length to the side-rod A, from *e* to the point also of its connection with the side-lever. These rods will remain during the working of the engine parallel to each other, and consequently the rod *ef* will continue parallel to the axis of the side-lever in all positions of the stroke. It must, however, be remarked that the parallelism is not absolutely correct; but is true only within certain, though narrow limits, giving an approximation sufficiently near for common practice.

Fig. 176 shows a form of parallel motion, sometimes adopted in land engines of the smaller class. It is susceptible of great accuracy, and admits of several modifications.

In this figure, A is the cylinder of the engine, B the beam, supported on a rocking-bar having a movable centre at D. The radius-bar has its fixed centre at P attached to the framing of the engine, and is centred to the beam at a point *c*, equidistant from the main centre F, and the point of at-

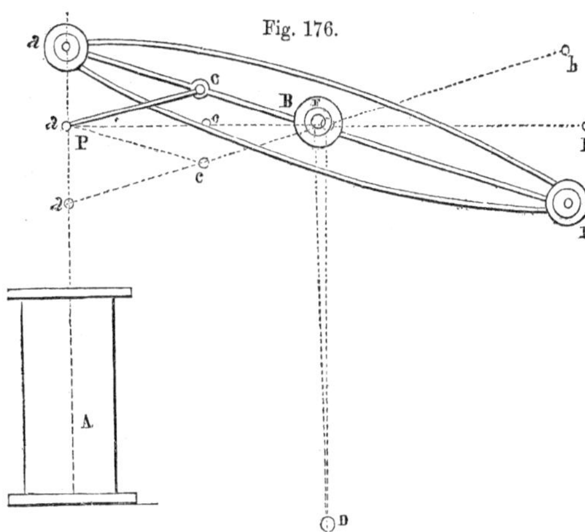

Fig. 176.

tachment of the piston-rod. Now, the radius-rod being equal to half the radius of the beam, and the radius-bar having a fixed centre at P, the point *c*, of the beam, must of necessity describe the arc *ccc*, during each stroke of the piston. Now, in describing this arc, it is plain that the main centre F, of the beam, must describe simultaneously an arc about the centre D upon which it is carried. But the radius FD being great in comparison to radii F*c* and P*c*, the motion of the main centre may be supposed, without sensible error, to be in a right line, as if it were free to slide in a horizontal groove. But the centre F being constrained to move horizontally through a given space during a stroke of the piston, the end *a* of the beam will travel horizontally through an equal space in the same direction, and will, therefore, instead of describing an arc about the centre F, describe the chord *aaa* of that arc, parallel to the chord of the arc *ccc*, which is the thing wanted.

This motion and its modifications are founded on the principle that if the arc of a semicircle be

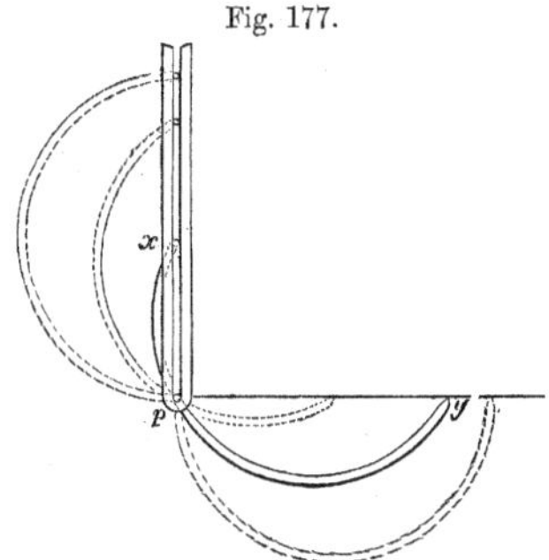

Fig. 177.

made to slide against a fixed point *p*, while one of its extremities *x*, is constrained to move in a straight line *x*, *p*, the other extremity *y*, will describe another straight line *p; y*, at right angles to the first.

To exhibit this principle in a practicable form, let *mn* be a rigid bar, having the end *n* guided in

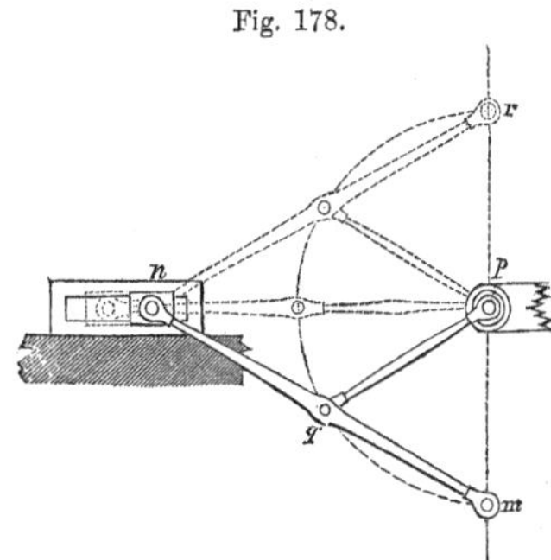

Fig. 178.

a horizontal groove, in which it can slide freely; and let *pq* be also a rigid bar, jointed to the former at *q*, and having a fixed centre at *p*. Let this bar be half the length of the bar *mn*, and let $mq = nq$; it is then evident, from the principle stated above, that, as the groove at *n*, and the fixed centre at *p*, control the motion of the bar *m n*, the end *m* is constrained to move in a straight line *mpr*, at right angles to *pn;* which is the condition to be fulfilled.

In Fig. 178, instead of the slot at *n*, the main-centre is allowed to traverse a small arc, which, deviating very little from a right line, fulfils the condition with considerable exactness. The same principle may be applied in various ways.

The course of the piston-rod deviates from the straight line bisecting the versines of the arcs described by the beam and radius-bar.

Let $QC = 85$: $Qn = 40$, the sine of the angle QCn, to radius AC. Put $Oz = 13$, the sine of the angle OCG; $Bm = 26$; $Am = 13$; $AB = 39$.

$$\sqrt{85^2 - 40^2} = 75 = Cn.$$

$$\therefore An = 85 - 75 = 10.$$

$$mg = \frac{10}{2} = 5 = mh.$$

$$Am : mh :: AB : Bt, \text{ that is,}$$

$$13 : 5 :: 39 : 15 = Bt = qA.$$

$$qA - nA = 15 - 10 = 5 = qn = fg.$$

And it is easily shown that,

$$qn = As;$$

$$BJ = tL;$$

$$fg = hi.$$

$$qs = BL = 5 + 10 + 5 = 20.$$

It is also easily shown that,

$$Qn = RL;$$

$$\therefore DB = \tfrac{1}{2}\left(\frac{RL^2}{BL} + BL\right) = \tfrac{1}{2}\left(\frac{40^2}{20} + 20\right) = 50.$$

Calculations similar to these have been made

Fig. 179.

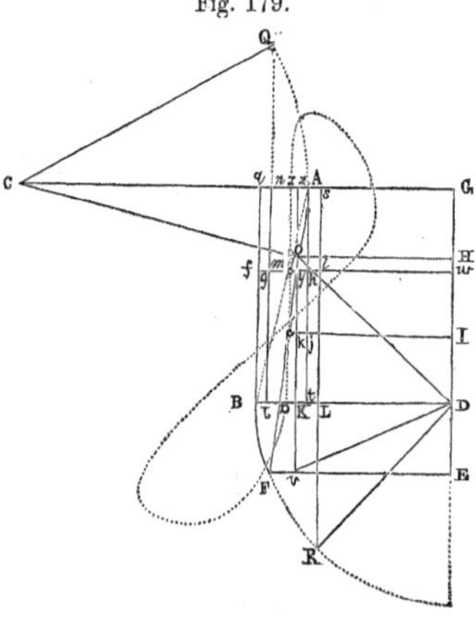

before, with respect to well-known properties of the circle. However, referring to Fig. 179, we have

$$Cz = \sqrt{CO^2 - Oz^2} = \sqrt{85^2 - 13^2} = 84.$$

$$Az = 85 - 84 = 1.$$

$$BD - Aq = AG = 50 - 15 = 35.$$

$$OH = zG = AG + Az = 35 + 1 = 36.$$

$$Bq = zK = \sqrt{AB^2 - Aq^2} = \sqrt{39^2 - 15^2} = 36.$$

$$HD = OK = zK - zO = 36 - 13 = 23.$$

The remaining calculations are to be made upon $OHIP$ and $OHEF$, which is represented in Fig. 180, for the sake of clearness.

Fig. 180.

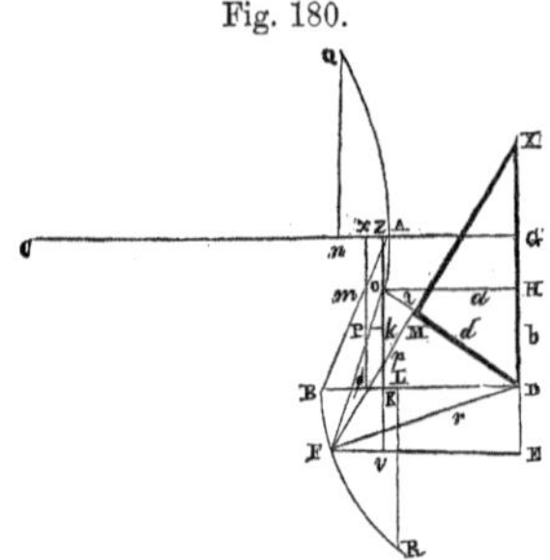

Put $OH = a = 36.$

$HD = b = 23.$

$FD = r = 50.$

$OP = c = 13 = Am.$

$OF = e = 39 = AB.$ Draw FM perpendicular to OD, and continue it to meet EH in X; then, if p be put for the perpendicular FM, and $d = MD$, $l = OM$, the segments of the base of the known triangle OFD.

Then, because the triangle MXD, is similar to both the triangle OHD and FXE, we have

$$b : a :: d : \frac{ad}{b} = MX.$$

$$\therefore FX = p + \frac{ad}{b} = \frac{pb + ad}{b}.$$

$$d + l : b :: \frac{pb + ad}{b} : \frac{pb + ad}{d + l} = FE.$$

$$\frac{pb + ad}{d + l} - a = \frac{pb - al}{d + l} = Fv.$$

$$OF : OP :: Fv : Pk.$$

$$e : c :: \frac{pb - al}{d + l} : \frac{c}{e}\left(\frac{pb - al}{d + l}\right) = Pk.$$

When Pk becomes known, we have the distance of the point P from $x\phi$, the line dividing the versines An and BL into two equal parts. Since the three sides of the triangle OFD are given, its area may be found by a common rule in mensuration, from which the perpendicular $FM = 37.7220984613$ is readily found.

$$OD = \sqrt{36^2 + 23^2} = 42.7200187266 = l + d.$$

The segments into which the perpendicular FM divides OD are easily found, as the sides OF and FD are known.

$$OM = 9.9016810529 = l.$$

$$MD = 32.8183376737 = d.$$

$$\therefore \frac{c}{e}\left(\frac{pb - al}{d + l}\right) = 3.9883545774 \quad Pk.$$

$Ax - Pk - Az = .0116454226$, this is the required distance that the point P is out of the straight line $x\phi$.

In Fig. 181, let thirteen inches of the up-stroke be made, then

Fig. 181.

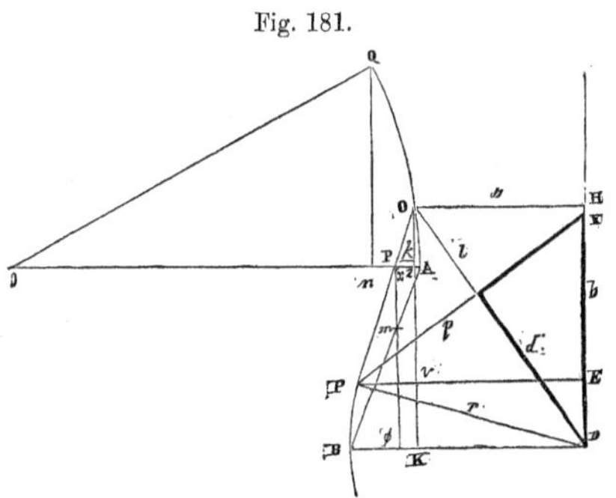

$$DH = 36 + 13 = 39 = b.$$
$$OH = 50 - 10 - 5 + 1 = 36 = a,$$
as before, for
$$OH = BD - B\phi - Ax + Az.$$
$$OD = \sqrt{36^2 + 39^2} = 53.075478 = d + l.$$

As in the first case, the three sides of the triangle OFD being known, its area may be found, and the perpendicular p is equal to twice the area divided by $d + l$.

$$p = 34.932157$$
$$l = 17.314984$$
$$\therefore \frac{c}{e}\left(\frac{pb - al}{d + l}\right) = 4.641287 = Pk.$$

Fig. 182.

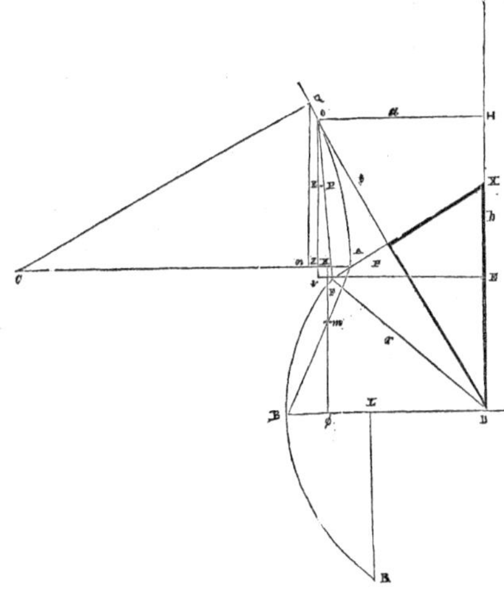

$\therefore\ Pk + zA = 5.641287$, and hence the point P is beyond the line $x\phi$, bisecting the versines .641287, which is considerable; but this case can never occur in practice.

In Fig. 182, let thirty-six inches of the stroke above the horizontal CA, be made; then

$$DH = 36 + 36 = 72 = b.$$
$$OH = 50 - 10 - 5 + 8 = 43 = a;$$
for, as before,
$$OH = BD - B\phi - Ax + Az. \quad \text{See Fig. 182.}$$
$$Cz = \sqrt{85^2 - 36^2} = 77.$$
$$\therefore Az = 85 - 77 = 8.$$
$$OD = \sqrt{72^2 + 43^2} = 83.863.$$

The three sides of the triangle FOD are 39, 83.863, and 50 respectively, from which we find the area to be 619.3666, and the perpendicular

$p = 14.771$ and
$l = 36.095$ the remaining side of the right-angled triangle.

Or, p and l may be thus found,

$$l = \frac{OD^2 + OF^2 - FD^2}{2\,(d + l)};\ \text{and}$$
$$p = \sqrt{OF^2 - l^2}.$$ If the numbers above given be substituted,
$$OD^2 = a^2 + b^2 = 72^2 + 36^2 = 7033.$$
$$l = \frac{7033 + 39^2 - 50^2}{2\ \sqrt{7033}} = 36.095.$$
$$p = \sqrt{39^2 - (36.095)^2} = 14.771.$$

In some cases this method will be found more convenient than that in which the area of the triangle OFD is found.

$$Pk = \frac{c}{e}\left(\frac{pb - al}{d + l}\right) = \frac{13}{39}\left(\frac{14.771 \times 72 - 36.095 \times 43}{83.863}\right)$$
$$= 1.943.$$

In this case the expression becomes

$al - pb$, for al is greater than pb.
$$Az - Pk = 8 - 1.943 = 6.057,$$
which shows that the point p is beyond the line $x\phi$ bisecting the versines.

The deviation of the piston-rod from a straight line, when a parallel motion is employed, is here for the first time accurately and directly determined, without involving calculations higher than that of extracting the square root. Many engineers and writers have attempted the solution of this problem, but all their labors failed, and ended in some clumsy indirect approximation or other.

MECHANICAL PRINCIPLES, RULES, LAWS, DEFINITIONS, AND DATA.

1. BY FORCE, we understand any cause which tends to impress or destroy motion. As we have no means of estimating force except by its effects, it is differently measured in statics and dynamics. In statics, force is measured by the pressure which it causes a body, when at rest, to exert against another with which it is in contact. Thus, when a heavy body is supported by the hand, it exerts a pressure downwards on the hand, and is sustained by the pressure of the hand upwards. The former pressure is called the *action*, and the latter the *reaction*, and they are evidently equal to each other.

In dynamics, FORCE is measured by the velocity uniformly generated in a given time. Thus, if a heavy body be not supported by the hand, it will fall towards the earth; and the velocity which it acquires in a given time is taken as the measure of the FORCE of gravity. The means and instruments by which different forces are compared and measured, will hereafter be very fully discussed.

THE PARALLELOGRAM OF FORCES.

If two forces (P, Q) act at the same point (A), the force which is equivalent to the two is ex-

Fig. 183.

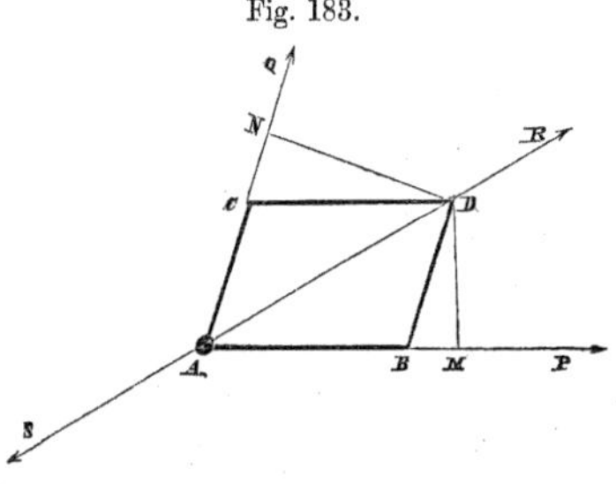

pressed in magnitude and in direction by the diagonal of the parallelogram (AD), of which the sides (AB, AC) represent the magnitude and direction of the component forces (P, Q).

Let the angle $BAC = a$, = Angle MBD.

In the two right-angled triangles ADM, BDM, let $AD = 40$, $BD = 25$, $MD = 24$, $AM = 32$, and $BM = 7$.

$\frac{DM}{AD} = \frac{24}{40} = .6000000 =$ sine of the angle DAM.

The common logarithm of this number (.6000000) is—1. + .7781513, which is written $\bar{1}.7781513$, the index 1 being negative and the decimal part positive. To the index add 10. then we have

9.7781513,

which is termed the *log.* sine of the angle DAM.

$\frac{AM}{AD} = \frac{32}{40} = .8000000 =$ cosine of the angle MAD.

Log. cos. of this angle = 9.9030900.

$\frac{MD}{AM} = \frac{24}{32} =$ .7500000 = tangent of the angle DAM. The *log. tan.* of this angle is 9.8750613.

$$\frac{BM}{BD} = \frac{7}{25} = .2800000 = cos.\ a.$$

$AD^2 = AC^2 + CD^2 - 2\,AC \times CD\ cos.\ ACD = AC^2 + AB^2 + 2\,AC \times AB\ cos.\ BAC.$

Or, which is the same thing,

$$R^2 = P^2 + Q^2 + 2\,PQ\ cos.\ a.$$

Also;

$$R : Q :: sin.\ a : sin.\ BAD.$$
$$R : P :: sin.\ a : sin.\ CAD.$$
$$P : Q :: DN : DM.$$

If three forces, P Q, S, act on a point and keep it at rest, each of these forces is proportional to the sine of the angle made by the other two. Let the forces P and Q be equivalent to the force R, then, since P and Q balance the force S, the force R will also balance the force S, and, therefore, R is equal and opposite to S. Hence

$$S \text{ or } (R) : P :: sin.\ a : sin.\ CAD \text{ or } sin.\ QAS.$$
$$S \text{ or } (R) : Q :: sin.\ a : sin.\ BAD \text{ or } sin.\ PAS.$$
$$\therefore S : P : Q :: sin.\ a : sin.\ QAS : sin.\ PAS.$$

If the three sides of any triangle be parallel to three forces which act on a point and keep it at rest, these forces will be proportional to the sides of the triangle. This proposition, which is known by the name of the *parallelogram of forces*, is the foundation of the whole doctrine of equilibrum.

Bernoulli, D'Alembert, Laplace, Poisson, Duchayla, &c., and other eminent philosophers, have given proofs of this important theorem.

2. If R be the resultant of two parallel forces P, Q, acting in the same direction upon the rigid straight line AB, then

$$R = P + Q \text{ and}$$
$$P : Q : R :: BC : AC : AB.$$

So that each of the three forces P, Q, R, is proportional to the line intercepted between the directions of the other two.

Fig. 184.

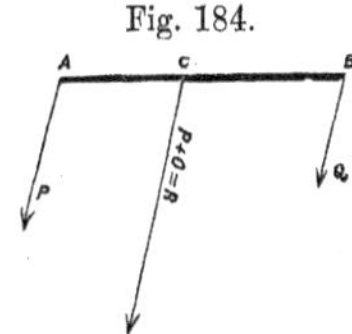

If R be the resultant of two parallel forces P, Q, acting in opposite directions upon a rigid straight line, then

Fig. 185.

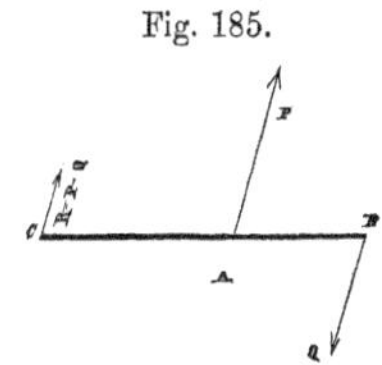

$$P - Q = R; \text{ and}$$
$$R : Q :: AB : AC, \text{ then}$$
$$AC = \frac{Q}{R} AB = \frac{Q}{P - Q} . AB.$$

Hence, when $P = Q$, the resultant $R = o$, and the distance AC becomes infinitely great. In this case no single force could produce the effect of the two equal forces P, Q. Their tendency would be to turn the system round in the plane in which they are.

3. The product of a force, and the perpendicular distance of a given point from its direction, is called the *moment of the force with respect to that point.* And if through this point an axis be drawn at right angles to the plane, passing through the point and the direction of the force, the product, which is the same as before, is called the *moment of the force* with respect to the axis.

By combining, compounding, and developing these simple propositions, numerous theorems and properties are established; large volumes are filled with them; they are termed works on Statics. Of the deductions of statics, in this place, we shall give but one more.

4. The moment of the resultant of any number of forces acting at a point A, with respect to a point P in the same plane, is equal to the sum of the moments of the component forces with respect to the same point P.

PARALLELOGRAM OF VELOCITIES.

5. A motion is uniformly variable when its velocity either increases or diminishes by a constant amount in equal times taken as small as we please. Any change in the velocity of a body is called *acceleration;* it is either positive or negative, according as there is increase or diminution of the velocity.

Suppose a locomotive to move at the rate of 80 feet a second, which, for convenience, is termed an 80-feet velocity, and is so retarded by friction, the atmosphere, and other causes, that, in each second, it loses 7 feet velocity; what is its velocity after 5 seconds?

In this case, 80 feet is the initial velocity; and the acceleration is negative 7 feet, (-7).

$$\therefore 80 - 7 \times 5 = 45; \quad . \quad . \quad \text{(A.)}$$

hence, the terminal velocity, at the end of 5 seconds, is 45 feet.

Let the initial velocity, 80 feet $= a$, the terminal velocity 45 feet $= v$, the acceleration in one second, -7 feet $= -p$, and the time the body is observed in motion, 5 seconds $= t$. Then (A) becomes

$$a - pt = v; \quad . \quad . \quad . \quad \text{(B.)}$$

This formula will hold for all uniformly retarded velocities.

A railway car rolling down an inclined plane with an initial velocity $a = 63$ feet a second, and acquires, in the course of each second, 4 feet additional velocity; its velocity at the end of 8 seconds will be

$$63 + 4 \times 8 = 95 \text{ feet.} \quad . \quad . \quad . \quad \text{(C.)}$$

the terminal velocity. When generalized, as in the former example (C), becomes

$$a + pt = v. \quad . \quad . \quad . \quad . \quad \text{(D.)}$$

which will hold for all uniformly accelerated motion.

The acceleration of a body falling freely in vacuo, at Washington, is $32\frac{2}{13}$ feet in a second, moving from a state of rest, what velocity will it acquire in 7 seconds?

$$32\tfrac{2}{13} \times 7 = 225\tfrac{1}{13} \text{ feet.}$$

And the general formula for the terminal velocity, in such cases, becomes

$$v = pt, \quad . \quad . \quad . \quad . \quad \text{(E.)}$$

as the initial velocity = zero.

6. In uniform motion, the space is equal to the product of the velocity and the time; thus a locomotive, going with a velocity of 10 feet a second, passes over 730 feet in 73 seconds; for

$$730 = 10 \times 73.$$

$$\text{Space} = \text{velocity} \times \text{time}. \quad . \quad \text{(F.)}$$

In the next place, we will show that the space (s), described in the time (t), with a uniformly accelerated motion is, $= \frac{vt}{2}$, that is,

$$s = \frac{vt}{2}; \quad . \quad . \quad . \quad . \quad . \quad \text{(G.)}$$

v being the terminal velocity. So that, if a body moved uniformly with a given velocity and for a given time, the space described is twice as great as that described by a body uniformly accelerated for the same time, and having the given velocity at the termination. This is easily seen by comparing (F) and (G).

It is easily seen, although writers on mechanics take out-of-the-way methods to prove it, that as the velocity uniformly increases from o to v, the mean $\frac{o+v}{2}$, multiplied by the time t, gives the space described.

$$\therefore \frac{o+v}{2} \times t = \frac{vt}{2} = s,$$

7, which we proposed to prove. Large books are filled, combining the simple principles and formulas laid down in the last two articles; they are termed works on Dynamics.

However, in this place, we will establish only a few of the more useful expressions, by mere transposition, without involving any additional principles.

Take (F) the expression for all uniform motions, and it immediately follows

$$\text{time} = \frac{\textit{space}}{\textit{velocity}}; \text{ and, velocity} = \frac{\textit{space}}{\textit{time}}.$$

Expression (E) in uniformly accelerated motion, the initial velocity being = o, the terminal velocity

$$v = pt$$

the product of the acceleration p, and the time t.

$$\therefore p = \frac{v}{t}; \text{ and } t = \frac{v}{p}.$$

From (G) we obtain directly

$$v = \frac{2s}{t} \text{ and } t = \frac{2s}{v}.$$

Substituting the value of $v = pt$ in $s = \frac{vt}{2}$, we obtain,

$$s = \frac{pt^2}{2}. \quad . \quad . \quad . \quad . \quad \text{(H.)}$$

And if the value of $t = \frac{v}{p}$, taken from the first of these expressions, be substituted in the second, we find

$$s = \frac{v^2}{2p}. \quad . \quad . \quad . \quad . \quad . \quad \text{(I.)}$$

(H) shows that the space described is the product of half the acceleration and the square of the time. (I) shows that the space is found by dividing the square of the terminal velocity by twice the acceleration.

8. By comparing two uniformly accelerated motions we obtain

$$V = PT; \; S = \frac{PT^2}{2};$$

$$v = pt; \; s = \frac{pt^2}{2}; \text{ and}$$

$$\frac{v}{V} = \frac{pt}{PT}; \frac{s}{S} = \frac{pt^2}{PT^2} = \frac{vt}{VT} = \frac{v^2P}{V^2p}.$$

If $T = t$, then

$$\frac{v}{V} = \frac{p}{P}; \; \frac{s}{S} = \frac{p}{P} = \frac{v}{V}.$$

which shows that the spaces described are to each other as the accelerations; or as the terminal velocities. If $P = p$ then

$$\frac{v}{V} = \frac{t}{T}; \quad \frac{s}{S} = \frac{t^2}{T^2} = \frac{v^2}{V^2};$$

so that, in like accelerations, and also in one and the same uniformly accelerated motion, the terminal velocities are proportional to the times, and the spaces described to the squares of the times, and also to the squares of the terminal velocities.

If $V = v$ then,

$\frac{p}{P} = \frac{T}{t}$ and $\frac{s}{S} = \frac{t}{T}$ hence, with equal terminal velocities the accelerations are inversely, and the spaces directly proportional to the times. When $S = s$.

$$\frac{p}{P} = \frac{T}{t} = \frac{v}{V}.$$

8. In uniformly accelerated motion, commencing with a velocity a, as the space (at) belongs to the initial velocity a, and the space $\frac{pt^2}{2}$ to the acceleration p, then

$$s = at + \frac{pt^2}{2}. \quad . \quad . \quad . \quad . \quad \text{(J.)}$$

is the space passed over in the time t, with an acceleration p, and an initial velocity a. It is easily shown that

$$s = at - \frac{pt^2}{2}. \quad . \quad . \quad . \quad . \quad (K.)$$

in a uniformly retarded motion.

By combining (J) and (D) by eliminating p, and then t, we find

$$s = \frac{a+v}{2}\, t \text{ and } s = \frac{v^2 - a^2}{2p}.$$

From (B) and (K) may be adduced

$$s = \frac{a+v}{2}\, t \text{ and } s = \frac{a^2 - v^2}{2p}.$$

9. A magnet falls more quickly to the earth than another body, when a mass of iron is immediately below it. The acceleration which the magnet experiences, in consequence of the iron, may be considered invariable, when the height from which it falls is small and the iron great, as in the case of an extensive layer of magnetic iron ore. If the acceleration due to the iron ore be 4 feet, and that due to the force of gravity $32\frac{2}{13}$, the magnitude would fall with the velocity $32\frac{2}{13} + 4 = 36\frac{2}{13}$ feet at the end of the first second. In this case, the acceleration in a second being $36\frac{2}{13}$; the body will fall through a space in three seconds $= \frac{36\frac{2}{23} \times 9}{2} = 162\frac{9}{13}$ feet, according to (H). The principle here introduced in a numerical form, may be thus stated in general terms.

Should one and the same body have, in addition to the primary velocities V and v, the constant accelerations P and p, then the corresponding spaces in the time t, will be

$$Vt;\; vt;\; P\frac{t^2}{2};\, p\frac{t^2}{2}.$$

When the velocities and accelerations are in the same direction, the whole space s passed over will be

$$s = Vt + vt + P\frac{t^2}{2} + p\,\frac{t^2}{2} = (V + v)t + (P + p)\,\frac{t^2}{2}.$$

Hence, not only the velocity of the resulting or compound motion is made up of the sum or difference of the simple velocities, as the case may be, but also the sum or difference of the accelerations, as the case may be, give the resulting acceleration, a fact worth being remembered.

10. The diagonal AD of a parallelogram, whose sides AB, AC represent the magnitudes and directions of two velocities, gives the direction, and represents the magnitude of the resulting motion. This parallelogram is called *the parallelogram of velocities.* The simple velocities V, v, are called the components, and the compound velocity W, the resultant. As in the parallelogram of forces

$$W^2 = V^2 + v^2 + 2\, Vv \cos. S$$
$$S = m + n.$$

Any given velocity may be supposed to consist of two components, and can be resolved into them by the expressions,

$$V = \frac{W \sin. m}{\sin. (n + m)} \text{ and } v = \frac{W \sin. n}{\sin. (n + m)}.$$

In practical cases, the two velocities are generally at right angles to each other, then $(n + m) = 90°$, and $\sin. 90 = 1$.

Hence $V = W \cos. n$ and $v = W \sin. n$.

Fig. 186.

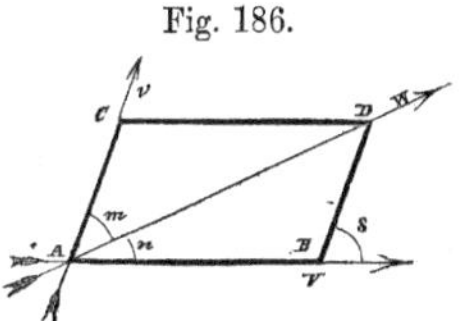

Let velocity $W = 30$ feet, be resolved into two components, which deviate from its direction by the angle $m = 51°$ and $n = 23°$

$$\sin. 51° = .7771460\,;\ \sin. 23° = .3907311\,;$$
$$\sin. (51° + 23°) = .9612617.$$
$$V = \frac{30 \times .7771460}{.9612617} = 24.254 \text{ feet.}$$
$$v = \frac{30 \times .3907311}{.9612617} = 12.195 \text{ feet velocity.}$$

THE PARALLELOGRAM OF ACCELERATIONS.

11. Two uniformly accelerated motions, beginning with the velocity zero, or 0, produced, when combined, a uniformly accelerated motion in a straight line. Let $P\,p$, be the accelerations in the directions AM, AN.

Then at the end of any time t,

$$AM = \frac{Pt^2}{2}, \text{ and } AN = \frac{p\, t^2}{2}.$$

$$\therefore \frac{AM}{AN} = \frac{Pt^2}{p\, t^2} = \frac{P}{p},$$ which is a constant ratio, not depending on the time; hence, the compound

Fig. 187.

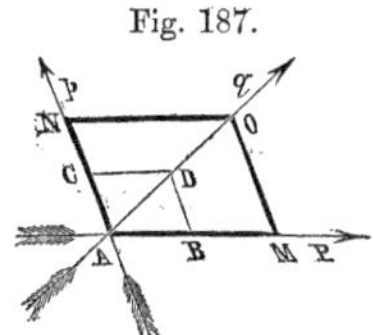

motion is rectilinear, and in the direction of the diagonal AO. Let $AB = P$, and $AC = p$, and from the similarity of the parallelograms,

$$\frac{AO}{AD} = \frac{AM}{AB} = \frac{\frac{1}{2}Pt^2}{P} = \frac{1}{2}t^2.$$

$$\therefore AO = AD \times \tfrac{1}{2}t^2.$$

Hence, the path AO, described by the compound motion, is proportional to the square of the time. The compound motion is uniformly accelerated, and the acceleration is represented by the diagonal AD, of the parallelogram composed of the simple accelerations $P\,p$.

THE PARALLELOGRAM OF VELOCITIES AND ACCELERATIONS.

12. When the directions of the motions do not coincide, the combination of a uniformly accelerated, and a uniform motion, the path described is a curve, called a *parabola*.

Met $AN = y$, and let it be described in the time t, by a uniform velocity v, then

$$AN = y = vt.$$

In the same time, with a uniform acceleration,

Fig. 188.

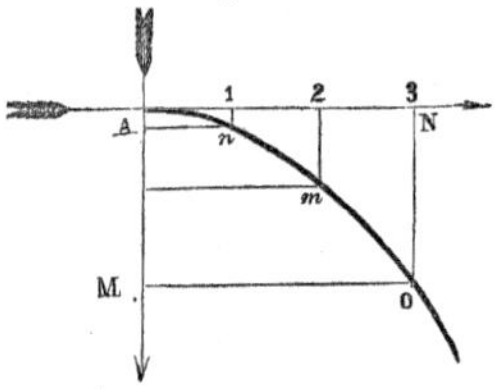

p, and in the direction AM, at right angles to the track AN, $\frac{p\,t^2}{2}$ will be described, which call x.

It is clear that the body is not always in one and the same straight line, for if from the first equation we take $t = \frac{y}{v}$, and substitute it in the second $x = \frac{p\,t^2}{2}$, we obtain

$$x = \frac{p\,y^2}{2\,v^2},$$

which is the equation to a parabola $AnmO$, of which the co-ordinates are x and y. In this way the equation to any curve forming the diagonal of the parallelogram may be found. However, by combining several velocities and several invariable accelerations a parabolic motion is produced, for the velocities may be united into a single one, and the accelerations into a single one likewise; the resultant, therefore, is of only one uniform, and one uniformly accelerated motion. Variable accelerations can also be united into a mean acceleration, for each of them may be considered invariable for an infinitely small space of time, and the corresponding motions during that short space of time, as uniformly accelerated. But after this very small space of time, the resultant and its component accelerations must be considered variable. By combining the resulting acceleration, obtained for the infinitely small space of time, with given or resultant velocities, it is possible to deduce a small curve, the path of the motion during the short time. In the same manner, for the next small portion of time, if the mean acceleration and velocity be combined, we obtain a new curve; and by continual repetitions we obtain the whole course of the motion.

A small portion of any curve may be taken as part of a circle. This particular circle at any point is termed the *circle of curvature*, and its radius, the *radius of curvature*. Hence the course of body moving in any curve, may be supposed to be composed of a series of arcs of the circles of curvature.

The whole theory of mechanics rests on the foregoing TWELVE short articles.

CENTRAL FORCES.

13. Centripetal and centrifugal forces are sometimes called central forces. When a material point or body moves in a circular arc, the normal force, acting in the direction of the radius inwards is termed the *centripetal force;* and the force which acts in the direction of the radius outwards, has received the name of *centrifugal force*.

Let a body describe Ab uniformly in a unit of time; then, if no force were to act on the body, it would in the next unit of time go on to B, in the same straight line describing $Bb = AB$. But when

Fig. 189.

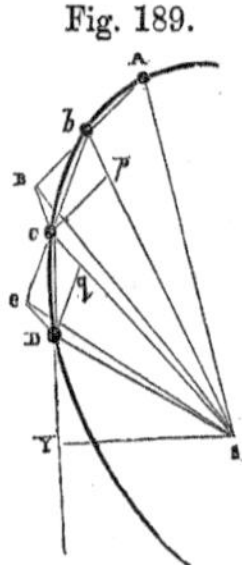

the body comes to b, let a force tending to the centre S act on it, and by a single impulse, cause it to describe bp, in a unit of time, if this force alone acted upon it. Complete the parallelogram Bb, Cp, and join SC, SB. Because the body would describe Bb, in consequence of the original motion, and bp from the attractive force at S, by combining the two motions, the body will describe bC, the diagonal of the parallelogram. As CB is parallel to Sb, the triangle $SbC = SBb, = SbA$, because $Bb = BA$.

In like manner, if an impulsive force act on the body at C, in the direction CS, the body will describe an area, in the next unit of time, equal to the areas in each of the two preceding units; and so on successively. If the unit of time be diminished, and the number of units increased indefinitely, the areas described in these units will still be equal to each other. And the polygon $AbCD$, &c., will ultimately become a curve line, and the forces which were supposed to act by impulses at b, C, D, &c., will be a continuous force acting at every point of the curve. And because equal areas are described in all equal times, it is clear that, in different times, the areas will be in proportion to the times. In this proof, we only employ the parallelogram of velocities, and the 37th proposition of the first book of Euclid. The velocity at any point D, is inversely as the perpendicular SY, drawn from S to the tangent DY. For if v be the velocity at D, and $SY = p$; $t =$ the time of describing CD, then $CD = vt$. The area of the triangle $SCD = \frac{1}{2}\ CD \times SY = \frac{vtp}{2}$. Now if a be the area described in a unit of time, $a\,t$ will be the area described in the small time, at the point of contact D,

$$\therefore \frac{vtp}{2} = a\,t; \text{ and}$$

$$v = \frac{2a}{p}.$$

So that the velocity v is as the perpendicular p, on the tangent.

It is a well-known property of the circle, Euclid 8, book vi.; on account of the similarity of the triangles MBD, MBA (Fig. 190); any (chord $MB)^2 = MA \times MD$.

14. If a body describe the circumference of a circle uniformly in consequence of an attractive force placed in its centre; the accelerating force which acts upon the body is measured by the square of the velocity divided by the radius of the circle.

Let the body come to M, and let it describe the arc Mm, uniformly with the velocity v, in the time t; then $vt = Mm$. Now the body would describe the tangent MN uniformly with the velocity v, were it not acted upon by the force at the centre C. But as it describes the arc Mm, it is evident that the accelerating force at C, acting upon the body at M, would make it describe a space equal to $Nm = Mp$ in the time t. Let f be the accelerating force at M; then since this may be considered constant through the indefinitely small space Nm, we have

Fig. 190.

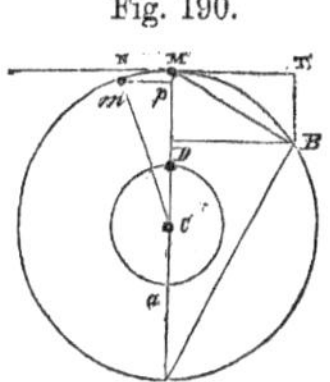

$$Nm = Mp = \frac{ft^2}{2} \text{ (Article 7).}$$

But by the property of the circle just quoted, $Mp \times MA =$ (chord $Mm)^2 =$ (*arc* $Mm)^2$, when it has no length, but the mere form of length; in fact, when the arc Mm becomes a mathematical point.

Let $r = CM$; and we have shown that $mM = vt$, and $Mp = \frac{ft^2}{2}$.

$\therefore Mp \times MA =$ (*arc* $Mm)^2$, becomes

$\frac{ft^2}{2} \times 2\,r = v^2\,t^2$, and consequently, $f = \frac{v^2}{r}$, (A.)

which we had to prove. The reasoning is extremely simple, as it only involves a single proposition of Euclid, and the parallelogram of velocities. The length of an arc of a circle of 180°, is generally represented by π, the radius $= 1$.

$$\text{Then } \pi = 3.14159265358979.$$
$$\pi^2 = 9.8696044010893586.$$
$$\sqrt{\pi} = 1.772453850905516.$$
$$\frac{1}{\pi} = .31830988618379.$$

These numbers are often required, and on that account only they are inserted here. To return to the motion of a body in a circle, let T be the time of an entire revolution, then the circumference of the circle will be

$$Tv = 2\,\pi\,r \text{ (B).}$$

since the velocity v, is uniform; and, as $2\,\pi$ is the circumference to radius 1, $2\,\pi\,r$ is the circumference to radius r. From (B) we have $v^2 = \frac{4\pi^2 r^2}{T^2}$, which, when substituted in (A), the result is

$$f = \frac{v^2}{r} = \frac{4\pi^2 r}{T^2} \quad . \quad . \quad . \quad . \quad (C.)$$

Long before NEWTON was born, what we have established in this 14th article was known and demonstrated; truths not very profound, the parallelogram of velocities, and a proposition in Euclid.

Let another body D, describe the circumference of the circle Da, in the same manner, in the time T_1. And let F represent the accelerating force at D, and $R = DC$, the radius of the circle. Then, from the formula marked (C),

$$F = \frac{4\pi^2 R}{T_1{}^2}.$$

$$\therefore f : F :: \frac{r}{T^2} : \frac{R}{T_1^2} \quad . \quad . \quad . \quad (D.)$$

Now the third law, discovered by Kepler, shows that the squares of the times are as the cubes of the distances from the centre C; hence, if we put r^3 for T^2 and R^3 for T_1^2, then (D) becomes

$$f : F :: \frac{1}{r^2} : \frac{1}{R^2} \quad . \quad . \quad . \quad (E.)$$

Showing that the forces f, F, are inversely proportional to the squares of the distances r, R. To secure the honor of Kepler's discoveries, and all that depend on them for an Englishman, the property expressed by (E), so easily deduced when Kepler's laws became known, was selected and called the great discovery of Newton. The author of this work has been often amused with the consummate skill displayed by English writers on mechanics, to uphold this great Newtonian hoax; it would be very harmless, and quite English, but by so doing, their works are rendered very difficult. It must not be forgotten that Kepler also discovered that the line drawn from the sun to any of the planets, passes over equal areas in equal times. (Art. 13.) English writers make use of such expressions as, "It was conjectured by the immortal Newton, and afterwards demonstrated by him, that bodies attract one another inversely as the squares of their distances;" "The law of universal gravitation was discovered by our own Newton;" &c. &c. The way in which this falsehood is perpetuated, and how it was established, are truly laughable. Fancy an English fat philosopher solemnly declaring, "It was the immortal *Stubbs* that discovered 5 was contained in 30, just 6 times and no more; after it was ascertained that 5 times 6 make 30." This was about the amount of skill required to find (E), when (C) and Kepler's laws were known.

Let a be the angular velocity, or the arc described in a unit of time, on a circle having the same centre C, whose radius is 1. Then,

$$a\,T = 2\pi;$$

and referring to equation marked (C),

$$f = \frac{v^2}{r} = \frac{4\pi^2 r}{T^2}, \text{ becomes } ra^2.$$

15. There are two ways in which the effects of forces may be estimated; one by comparing their velocities, and another by comparing their momenta. *Accelerating force* is measured by the velocity uniformly generated in a given time, no regard being had to the quantity of matter moved. *Moving force* is measured by the momentum or quantity of motion uniformly generated in a given time, and is equal to the product of the accelerating force and the quantity of matter. In another place, these methods of comparing and measuring forces will be more fully discussed; they are alluded to here, to show that the acceleration is the most material element, when motion is considered. For, when the acceleration becomes known, all other circumstances respecting the motion are readily obtained. With respect to circular motions, and all curvilinear motions can be reduced to a series of circular motions (Art. 12), we have shown that the accelerating force f in the direction of the radius can always be expressed by $\frac{v^2}{r}$. That is, the *centripetal* (art. 13) force is represented by $\frac{v^2}{r}$; it is clear that the centrifugal force may also be measured by $\frac{v^2}{r}$, for in a circle it is equal and opposite the *centripetal*, since the body always maintains the same distance from the centre of force.

Suppose the radius of the earth to be 3956 miles, and the distance of the moon from the centre of the earth to be 60.24 times the earth's radius. What is the accelerating force at the moon, which causes it to revolve round the earth in an orbit nearly circular in 27 days 7 hours 43 minutes; the earth supposed to be at rest. Taking the second for the unit of time, and the foot for the unit of space, we have

$$f = \frac{4\pi^2 r}{T^2} = \frac{4\pi^2 \times 60.24 \times 3956 \times 5280}{(39343 \times 60)^2}$$

$= .008914$ feet.

Now, without Kepler's laws, or of Newton's mock discoveries, this very rough calculation shows that the force of the earth's attraction, at the distance of the moon, is such that it would oblige a body after one second of time had elapsed, or at the end of the first second, to be moving at the rate of .008914 feet a second, supposing it to move in a straight line from a state of rest, to the centre of the earth. But the force of the earth's attraction at the surface is such, supposing it to be a globe, that it will cause all bodies to fall near its surface, so that at the end of the first second they will be moving with a velocity of about $32\frac{1}{3}$ feet a second. It is by comparing the numbers $32\frac{1}{3}$ and .008914, that the force of the earth's attraction is measured at the surface of the earth, and at the distance of the moon. This calculation is entered into, to illustrate numerically how forces are estimated by their accelerations.

In most works, the letter g is put for the acceleration of the force of gravity, in the same way that π is put for the length of an arc of a circle of 180°, radius $= 1$.

At Washington, $g = 32.155$ feet. But Washington is far above the surface of the globe, which we have imagined the earth to be, in the foregoing problem, and hence we assumed g, a little greater. By some writers, all accelerating forces are compared with the force of gravity, which is called 1; thus, a force which was equal to twice the force of gravity, was called 2; and so on.

The ratio 60.24 to 1, is nearly equal to 241 to 4, and the decimal .008914 is nearly equal to $\frac{11}{1234}$; therefore,

$32\frac{1}{3} : \frac{11}{1234} : : (241)^2 : \frac{(241)^2 \times 11 \times 3}{1234 \times 97} = 16$ very nearly. So that in this very rough way, it is clear that bodies attract inversely as the squares of the distances,

$$32\frac{1}{2} : \frac{11}{1234} : : (241)^2 : (4)^2.$$

This point is discussed at some length, as it is rendered very obscure by English writers; which, from all appearances, have no other object than that of concealing the Newtonian hoax. From the formula

$$f = \frac{v^2}{r} \text{ we have } r = \frac{v^2}{f};$$

by which the radii of curvature at any point in any curve may be found, when the velocity v, at that point, and the acceleration f, at right angles to the direction of motion, are known. If a body rotates in a circle of 20 feet diameter, and makes a complete revolution in 12 seconds, then the velocity v in each second is $\frac{2\,\pi \times 10}{11} = 5.712$ feet; and the normal acceleration, $f = \frac{(5.712)^2}{10} = 3.2627$ feet. If this body moves from M to B (Fig. 190), in $1\frac{3}{4}$ minutes, it will have receded from the tangent MT the distance $MD = TB = \frac{1}{2}\,ft^2 = 2.856\,(1\frac{3}{4})^2 = 4.996$ feet. (Art. 7.)

16. Let a body describe a curve line AMm, in consequence of a centre of force placed at S (Fig. 191); and let another body descend in the straight line AS towards S. And let the velocities of the two bodies at the equal distances SD, SM, be equal. Take an indefinitely small arc Mm, so small that it may be considered a straight line, and describe the circular arcs MD, md. From p, the intersection of SM, md, draw pq perpendicular to Mm. Let f be the accelerating force at D or M, towards S, and let $Dd = Mp$ represent this force. Then, according to the parallelogram of accelerations (Art. 11), the force Mp may be resolved into two Mq, qp; of which Mq alone is effective in accelerating the body's motion along the curve at M. Put the angle $SMm = a$; then the effective force Mq is evidently equal $f \cos. a$. Because the space Mm is indefinitely small, the increase of velocity from M to m

Fig. 191.

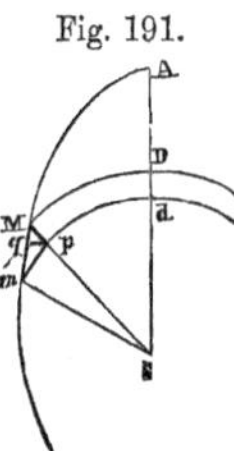

will be indefinitely small; and hence Mm, may be supposed to be described with a uniform velocity. And because the velocities at D and M are equal, if t be the time of describing Dd or Mp uniformly,

$$t \times \frac{Mm}{Mp} = \frac{t}{\cos. a},$$

will be the time of describing Mm, uniformly with the same velocity; for, in this case,

$$Mp : Mm : : t : t \times \frac{Mm}{Mp}.$$

Now the increase of velocity from M to m (Art. 5), is equal to the accelerating force $f \cos. a$, multiplied by the time $\frac{t}{\cos. a}$, but

$$f \cos. a \times \frac{t}{\cos. a} = ft.$$

which is equal to the increment of the velocity from D to d. Consequently, as the velocity at D in the direction of S, and at M along the curve are equal, and the increment of velocity from D to d, equal to the increment of velocity from M to m; the velocities at the equal distances d and m must also be equal. In like manner, it may be shown that the velocities at all other equal distances are equal; and if, instead of approaching the centre, the two bodies should recede from it, the same proposition is equally true of their velocities.

THE PRINCIPLE OF D'ALEMBERT.

17. This principle is of great importance in deducing the laws of constrained, from those of free motion, and it reduces the general principles of dynamics to those of equilibrium. The form in which this principle was expressed by D'Alembert, may be thus stated:—

If there be any system of bodies P, Q, R, &c., connected in any manner with each other, and acted on by given forces; and if, at any time, the additional velocities which these bodies would acquire in the succeeding instant be p, q, r, &c., whilst the velocities which the bodies would acquire in the same instant, were they all free from their mutual action, are a, b, c, &c.; then if the velocities p, q, r, &c., be such that the momenta Pp, Pp, are equivalent to Pa; the momenta Qq, Qq, are equivalent to Qb, and so on; then if the momenta Pp_1, Qq_1, Rr_1, &c., act on the system alone, it will be kept in equilibrium.

This principle may be given under another form more convenient for calculation. Since the momentum Pa is the resultant of Pp, Pp_1; it is evident that Pp_1, is the resultant of the momenta Pa and $(-Pp)$. Hence, it follows that there will be an equilibrium, if we suppose the momenta

$$Pa - Pp;\ Qb - Qq;\ Rc - Rr;\ \&c.,$$

to act upon the system. For example, let the body A impinge upon B, and let their velocities before impact be a and b; also, let v be their common velocity after impact.

Then we have

Weights of the bodies.	Impressed velocities.	Effective velocities.
A	a	v
B	b	v

Now if, at the moment of impact, the velocity v should be communicated to each of the bodies in an opposite direction, there would be an equilibrium. Hence, the forces which destroy each other, are

$$Aa,\ Bb,\ -Av,\ -Bv;$$

and, therefore, the sum of these momenta must be equal to zero; or

$$Aa + Bb - Av - Bv = 0, \text{ or } v = \frac{aA + bB}{A + B}.$$

Again, take two bodies hanging over a fixed pulley. Let P descend and draw up Q, and let v be their common velocity at the end of the time T; and $v + x$ their common velocity at the end of the time $T + t$; where t is supposed to be indefinitely small. Now if, at the end of the time T, the string should break, and the bodies be set free, their velocities after the instant t, would be $v + gt$ and $v - gt$ (see page 99). But their actual velocities at the end of this time is $v + x$. We then have

Weights of the bodies.	Impressed velocities.	Effective velocities.
P	$v+gt$	$v + x$
Q	$v-gt$	$v + x$

Hence, taking the momenta communicated in the time t, and putting a contrary sign before the effective velocities, we have

$$Pgt - Qgt - Px - Qx = 0, \text{ hence,}$$

$$\frac{x}{t} = \frac{P - Q}{P + Q}g = \text{the acclerating force.} \quad g = 32\tfrac{2}{13}.$$

For it has been shown in Arts. 6 and 7, that the acceleration is equal to the velocity (x), divided by the time (t) in which it is acquired.

THE TRUE PRINCIPLES

UPON WHICH

PRACTICAL MECHANICS ARE BASED AND MACHINES OPERATE:

AN EXPOSITION OF THE FALSE MECHANICAL DOCTRINES PROMULGATED BY NEWTON, HUTTON, GREGORY, ROBISON, TREDGOLD, MORNAY, BARLOW, AND OTHER ENGLISH WRITERS; WHICH ERRONEOUS DOCTRINES ARE YET TAUGHT IN SCHOOLS AND COLLEGES, AND BY PUBLIC LECTURERS.

THE PROPORTIONS AND PROPERTIES OF SCREW PROPELLERS, AND THE OPERATIONS OF SCREW VESSELS.

MECHANICS had scarcely been subjected to mathematical investigation, when a dispute arose among mathematicians, Newton on one side, and on the wrong side; while Leibnitz, and Dr. Young of Trinity College, Dublin, and others, were on the right side. This dispute was about the measure of the force of a body in motion. Many eminent men took sides in the argument, for it lasted for more than fifty years, and was conducted with more acrimony, earnestness, and zeal than could be supposed possible in such hands, and of so abstract a nature. And after all it was rather dropt than ended, much to the discredit of English mathematicians.

Let w represent the weight of a body, and v, its velocity.

On one side of the dispute it was contended that the true measure of the force is found by $w \times v$, which represents the weight multiplied by the velocity; and on the other side it was maintained that the right measure was $w \times v^2$, or in words, the weight multiplied by the velocity squared. When theory was reduced to practice, it was observed that the different properties expressed by

$$w \times v, \text{ and } w \times v^2,$$

were not at variance, and the introduction of the terms *momentum* and *impetus*, with their synonyms removed the groundwork of dispute.

Practical men further found that neither impetus nor momentum had much to do with practical mechanics, since neither $w \times v$, nor $w \times v^2$, measure directly the efficiency developed in ordinary machines. The criterion of their efficiency is the force (F), multiplied by the space (S), through which it acts. And we have in another place (page 69) mentioned, that a dynamical unit is a force equal to that uniformly exerted to raise a pound one foot high against the force of gravity. It must be remembered that this definition is founded on the assumption that the resistance remaining the same at every new point of space, the pressure must also be exerted anew at every point through which the resistance is overcome. The dynamical unit, as before observed, termed a *horse-power*, is 33,000 lbs., or 528 cubit feet of water raised one foot high in a minute. The value of a horse-power in France is 75 kilogrammes raised one metre the second. The length of the metre is 3.2808992 American feet, or 39.3707904 inches, and is the ten-millionth of the quadrant of the globe, measured from the equator to the pole. A kilogramme is 2.204737 pounds.

So that 100 American horse-power is equal to 105 French horse-power nearly. This definition applies, but not directly, in the case of a body projected by an impulsive force. We place this matter in the strongest light, to fix the attention of the young machinist and engineer. If a body be projected upwards by the explosive force of gunpowder, or by any other impulsive force, the body ascends through a certain ascertainable space, proportioned to the force which may be said to be accumulated in the body when first started; but if a body be raised slowly by a rope, we cannot for an instant relax our exertion; for, if we do, the body at once begins to descend, in obedience to the force of gravity. Consequently, during the ascent, a new pressure is necessary to draw the body through every point of its path. In the same manner, if a certain amount of exertion be required to bore a hole an inch deep in a uniform block, it will require an equal exertion to bore through the next inch of the same block, and after each exertion the work will not go on unless the force be continued. And since every resistance may be expressed by a weight, and to overcome a resistance may be compared to or measured by raising a weight through a vertical space, always bearing in mind that the weight must remain at the point to which it is raised; hence we arrive at a convenient and simple method of comparing and computing the mechanical efficiency of steam, water, and other mechanical agents. From what we have stated, it follows that the laboring force exerted is proportional to the resistance and space conjointly, and may be expressed and measured by the product of two numbers $R \times S$; R, being the number representing the resistance, and S the number representing the space. To exemplify this, let it be found by experiment, that it takes the force of 200 lbs. to draw a carriage along a plank road; it is clear that

$$200 \times 60 = 12000, \text{ units},$$

is the power expended in drawing the carriage through 60 feet, and would be the same laboring force as that required to raise 200 lbs. through a perpendicular height of 60 feet. It is clear that the laboring force is independent of the nature of the work done. If the thrust of a screw propeller shaft, found by a dynamometer, be 5 tons, the effective or available horse-power of the engine $298\frac{2}{3}$, supposing the vessel to move at the rate of 10 miles an hour. For

$$1760 \times 10 \times 3 = 52800 \text{ feet in ten miles},$$

$$\frac{52800}{60} = 880 \text{ feet moved in a minute},$$

$$2240 \times 5 = 11200 \text{ lbs. in 5 tons},$$

$$\therefore \frac{11200 \times 880}{33000} = 298\tfrac{2}{3} \text{ horse-power}.$$

The steam-engine which turns this screw may be one of 1000 horse-power; consequently, more than 700 horse-power is uselessly expended. Laboring force is infinitely diversified by the mechanism and engine-work employed, but it is always equal to the sum of the effects produced; much of it may be uselessly expended or lost to useful purposes from friction and other causes. That machine is the best, which, for the longest time, transmits the power applied to it. The *modulus* of a machine is a fraction which expresses the relation of the work done to the work applied. If a machine only does three-fourths of the work that is applied to it, the *modulus* would be $\frac{3}{4}$ or .75. In the case of the screw-propeller engine just given, the modulus would be

$$\frac{298\frac{2}{3}}{1000} = .29866.$$

M. A. Morin, in his *Mecanique Pratique*, gives the following *moduli* of machines for raising water:—

Archimedian screw . . .	.70
Pumps for draining mines . .	.66
Chinese wheel	.58
Upright chain-pump . . .	.53
Bucket-wheel	.60
Inclined chain-pump . . .	.38.

How many cubic feet of water will be raised in an hour, by an upright chain-pump, to the height of 60 feet, by an engine of 100 horse-power.

$33000 \times 100 \times 60 = 198000000$ units of work applied each hour.

The modulus of this machine being .53, the units of work done in an hour will be $198000000 \times .53 = 104940000$. The work developed in raising a cubic foot of water, which weighs 62.5 lbs., 100 feet will be

$62.5 \times 100 = 6250$ units,

$\frac{104940000}{6250} = 16790.4$, the required cubic feet.

What is here stated, is equally true of any mechanism, however complicated. And, generally, if P be the pressure exerted by the motive power on the first part of the machine that moves, in the direction of its motion, and S the space through which it moves in any unit of time, then,

$$P \times S = p \times s + f;$$

if p be the pressure exerted by the last piece of mechanism upon the work, s the space through which it moves in the same given unit of time, and f the amount of power necessary to overcome the frictions and obstructions of the machinery. Let a train of railway carriages of 40 tons, move with a uniform speed of 30 miles an hour on a level rail; the resistance of friction of the rail 7 lbs. a ton. The resistance of the atmosphere upon the whole train 36 lbs., when the speed is 10 miles an hour, the area of the piston 100 inches, the length of stroke 2 feet, and the diameter of the driving-wheel 5 feet. When the speed of the train is 10 miles an hour, the resistance due to the blast-pipe 1.5 lbs. to each square inch of the piston, what is the pressure of the steam on the piston, the evaporation of the boiler, and the bushels of coal necessary for a distance of 720 miles, one bushel evaporating 11 cubic feet of water?

$$\left(\frac{30}{10}\right)^2 \times 36 = 324 \text{ lbs.}$$

supposing the resistance of the atmosphere to increase according to the square of the velocity.

$40 \times 7 + 324 = 604$ lbs. the resistance to the motion of the carriages.

$3.1416 \times 5 = 15.708$ feet moved over in one revolution of the driving-wheel.

$604 \times 15.708 = 9487.632$ units of work done in one revolution.

Let x represent the effective pounds pressure on an inch of the piston in one revolution of the driving-wheel; and as the locomotive has two cylinders, the piston of each makes two strokes for one revolution of the driving-wheel.

$x \times 100 \times 2 \times 4 =$ the units of work or effective pressure on the pistons during one revolution of the driving-wheel.

$$\therefore x = \frac{9487.632}{100 \times 2 \times 4} = 11.86 \text{ lbs.}$$

effective pressure on each square inch of the piston. For, according to the principle above stated,

$$x \times 100 \times 2 \times 4 = 9487.632.$$

The resistance due to the blast-pipe of a locomotive, is in proportion to the speed; hence,

$$1.5 \times \frac{30}{10} = 4.5 \text{ lbs.}$$

the resistance in this case.

$11.86 + \frac{1}{8} \times 11.86 + 1 + 15 + 4.5 = 34.34$ lbs. the total pressure of the steam on the piston, allowing 15 lbs. for the pressure of the atmosphere, 1 lb. for the friction of the machinery, and $\frac{1}{8}$th the effective pressure to overcome the friction of the engine when loaded.

$\frac{30 \times 5280}{60 \times 5 \times 3.1416} = 168$, the number of revolutions of the driving-wheel a minute.

$168 \times 4 = 672$, number of strokes of the piston a minute.

$\frac{100 \times 2 \times 672}{144} = 933$ cubic feet of steam discharged each minute. Now, from the formula, page 77, we find that a cubic foot of water produces 760 cubic feet of steam, of 34.34 lbs. pressure; hence, the cubic feet of water evaporated each minute, will be $\frac{933}{760} = 1.23$ nearly. And because one bushel of coal evaporates 11 cubic feet of water, the number of bushels of coal used a minute is $\frac{1.23}{11}$. Therefore, the number of bushels for 18 hours, or for 720 miles, will be

$$\frac{1.23}{11} \times 60 \times 18 = 121 \text{ bushels nearly.}$$

It is necessary to observe that the amount of laboring force corresponding to any given space, is not altered by altering the velocity of working, provided the pressures P and p remain constant. But it often happens that the pressure exerted changes with the change of velocity, and hence the power varies with the change in the rate of working, and in most cases there is a rate of working for which a particular power is a maximum. For instance, a water-wheel would have no mechanical efficiency at a velocity which would be just equal to that of the water that impels it. The horse-power, that moves a locomotive engine and train of T tons at the rate of M miles an hour, is represented by

$$\frac{T \times M}{37.5},$$

taking the friction at 10 lbs. the ton. It is easily seen that there is a maximum effect between the load that the engine is just capable of moving, and the speed which it would attain without any load. The conditions under which machines produce a maximum effect, may be considered with respect to the mechanical effect they are capable of taking from the prime mover or motive power, or with regard to the amount of mechanical effect which they are capable of developing with respect to the impelling force; and as these conditions are seldom separated, to obtain a maximum effect in one case, differs widely from the state of things that will produce it in the other case.

To obtain the maximum effect from a given expenditure of motive force, the machine must be adapted to receive the greatest amount possible of the motive force, and not permit any portion of it to be expended without producing its full effect in impelling the machine. This obviously depends upon the mechanical organs being perfectly proportioned to the forces that are to act upon them, according to the velocity, intensity, and direction of those actions, and must have reference to some particular velocity with which the motive force is required to impel the machine; but it is also equally obvious that each kind of motive force having some particular velocity at which it can act with the greatest advantage, if we exact from the machine a higher velocity of motion than is consistent with the activity of the impelling power, we can only obtain it by a sacrifice of mechanical effect. Thus the useful effect due to animal exertion decreases rapidly as the speed increases. A horse, for instance, cannot move its limbs quicker than a certain velocity, even if it had no resistance to overcome; and it is only when working at the most advantageous speed, that its mechanical effect can be valued at 33,000 lbs. raised 1 foot per minute. On the other hand, a resistance may be opposed so great that the animal cannot move at all; and in this case, as well as in that of excessive velocity, no mechanical effect is realized. In the same manner the natural currents of wind and water are limited in the rapidity of their motions, and will act as motive forces most efficaciously when the recipients are adapted to their respective velocities; that is, when the parts of the machine to which the motion is applied, act only at such velocities as to receive the whole force of the current. If the motion of the recipient be greater—should it approximate to that of the current—then a part only of the force will be realized; for the current, when it has passed from the machine will retain the same velocity as the parts upon which it acted, and consequently a motive force corresponding to that velocity, which has produced no useful effect upon the machine. In like manner, the elastic force of steam is limited in the velocity of the motion with which it can act upon the piston (in the steam-engine); and in the case of the locomotive engine, the velocity corresponding to the maximum effect may be passed. It is, however, to be remarked that this limit is brought greatly nearer by the practical necessity there is of contracting the apertures by which the steam is admitted into the cylinder; the motive force is thereby not permitted to act freely upon the piston; but only with a limited activity; and further, that certain of the resistances—the resistance, for instance, arising from the action of the atmosphere upon the train, and of the blast-pipe against the piston—increase with the velocity, so that at a certain speed, easily determined by calculation (where the data are determined), the augmented resistance becomes equal to the diminished motive force. This is the limit of velocity, for, there being no preponderance of motive power, there cannot be any acceleration; and a dynamical equilibrium being established, the motion will continue uniform. Did these conditions not exist—had the steam no contracted orifices to pass through, and were there no augmentation of resistance with increased speed—then the velocity of a locomotive, and the power of steam-engines generally, would be limited only by the rate of vaporization in the boiler.

In any moving body there is accumulated by the action of the forces from which its motion has resulted, an amount of power which it develops or reproduces upon any resistance opposed to it, and the resistance is measured by the effect produced upon the obstacle that opposes it.

Thus in a ball fired from a cannon there is an accumulated power ready to be expended upon any obstacle it may encounter in its flight; and in the water which flows through the channel of a mill-lead there is accumulated the power which is transferred (in part) to the undershot wheel. Similarly, a carriage descending an incline, if allowed to descend freely, accumulates a power sufficient to carry it a considerable distance up the next incline. [In those and analogous cases, the pressure for a time exceeds the resistance, and that surplus pressure is accumulated in the moving body; and it is easily shown that, in every case, the power accumulated is precisely equal to the power expended upon the body beyond that necessary to overcome the resistance opposed to its motion; a principle, indeed, which might almost be assumed as in itself evident.] It is likewise evident that the power accumulated in a moving body will be the same for the same velocity, under whatever circumstances that velocity has been acquired. Whether the velocity of a ball has been communicated by projection from a steam-gun, or by explosion from a cannon, or by being allowed to fall freely from a sufficient height, it matters not to the result, provided the same velocity, v, be communicated to it in all three cases; and it be of the same weight w, the power accumulated in it, estimated by the effect it is capable of producing, is evidently the same.

To estimate the power accumulated in a body moving with a given velocity v; because, to raise a pound slowly, one foot high, against the force of gravity is our unit of measure, let us suppose that the body is moving in a direction opposed to the force of the earth's gravity. Neglecting the resistance of the atmosphere, it will ascend to a height h, from which it must fall to acquire the velocity v. There must then, at the instant of projection, have been accumulated in the body a sufficient force to raise it to the height h. But we have before shown that the number of units of power or work required to lift a weight w, to the height h, is represented by $w \times h$. Now, since cause and effect are equal, $w \times h$ will also express the number of dynamical units accumulated in the body at the instant of projection. But, because h is the height from which the body must fall, to acquire the velocity v, then, according to the well-known law of falling bodies near the earth's surface. Art. 7, page 100.

$$v^2 = 2\,gh.$$

$\therefore h = \dfrac{v^2}{2\,g}$, and is often termed the height due to the velocity v.

$\therefore w \times h = w \times \dfrac{v^2}{2\,g} = \frac{1}{2}\dfrac{w}{g}v^2$, the number of dynamical units accumulated in the body at the instant of projection. It may be necessary here to state that the force of gravity is, in respect to the descent of bodies near the earth's surface, a constantly accelerating force, increasing the velocity of their descent by 32.2 feet in each successive second: in like manner if they be projected upwards, it becomes a constantly retarding force, diminishing their velocity by 32.2 feet each successive second of time. The letter g is commonly used to represent this number.

If a ball 24 lbs. weight leave a gun with a velocity of 500 feet a second, the units of work accumulated in this body, at the instant of projection, will be

$$24 \times \frac{(500)^2}{64.4} = 9316.7$$

$w = 24$; $v = 500$; $g = 32.2$ as usual.

What are the units of work if the velocity of this ball be 1000 feet a second.

$24 \times \dfrac{(1000)^2}{64.4} = 37266.8$ units, which is just four times the units last found. Hence a bullet, moving with a double velocity, will penetrate to four times the depth in a bed of clay of uniform consistence: a ball of equal size, but of one-fourth part of the weight, moving with a double velocity, will penetrate to an equal depth. Thus, also, when the resistance opposed by any body to a force tending to break it, is to be overcome, the space through which it may be bent before it breaks being given, as well as the force exerted at every point of that space, the power of the body to break it is proportional to its weight, multiplied into the square of its velocity. And from this it follows that, to double the velocity, we must apply four times the power. Thus, were it necessary to obtain a certain velocity by means of the descent of a heavy body from a height, to which we carried it by a flight of steps, we must ascend, if we wish to double the velocity, a quadruple number of steps, and this will cost four times as much labor.

These results are obtained by comparing the respective units of work developed. From what has been here laid down, it will be easily seen that the units of work which a body acquires when it passes from a lesser velocity v, into a greater v_2, or produces when it is compelled to pass from a greater velocity into a less, are equal to

$$w \times \frac{v_2^2}{2g} - w \times \frac{v_1^2}{2g} = w\left(\frac{v_2^2 - v_1^2}{2g}\right).$$

If a carriage of 1000 lbs. goes forward with a velocity of 20 feet, which is changed by a force acting upon it into a velocity of 30 feet, how many units of work are done by the force, or acquired by the carriage?

$$v_2 = 30,\ v_1 = 20,$$

$w\left(\dfrac{v_2^2 - v_1^2}{2g}\right) = 1000\left(\dfrac{30^2 - 20^2}{64.4}\right) = 776.5$, the units of work required.

This last rule is easily adapted to logarithmic computation, as $(v_2 + v_1) \times (v_2 - v_1) = v_2^2 - v_1^2$, $log.\ 2g = 1.8088858$. For example, let a body of 6000 lbs. go forward with a velocity of 15 feet, which is changed by a force acting upon it, to a velocity of 24 feet, how many units of work are done by the force?

Log. $(v_2 + v_1)$; . . .	$24 + 15 =$	1.5910646
Log. $(v_2 - v_1)$; . . .	$24 - 15 =$	.9542425
Log. w;	$6000 =$	3.7781513
		6.3234584
Log. g, subtract		1.8088858
Log. 32702		4.5145726

32702 are the units of work required, which is ascertained by common addition and subtraction, by employing logarithms. See the *Practical Model Calculator*, by the Author of this work, Mr. Oliver Byrne.

The mass M, of a body is equal to the weight w, divided by g, that is $M = \dfrac{w}{g}$.

Mv^2 or $\dfrac{w}{g}v^2$ is termed the *vis viva*, or living force, without attaching to the product any definite idea. And we have just shown that the units which a moved mass M, or weight w, acquires, are equal to half the *vis viva* of the same. Further, if a mass enters from a velocity v_1, into another v_2, the units of work done are equal to half the difference of the *vis viva* at the beginning, and at the end of the change of velocity. This law of the mechanical operation of bodies by means of their inertia, is called the principle of *vis viva*, or of *living forces*.

THE SCREW PROPELLER, AND THE PRINCIPLES CONCERNED IN THE OPERATION OF SCREW VESSELS.

Taken from Bourne on the Screw Propeller, with some alterations.

FLUID RESISTANCE.

The laws of Fluid Resistance are still involved in much obscurity; partly, no doubt, from the inherent difficulty of the subject, but mainly from the want of independent research on the part of the various authors who have undertaken the elucidation of the subject. It is an easier thing to copy than to think; and the mistakes incidental to the researches of Newton and other eminent philosophers, have, by the reverential acceptation of succeeding writers, been expanded into mischievous fallacies, which have at length overrun various departments of physical science, and are now found most difficult of eradication. Under these circumstances it becomes expedient to investigate, in a plain and practical way, a few of the leading principles of mechanics which bear upon the question before us, as there will be less trouble in taking a new course altogether, than in clearing away the errors with which the beaten track is found to be choked up.

Mechanical power is pressure acting through space; and the amount of mechanical power developed by any combination is measurable by the amount of the pressure, multiplied by the amount of space through which the pressure acts. A pressure of 10 lbs. acting through a space of 1 foot, represents the same amount of mechanical power as a pressure of 1 lb. acting through a space of 10 feet; and 10 lbs. gravitating through 1 foot, or 1 lb. gravitating through 10 feet, represents ten times the amount of mechanical power due to the gravitation of 1 lb. through 1 foot. In the same way, 1000 lbs. gravitating through 1 foot, is equivalent to 1 lb. gravitating through 1000 feet; and, in general terms, the weight or pressure multiplied by the space through which it acts, represents the power universally. If, therefore, a body falls freely through space by the operation of gravity, since it parts with none of its power during its descent, the whole power must be accumulated in the falling body in the shape of momentum; and, at the instant of reaching the ground, the body must have such an amount of mechanical power stored up in it as would suffice to carry it up again to the position from which it fell, if the power were directed to the accomplishment of that object. The amount of mechanical power, therefore, in any moving body, is measurable by the weight of the body, multiplied by the space through which it must have fallen by gravity, to acquire the velocity it possesses; and this fundamental law, if distinctly apprehended, and kept constantly in recollection, will insure exemption from the fallacies which prevail so generally among English authors in reference to such subjects. In Newton's "Second Law of Motion," it is maintained that "the change or alteration of motion produced in a body by the action of any external force, is always proportional to that force;" from whence it is inferred, that to produce twice the quantity of motion in a body, will require just twice the power; and this is the doctrine maintained by Robison, in his *Mechanical Philosophy*, and by Hutton, Gregory, and most other English authors who have undertaken to illustrate such questions. Nevertheless, there is no doubt whatever that the doctrine, though resting on the authority of Newton, is altogether erroneous, as was shown by Leibnitz at the time of its promulgation, and subsequently by Smeaton, and Dr. M. Young, of Dublin, who, by a series of carefully executed experiments, proved very clearly that it required four times the amount of mechanical power to double the velocity of a moving body that was necessary to put it into motion at first; and consequently that the momentum of moving bodies of the same weight varies as the squares of their respective velocities. The soundness of this conclusion is made manifest by a reference to the law of falling bodies, by which it will be found that it is necessary a body should fall through four times the height to double its ultimate speed: nine times the height, to treble its ultimate speed, and so on; showing that the height, and therefore the power exerted in creating the motion, must be as the square of the ultimate speed; and consequently, that the ultimate velocities of all falling bodies will be as the square roots of the heights from which they have respectively descended. In the case of two bodies of equal weight, therefore, moving in space, but of which one moves with twice the velocity of the other, the faster will have four times the amount of mechanical power stored up in it that is possessed by the slower; for it must have fallen from four times the height to acquire its doubled velocity, and the relative quantities of power capable of being exerted by bodies of the same weight, is measurable in all cases by the spaces through which the weight or pressure acts. A cannon-ball, moving with a velocity of 2000 feet a second, has four times the momentum of a cannon-ball, of equal weight, moving with a velocity of 1000 feet a second; and every particle of a stream of water moving with a velocity of 10 miles an hour, has four times the momentum of every particle of a stream of water moving with a velocity of 5 miles an hour. Every particle of the faster stream, therefore, will exert four times the effect in impelling any body on which it impinges, that is exerted by every particle of the slower stream. But in the faster stream, not only will every particle impinge with four times the force, but there will be twice the number of particles impinging in a given time; and a quadrupled force for each particle, and twice the number of particles striking in a given time, gives an effect eight times greater in a given time with a double velocity of the stream. Accordingly, it is found that in a water or wind mill, when the velocity of the current is doubled, the power exerted is about eight times greater than before; and it is also found that a steam-vessel, to realize a double velocity, requires about eight times the amount of power: but these results, it is obvious, have reference, not merely to the increased velocity of the particles of matter, but to the larger number of them brought into operation; and any *given quantity* of water, if flowing with a double velocity, would only exert four times the power exerted before. In the same manner a steam-vessel, to accomplish any given voyage in half the time, would require four times the quantity of coal previously consumed; for although eight times the quantity of coal would be consumed per hour, yet only half the number of hours would be occupied in accomplishing the distance. The number of particles of water to be displaced by a vessel in performing *any given voyage*, is the same, whatever the velocity of the vessel may be; but the number of particles displaced *in the hour* differs with every different velocity, and the power expended must consequently vary in a corresponding proportion. It may hence be asserted, generally, that the power or dimension of engine necessary to propel a vessel, increases as the cube of the velocity required to be attained; but the consumption of fuel will only increase as the square of the velocity, looking to the number of miles of distance actually performed.

It may be useful to compare with these doctrines the statements of some of the most eminent authors who have treated of Theoretical Mechanics. Robison, in his *Treatise on Mechanical Philosophy*, vol. ii. page 269, gives the following as the fundamental proposition of the doctrine of the resistance of fluids: "The resistances and (by the third law of motion) the impulsions of fluids on similar bodies, are proportional to the surfaces of solid bodies, to the densities of the fluids, and to the squares of the velocities jointly;" and Robison says that he has borrowed the demonstration from Newton's *Principia*, book ii. proposition 23. In Tredgold's work on the Steam-Engine, there is an Appendix on paddle-wheels by Mr. Mornay, where the same doctrines are propounded. At page 122, Mr. Mornay writes as follows: "In order to be able to calculate the absolute amount of power required to produce a given effect, it is necessary to be acquainted with the laws which govern the resistance of fluids to the motion of solid bodies in them, which are generally admitted to be based on the following theorem: If a plane surface move at a given velocity through a fluid at rest, in a direction perpendicular to itself, the resistance is proportional to the density of the fluid, and to the square of the velocity of the plane."

He adds: "It is assumed that the resistance to a plane moving in a fluid at rest, is equal to the pressure of the fluid on the plane at rest, the fluid moving in the same velocity and in the contrary direction to that of the plane in the former case; on which hypothesis the ratio of the square of the velocity is explained in two very different ways. The first is, that 'the resistance must vary as the number of particles which strikes the plane in a given time, multiplied into the force of each against the plane; but both the number and force are as the velocity; and consequently the resistance is as the square of the velocity.' The second explanation is, 'that the force of the fluid in motion must be equal to the weight or pressure which generates that motion, which it is known is equal to the weight of a column of the fluid, whose base is equal to the area of the surface and altitude, the height through which a body must fall to acquire the given velocity.'" These explanations, Mr. Mornay adds, are extracted from Dr. Gregory's *Treatise on Mechanics;* and in the works of Hutton, and most other English writers on theoretical mechanics, similar statements are to be found; yet it is quite certain that they are altogether erroneous, and their original promulgation is traceable to the accident of the mechanical force resident in moving bodies having been set down by Newton as measurable by the velocity, instead of by the square of the velocity, as is now known to be the case. If, therefore, the resistance varies as the number of the particles multiplied by the force of each particle, it must vary as the cube of the velocity; for the number of particles varies as the velocity, and the force of each particle varies as the square of the velocity; and the velocity, multiplied by the square of the velocity, is obviously the cube of the velocity. It consequently cannot be true that the impact of a fluid in motion will produce a pressure only equal to that due to the head of fluid that will produce the motion, as was long ago perceived by Daniel Bernouilli. For, as water issuing from a reservoir has the same velocity as any heavy body would acquire by falling freely from the level of the surface of water in the reservoir to the level of the issuing stream, and as, by the laws of falling bodies, the ultimate velocity of a falling body is just double its mean velocity, it is clear that a jet issuing horizontally, after having acquired the ultimate velocity due to the head, will pass through a distance equal to twice the distance that a body would pass through in descending from the level of the water-surface to the level of the orifice. Hence Bernouilli inferred that the accumulated hydraulic pressure by which a vein of heavy fluid is forced out through an orifice in the side or bottom of a vessel, is equal to the weight of a column of the fluid, having for its base the section of the vein, and for its height *twice* the fall productive of the velocity of efflux.

Bernouilli's theory was adopted and still further developed by Euler, who gives a formula for ascertaining the percussive effect of a jet of water on a plate, which is as follows:—

Let R = force of impact in permanent percussion.
a = area of vein.
H = height due to actual velocity of jet.
h = height due to velocity of reflected water.
ϕ = angle of reflected water to axis.

$$\text{Then } R = 2aH\left(1 - \frac{\sqrt{h}}{\sqrt{H}} \cos.\ \phi\right).$$

The experiments of Morosi and Bidone lend material confirmation to the doctrines of Bernouilli and Euler on this subject. Euler says, that the theoretical value of the percussion of a fluid vein may increase until it is equal to the weight of a fluid column of the same base as the section of the vein, and of a height four times greater than that due to the velocity of the vein. Bidone found that the sudden shock of a jet upon a plate is to the force of the jet, when permanent, as 1.84 to 1; but this effect may be in some measure attributed to the momentum acquired by the parts of the instrument by which the percussive force was measured.

According to the results of the experiments made by Colonel Beaufoy, for ascertaining the resistance of bodies moving through water, it appears that at low speeds, such as two knots an hour, the weight necessary to draw the body varies as the square of the velocity; but at higher speeds, such as eight knots an hour, the weight necessary to draw the body does not increase in quite so great a proportion as the square of the velocity. The weight necessary to overcome the friction of a body moving in water, appears to vary at about the 1-7th power of the velocity; but the proportion appears to diminish slightly with an increase of speed. The friction upon a square foot of plank, moving through the water in the manner of the bottom of a ship, was found to be equal to a weight of .014 lbs. with a velocity of one nautical mile an hour; or, in other words, it would require a weight of .014 lbs., acting on a string passing over a pulley, to overcome the friction of a square foot of plank, when passing through the water at a velocity of one nautical mile per hour. At a speed of two nautical miles per hour, the friction was found to be equal to a weight of .0472 lbs.; three miles an hour, .0948 lbs.; four miles an hour, .153 lbs.; five miles an hour, .2264 lbs.; six miles an hour, .3086 lbs.; seven miles an hour, .4002 lbs.; eight miles an hour, .5008 lbs.; and, by carrying the law up to thirteen nautical miles per hour, the weight necessary to overcome the friction upon each square foot is found to be about 1.2 lbs. At two nautical miles per hour, the weight necessary to overcome the friction varies as the 1.823 power of the velocity. At eight nautical miles per hour, the weight necessary to overcome the friction varies as the 1.713 power of the velocity. In the gross, it may be asserted that the weight necessary to draw any body through the water, varies nearly as the square of the velocity; but the distance through which the weight descends varies also as the velocity, so that the *power expended* in any given time, varies nearly as the cube of the velocity. It does not, however, follow that the resistance is made up in the manner supposed by Newton's hypothesis; for water does not consist of little balls which strike independently of one another, and the mutual interference of the particles when the water is reflected from the body struck, the viscidity, friction, and other elements, introduce different conditions from those which that theory supposes. Indeed, it is nearly certain that, while the aggregate resistances vary in the manner which has been stated, with such speeds as those usual in steam-vessels, the elementary resistances of which this aggregate is made up, follow different laws altogether. Don Georges Juan, one of the ablest authors who has treated of the theory of naval architecture, and one whose works are but little known in this country, after recapitulating the errors of preceding writers, lays down a new theory of the resistance of fluids, which he states is in perfect accord with fact, and with the known principles of science. He states that the resistances of bodies moving in fluids vary as the densities of the fluids, as the surfaces of impact, as the square roots of the depths to which they are submerged, as the simple speeds, and as the simple sines of the angle of incidence under which the surfaces are struck. This is the law which is followed when the surface is completely immerged in the fluid, and where the anterior part of the body resembles the posterior part. But when one part of the surface is out of the fluid, there is a new quantity to consider in the resistances which depend in no degree upon the surface struck, but which proceed simply from the velocity; and this quantity is neither as the simple velocities, nor as their squares, but as their fourth powers. In certain cases, there ought yet to enter a third quantity into the expression of the resistance, which is as the squares of the velocities, and as the surfaces struck; and, finally, there are circumstances under which it is necessary to have regard to a fourth quantity, which does not in any degree depend upon the speed, but only upon the surfaces struck. According to this theory, therefore, the resistances depend upon four distinct quantities, of which some vanish in certain cases; and in researches respecting sailing ships, these quantities reduce themselves usually to one, which is the first of those which have been mentioned. Nevertheless, in cases of a great velocity, it is necessary to take the second quantity into account; whilst to the third, which heretofore has been the only one which has claimed attention, it is usually unnecessary to pay regard.

It is also stated by this very able author, that it follows from his theory, that ships may not merely sail as fast as the wind, but faster than it; a result well known to nautical men to be sometimes attained. He states, also, that his theory accords with the results of experiments made with kites, and also with the results of Smeaton's experiments to determine the force with which water acts to turn water-wheels. And the errors in the previously accepted law of the resistance of fluids, vitiate, he says, all the calculations which had been antecedently made touching the angle which the sail should make with the keel and with the wind, the pressure upon the sail with reference to stability, and other questions of that nature. In previous theories, the curve of the sail, and the angle which the vessel assumes from the side pressure of the wind, had been disregarded, and the pitching and rolling motions of the vessel had been considered as referable to the laws which govern the operation of pendulums; whereas, those motions are, in fact, mainly governed by the movements and dimensions of the waves. Prows of the form of the solid of least resistance, which had often been recommended by mathematicians as advantageously applicable to ships, would have, he says, this difficulty attending them, that in an agitated sea they would cause the bow to be buried in the waves; and, to say nothing of other objections, the shocks of the sea, and the increased immersion, would cause a diminution of speed which would neutralize the benefit resulting from the finer form. This objection, however, it is obvious, chiefly holds where the bow is made sharp without a corresponding sharpening of the stern.

When the sail of a vessel, considered as a plane surface, is struck by the wind, the direction in which the sail would move, if not resisted, is in a line perpendicular to its surface. This line is called the line of moving force; and the line which would be followed by the aggregate sails of a ship standing at different inclinations, is called the mean line of moving force. If the vessel was subjected to no other force or impediment than that which she receives from the sails, she would always follow the direction of the mean line of moving force, and the same result would follow if the hull consisted of a portion of a cylinder or sphere. But in a vessel of the ordinary form, the resistance of the water against that side which the vessel presents most to the impulsion of the water being greater than that sustained on the opposite side, it is manifest that this inequality of resistance will turn the vessel out of the mean line of moving force. It is also clear that, if this resistance was infinite in reference to that encountered by the stem, or, what comes to the same thing, if the vessel did not experience any resistance or difficulty in cleaving the water, she would go along the line of the keel, whatever position it occupied in relation to the mean line of moving force. Since, however, the resistance which the water makes to the bow is neither nothing, nor infinitely small in relation to that which is encountered by the side, it is natural to suppose that the course of the vessel will follow neither the line of the keel nor the line of moving force, but will follow a third line intermediate between the two preceding, making with the keel the angle which is called the angle of lee-way. In vessels with the same lateral resistance, the amount of lee-way will mainly depend upon the facility with which the vessel passes through the water; and as an auxiliary screw virtually diminishes the resistance encountered by the hull, screw vessels will be more weatherly than ordinary sailing vessels. In light beam winds, also, the screw will operate advantageously in bringing the vessel continually into a new stream of wind; so that the wind will not stagnate against the sails, and such of its power as is really brought to act, will also be more effectually used up. To obtain a maximum effect from a given quantity of wind, the sails should move with about half the velocity of the wind itself; and if the vessel moves with a very small velocity, the wind will be reflected from the sails with nearly the same velocity it had at first, and only a small amount of power can be communicated in such a case. It follows, consequently, that vessels maintaining a considerable rate of speed through the water, whether by the aid of steam or otherwise, will, under most circumstances, utilize or use up a larger proportion of the power of the wind than slow vessels, from the sails of which the wind is reflected with nearly its original force. Whatever power or velocity the wind loses the vessel acquires, and the object which should be sought to be attained, therefore, is to intercept as large a column of the wind as possible, and to cause it to be reflected from the sails with the least possible force. The size of the column, and the difference between the initial and residual velocities, represents the power gained by the ship.

It would be foreign to the design of the present work to enter further into the discussion of these topics, than to show the doubt and discrepancy which still hangs over the question of fluid resistance, and to indicate, in a general manner, certain laws or axioms which may be accepted as an approximation to the truth, having been derived, not from theoretical considerations, but from experiments frequently repeated upon actual vessels, of different forms and of different proportions of power. And whatever theory of fluid resistance may be eventually adopted, it is at least certain that, in the case of ordinary vessels and ordinary velocities, the power necessary to accomplish any particular speed which may be prescribed, is ascertainable by the equation $\frac{S^3 A}{C} =$ horse-power where S is the speed in miles per hour, A the immerged sectional area of the vessel in square feet, and C a certain number, or coefficient, which varies with the form of vessel employed. This coefficient, as set down in the table, is obtained by multiplying the cube of the speed, in nautical miles per hour, by the immerged midship section of the vessel in square feet, and dividing by the indicated horse-power of the engine; and a number is thus obtained, by the aid of which the power necessary to accomplish others peeds, with a similar form of hull, may be approximately found.

Tons displaced by different vessels.	Value of the coefficient C.
2828	229.8
3090	348.2
2025	283.5
1238	515.3
2444	531.1
2790	154.7
1443	414.5
2241	257.4
2251	467.6
2350	404.3
2480	446.7
1405	470.3
1393	541.7
1393	697.4
98	238.3
1192	509.6
1290	434.8
168	464.8
196	428.9
1835	513.8
1865	538.1
3054	480

In all cases of the impact of water upon a solid body, the water is reflected or rebounds from the surface of the body with a certain velocity, occasioning thereby a corresponding loss of power, if the force or reaction of the water has to be employed for any purpose. In undershot water-wheels, which are driven by a stream of water, and also in paddle-wheels, especially if they strike the water with any considerable shock, a material diminution in the useful effect is produced from this cause. Bidone concludes, from his experiments, that water giving out its power by impact, will only produce half the effect that is due to its weight and velocity. In undershot water-wheels, it is found that somewhat less than half the theoretical power of the stream is on the average available in turning round the wheel; and in steam-vessels, propelled by common paddle-wheels, in which the float surface is generally too small, it is found that not much more than half the power of the engine is available in the propulsion of the vessel, the residue being lost in creating a disturbance of the water. It consequently becomes important, in every kind of propelling apparatus, to take care that the least possible disturbance of the water shall be occasioned; that in forcing the vessel forward through any given distance, the water upon which the propeller reacts shall be forced backward through the least possible distance; and, other things being equal, that species of apparatus will be the most efficient in propelling, which most effectually fulfils this condition. The whole of the engine power must be expended in some shape or other, and all the power which is not expended in disturbing the water, must be expended in propelling the vessel. In paddle vessels, the larger the floats are made, as a general rule, the less will the water be disturbed, and the more will it approximate in resisting power to a solid. It consequently becomes an important indication, both in screw vessels and in paddle vessels, to make the pushing or resisting area of the propeller as large as possible, as the slip of the propeller will be less the larger the hold it has of the water, and the speed of the vessel will be correspondingly increased. There are practical limits, however, to the dimensions of the floats in paddle vessels, which greatly add to the difficulty of obtaining high rates of speed through the instrumentality of paddles alone; for it will not answer well to make the floats very deep, else the water will not gain access to the heart of them, and there are obvious objections against making them very long.

When a locomotive is put in motion on a railway, the force with which the driving-wheel revolves will be less than the force urging the piston, just in the proportion in which its velocity is greater; and if the circumference of the driving-wheel is twenty feet, and the double stroke of the piston two feet, then every 100 lbs. of pressure on the piston will be balanced by 10 lbs. pressure on the driving-wheel. If, therefore, 11 lbs. of counteracting pressure were to be applied to the driving-wheel for every 100 lbs. pressure upon the piston, the engine would first be brought to a state of rest, and would then revolve in the opposite direction. If, however, instead of applying a greater counteracting pressure, the carriage were held fast, and the wheels suffered to revolve upon the rails, the velocity of the engine would go on increasing, until the resistance occasioned by the friction of the revolving wheels just balanced the pressure upon the pistons, and at this speed the wheels would continue to revolve so long as the supply of steam was maintained. In a steam-vessel, the operation of the engines upon the paddle-wheels or screw, is much the same as in the case just recited. If a steam-vessel be tied at the stern, and the engines be then set into revolution, their velocity will go on increasing until the resistance at the centre of pressure of the paddle-wheels just balances the pressure on the piston—the centre of pressure being a point in the depth of every float at which the pressure above and below it is the same, or at which the aggregate pressure may be supposed to be collected. Now, as the resistance at the centre of pressure must just balance the pressure upon the piston, it follows that the pressure urging forward the vessel will be the same, whether the vessel is at rest or in motion, supposing always that the engines are adequately supplied with steam; and the resistance created at the centre of pressure will be the same, whether the paddle-floats are large or small—only, if they be small, a greater velocity of revolution will be necessary to create the resistance requisite to balance the pressure upon the pistons, and a larger consumption of steam will be occasioned, without any countervailing advantage. If, however, the wheel be diminished in size, the pressure upon every paddle-float will be increased, for a larger resisting area will then be necessary to balance the pressure upon the pistons, in consequence of the diminished length of leverage acting against that area; and when a small diameter of wheel is employed, either a larger area of float is necessary, or else the centre of pressure will pass with a greater velocity through the water, which is tantamount to saying that the slip will be increased. In the case of the screw, similar results will be found to ensue. Setting aside the loss of power occasioned by the friction of the screw when revolving in the water, and the resistance occasioned by its cutting edge, it will be obvious that the forward thrust of the screw-shaft will be the same whatever the dimensions of the screw itself may be, for the velocity of rotation will go on increasing until the resistance which the screw encounters balances the pressure on the pistons; and if the pressure on the pistons be considerable, so will be the thrusting or pushing force of the screw. If the screw, however, be of inadequate dimensions, then the velocity of its rotation will be much greater than what answers to the speed of the vessel, and there will be a larger consumption of steam by the engine than would be necessary, if the screw were of a larger size. It is hence obvious that a very small diameter of screw, relatively with the midship section, or with the resistance to be overcome, is inadvisable, just as a small area of float-board is inadvisable in the case of a paddle-wheel. Nevertheless, it is possible to make a screw too large, just as it is possible to make a vessel too sharp; and that point will be attained when the friction consequent upon the increased diameter, the resistance arising from the extension of the cutting edge, and other analogous sources of loss, more than balance the loss arising from the slip. From some experiments which were made by Mr. Brunel at Bristol, in 1840, with half a disc of metal 5 feet 9 inches diameter, set on a shaft revolving in water, it appears that it took 6.4 horse-power by the indicator to give the shaft a velocity of 101 revolutions per minute, when the semi-disc revolved in air without the contact of water; and that it took 9 horse-power by the indicator to give the shaft a velocity of 100 revolutions per minute, when the semi-disc revolved in water. Hence it was inferred that the resistance to the semi-disc, which a screw with an equal amount of surface, and an equal length of cutting edge, suffers from the water at a speed of 100 revolutions per minute, will be overcome by about 3 horse-power of the engine. This is equivalent to a weight of about 55 lbs. at the end of the arm, or at the circumference of the disc, hindering its revolution for 5 feet 9 inches, or 69 inches $\times$ 3.146 $\div$ 12 = 1806.42 feet per minute, and 3 times 33,000 lbs. or 99,000 lbs. $\div$ 1806.42 = 55 lbs. very nearly; but the weight will of course be greater than this at the centre of effort of the screw. Probably the resistances were somewhat underrated in these experiments, as no adequate precautions seem to have been taken to prevent the water in which the half disc revolved, from itself acquiring some rotatory motion. Beaufoy's experiments, already mentioned, enabled an approximate estimate of the friction to be made; and such a result may be also arrived at by comparing the actual with the theoretical discharge of water through pipes. The theoretical velocity of water flowing from a pipe is the same as that of a heavy body falling from the level of the water in the cistern to the level of the orifice. The actual velocity is ascertainable by the following rule: Multiply 2500 times the diameter of the pipe in feet by the height in feet, and divide the product by the length in feet, increased by 50 times the diameter; the square root of the quotient will be the velocity of discharge in feet per second. If we take the rubbing surface of the screw, reduced to an equivalent number of square feet, moving with the same average velocity, and if we take a pipe of such a diameter that a pound of water just covers a square foot of its internal surface, then, if this pipe be set at such a declivity that the velocity of the water within it comes up to the velocity of the screw, but does not exceed it, it is clear that the gravitation down the plane of the water in a foot length of pipe will be the same as the friction in pounds upon a square foot of its internal surface, which again is equal to the mean friction in pounds upon a square foot of the surface of the screw. All rivers which flow with a uniform velocity have the gravitation of the water down the incline plane of the bed balanced by the friction of the water upon the bottom and sides of the channel; and with any given declivity of bed, the velocity of a river will increase in proportion to its depth and size, there being relatively less rubbing surface when the volume of water is great.

It will be obvious from the general tenor of the foregoing observations, that the laws of fluid resistance have not yet been ascertained in so conclusive a manner as to warrant reliance upon them in any case which differs materially from cases commonly occurring in practice. In steam-vessels of the usual form, and with the ordinary rates of speed, the resistance of the vessel, or what comes to the same thing, the amount of thrust necessary to be imparted by the paddle or screw-shaft, increases very nearly as the square of the velocity; and as, in order to communicate twice the velocity to the vessel, the engines must not merely be able to work against four times the load, but must also move with twice their previous speed, the power expended in a given time will be nearly as the cube of the velocity of the vessel. Contrariwise, if the engine-power of a vessel be increased while her immersion and other elements remain without alteration, her speed will be increased in the proportion of the cube root of the increased power. If, therefore, the engine power of a given vessel be doubled, her speed will be increased in the proportion of the cube root of 1 to the cube root of 2, or in other words, in the proportion of 1 to 1.25. If the original speed of the vessel, therefore, were 10 knots an hour, the effect of doubling the power would be to raise the speed to 12½ knots an hour. While, however, this result may be confidently expected in the case of such speeds as 10 or 12 knots per hour, it does not follow that the law will apply in the case of such speeds as 18 or 20 miles an hour, supposing the same form of vessel to be retained. Indeed, it is well known that at high velocities the resistance of any given vessel increases in a higher ratio than the square of the speed. The main cause of this accelerated increase in the resistance in the case of high speeds, is traceable to the inability of the water to close in at the stern of the vessel with sufficient rapidity to impart its proper pressure thereto, and in addition, therefore, to the ordinary resistances, the vessel has under such circumstances to encounter the hydrostatic pressure due to the deficient gravitation of the water against the stern. At high speeds it is consequently indispensable to make the stern very fine, else the vessel in passing through the water may leave a vacant space behind her, and the resistance will be enormously increased thereby. Each different speed, indeed, has a corresponding form of vessel, which will make the resistance a minimum. A vessel with any given amount of power, and with any given displacement, may be sharpened so much that an additional sharpening would increase the resistance, by increasing the friction of the bottom in a greater ratio than the bow and stern resistances were diminished. And when, by adopting such an amount of sharpness as gives the best result the total resistance is brought to a minimum for one particular amount of power, it will be found that a further sharpening is necessary to make the resistance a minimum for an increased amount of power. In practice cases have occurred where a vessel has been made too sharp, since with the same engine-power placed in a blunter vessel a better speed was obtained. But with an increased power the sharper vessel would have afforded the best result.

The disadvantage of a deficient sharpness of the stern is materially aggravated if the vessel be set to ply in shallow water; for in such circumstances the friction of the water upon the ground retards its entrance into the vacant space caused by the motion of the vessel through the water. Practically, therefore, the existence of shallow water is tantamount to an increased fulness of the stern. In other words, if two vessels of the same speed be taken, and one of them be set to ply upon shallow water, then the velocity will be so much reduced, from the difficulty of the water flowing in at the stern, as will be equivalent to the retardation caused in the other vessel by increasing the fulness of the stern. Whatever sharpness of the stern, therefore, it may be found advisable to give to ordinary vessels moving with a given speed in deep water, must be very much increased in the case of vessels intended to move with the same speed in shallow water. In all cases it is found that vessels plying in shallow water attain the best speed when trimmed very much by the head. The stern is thus partially raised out of the water, and made virtually finer than before; and vessels intended to ply upon shallow lakes or rivers should not merely be made very sharp at the stern, but the greatest immersion should be near the bow, from whence the keel should rise gradually upward towards the stern until it comes out of the water altogether. The higher the speed that is intended to be maintained the more imperative becomes the condition of giving extreme sharpness to the stern; and by no other known method of construction is it possible to navigate shallow waters at a considerable rate of speed.

CONFIGURATION AND PROPORTIONS OF THE SCREW PROPELLER.

The screw propeller, as now commonly applied to the propulsion of vessels, consists of two or three helical or twisted blades set upon a shaft or axis, revolving beneath the water at the stern.

The shaft where it protrudes through the stern of the vessel is surrounded by a stuffing-box, containing hemp-packing, whereby the entrance of the water into the vessel is prevented, and the extremity of the shaft in the rear of the screw is supported in a socket or bearing attached to the rudder-post. This post rests upon the keel, and from it the rudder is suspended. The screw revolves in that thin part of the stern of the ship which is called the deadwood, in which a hole of suitable dimensions is cut for its reception; and the thrust or forward pressure caused by the action of the screw upon the water is transmitted to some point within the vessel, which can be amply lubricated. The most perfect lubrication of this point is indispensable to counteract the friction caused by the combined thrust and rotation of the shaft, and cases have occurred in practice in which the end of the shaft became white hot even with a stream of water playing upon it, and actually welded itself to the steel plate against which it pressed. It is the thrust of the shaft which is operative in propelling the vessel, and the amount of this thrust can be measured by means of a dynamometer applied to the end of the shaft within the vessel.

The diameter of the screw is the diameter of the circle described by the arms; and the length of the screw is the length which the arms occupy upon the revolving shaft. If a string be wound spirally upon a cylinder it will form a screw of one thread. If two strings be wound upon a cylinder with equal spaces between them they will form a screw of two threads. Three strings similarly wound will form a screw of three threads, and so of any other number. If instead of strings flat blades be wound edgewise round the cylinder, and if each blade has one of its edges attached to the cylinder by welding, soldering, or otherwise, then if a slice be cut off the end of the cylinder, there will be only one piece of blade attached to that slice if the screw be of one thread, two pieces of blade if the screw be of two threads, three pieces of blade if the screw be of three threads, and so of any number. The number of blades, therefore, of any screw determines the number of threads of which it is composed; and this indication equally holds, however thin the slice cut off the end of the screw may be.

The pitch of a screw is the distance measured in the direction of the axis between any one thread and the same thread at the point where it completes its next convolution. Thus a spiral staircase is a single-threaded screw, and the pitch of such a screw is the vertical distance from any one step to the step immediately overhead. Ordinary screw propellers are not made nearly so long as what answers to a whole convolution, and in speaking of their pitch, therefore, it is necessary to imagine the screw to be continued through a whole convolution at the same angle of inclination with which it was begun. Of this whole convolution any given proportion may be employed as a propeller, and the length of a screw, therefore, cannot be determined from the pitch.

The screw employed in this country has from five to two blades or threads. The pitch of the screw is usually made equal to its diameter, or a little more, and the length of the screw is usually made equal to one-sixth of the pitch. The thrusting surface of the screw is measured by the area of the circle described by the arms, which is termed the area of the screw's disc. The screw's disc should have about 1 square foot of area for every $2\frac{1}{2}$ or 3 square feet in the immersed transverse section of the vessel. Thus, a vessel with 226 square feet of immersed section should have a screw of such diameter, that the disc will have an area of about $75\frac{1}{2}$ square feet. This answers to a diameter of screw of 10 feet. The pitch of such a screw should be about 11 feet, and the length of the screw about 1 foot 10 inches. These proportions are those proper for screws with two blades, but they will also apply to screws with three blades. The more numerous the blades are, the smaller may be the diameter of the screw and the coarser the pitch; but screws of many blades are not well calculated for the attainment of high speeds.

POSITIVE AND NEGATIVE SLIP OF THE SCREW.

By slip, it will be recollected, is meant the difference between the actual advance of the propeller through the water and the advance which would be accomplished if there were no recession of the water produced by the pressure of the propelling surface. A screw of 10 feet pitch, if working in a stationary nut, would advance 10 feet for every revolution it performed; but, when such a screw acts in the water, it may only advance 9 feet for every revolution—the water being, during the same time, pressed back 1 foot, from its inertia being inadequate to resist the moving force. In such a case, the slip is said to be 1 foot in 10, or 10 per cent. With every kind of propeller which acts upon water, there must be a certain amount of slip; for any force, however small, will overcome the inertia of the water to a certain extent; but, by so proportioning the propelling apparatus that it will lay hold of a large quantity of water, the backward motion of the water will be small relatively with the forward motion of the vessel—or, in other words, the slip will be reduced to an inconsiderable amount.

One of the most remarkable phenomena connected with the action of the screw is, that under some circumstances its apparent progress through the water is not only as great as that of the ship, but greater. In some of the early voyages of the "Archimedes," when the vessel was proceeding under the joint action of steam and sails, it was found that the progress made by the vessel through the water was greater than if the screw worked in a solid nut. It was from hence inferred that the ship must be overrunning the screw; yet that, it was also plain, could not be the case, as the engine was all the while well supplied with steam, and had the usual load upon it. The engine was, therefore, evidently driving *something*, and it was certain that the mere friction of the machinery and of the screw in the water could not consume all the power. There was also the usual thrust upon the screw-shaft, so that the screw, although moving slower than a patent log would do, if put over the stern, was nevertheless propelling the vessel. Shortly afterwards, the vessel was fitted with a number of different screws, and it was ascertained that with some of these screws the vessel went faster without the aid of sails, than if the screw had been working in a solid nut. In various other vessels the same action has since been observed; and if the pitch of the screw be made much less than the diameter of the screw, this action is very likely to follow. At first, the phenomenon appeared so paradoxical as to be pronounced incredible; but it is now known to be mainly a question of relative velocities between the screw and a column of water which follows the ship, and that column and the water of the sea.

When a strong current of water runs through the arches of a bridge, the water may be observed to curl around those ends of the piers which stand lowest in the stream; and if a chip of wood be thrown into that spot, it will not be carried off by the stream, but will remain at rest, showing that the water is not in motion at that place. Now, if we suppose a screw to be placed in this stationary water, it will be obvious that *any* movement of rotation given to it will produce some thrust upon the screw-shaft; whereas, if the screw were placed in the stream, it would require to revolve faster than the stream runs, before any thrust upon the screw-shaft could be produced. If, now, we suppose the pier to be a ship, the other circumstances we have specified will not be altered thereby; and it is conceivable that a screw acting in this dead water, might enable the vessel to stem the current, even though the screw moved with a less velocity than that of the current itself. That the screw will exert some reacting force upon this dead water, even with *any* speed of rotation, is obvious enough; but whether, with a speed inferior to that of the stream, it will produce a sufficient thrust to enable the vessel to stem the current, will depend very much upon the shape of the vessel and the dimensions of the screw employed. If the pitch be fine, and the number of revolutions answering to a given speed of vessel be great, there will be a tendency to pile up the water at the stern, owing to the adhesion of the water to the rapidly-revolving blades, and the consequent acquisition of a considerable centrifugal force by the water. Where this action occurs, the vessel will be forced forward, to some extent, by the hydrostatic pressure produced by the elevation of the water at the stern, and this pressure will aid the thrust of the screw. If, then, by such an arrangement, a vessel could be made to stem a current, she could obviously, under like conditions, be made to move through still water. All vessels carry a current in their wake, which answers to the dead water in the case of the bridge; and if the screw acts in this current, then the *apparent* slip will be positive or negative, just as the *real* slip or the velocity of the current may preponderate. In every case, the screw must have some slip relatively with the water in which it acts; but if that water has itself a forward motion, the result cannot be the same as if the water were stationary, and it will be necessary to reckon the forward motion of the current as well as the forward motion of the ship. Thus, if the real slip of the screw be three miles an hour, and the following current runs at the rate of three miles an hour after the ship, then there will appear to be no slip, if the comparison be made with the open ocean on each side of the vessel; or there will appear to be a *negative* slip, as it is termed, of one mile an hour, if the following current runs at the rate of four miles an hour. The whole perplexity vanishes, if we consider that a current follows the ship at a rate which may be either greater or less than the slip of the screw. This current is confined to the water very close to the ship; so that a log, whether of the ordinary or the patent kind, will not take cognizance of it, if thrown over the stern. But if a patent log were to be set in the spot where the screw revolves, it would show the velocity with which the vessel leaves the current, and the real slip of the screw would then be ascertained. In all screw vessels, I believe the slip to be greater than it is commonly reckoned, for in all of them there is a following current in which the screw works; and as, in some cases, this current makes the apparent slip to disappear altogether, so it will, I believe, in every case, reduce the visible slip to a less amount than the real slip, and it is the real slip which it concerns us to determine. There is no benefit derived from the existence of a following current in screw vessels; for to produce the current requires a large expenditure of power; and in screws so proportioned as to produce a negative slip, a worse performance has been obtained than in cases in which screws producing an apparent slip of 10 or 12 per cent. have been employed.

CENTRIFUGAL ACTION OF THE SCREW.

In the ordinary form of screw with helical blades standing at right angles with the axis, there is some loss of power from the centrifugal velocity given to the water, even under the most favorable circumstances which can attend its operation. But when the speed of the vessel is arrested by head winds or otherwise, a large proportion of the engine power is thus uselessly dissipated. At no time is the water thrown back in a cylindrical column from such a screw; but the water has the figure of the frustum of a cone, with the smallest end against the screw, even when the vessel is proceeding with little slip. If, however, the course of the vessel through the water be resisted, so that the screw has less of a progressive motion in the water, the arms act like a centrifugal fan, and the central part of the screw becomes in all probability a hollow space in which there is no water at all. The result of this operation is, that the screw moves with nearly the same velocity as if there were no extra impediment; yet there is no increased thrust upon the screw-shaft, and power is lost by slip to a very serious extent. These defects are more conspicuous in vessels of shallow draft, and using screws of small diameter, than in deep vessels with large screws; and in cases where the screw is above the water, when the vessel is stationary, it becomes covered so soon as the vessel gets under weigh, owing to the volume of water thrown upward by its centrifugal action. It is found, also, that in small and shallow screw vessels, the engines, if set on at their full power when the vessel starts, instead of moving slowly at first, until the inertia of the vessel is overcome, as in the case of paddle vessels, actually *run away*, if permitted, and throw up a cascade of water at the stern. Such a result, if it only happened when the vessel was being started, would not be of much consequence; but it also occurs, to a greater or less degree, when the vessel is resisted by a head wind or sea; and this peculiarity of the screw renders it much less eligible than the paddle for propelling vessels head to wind. To some extent, this fault may be corrected by bending back the arms of the screw towards the stern. But this will not be sufficient of itself to cure the defect, and the proper remedy appears to lie in sinking the screw deeper in the water. I consider that in no screw vessel has the screw yet been sunk sufficiently deep in the water. If the screw be but little immerged, it follows that the water is thrown backwards or outwards faster than the particles of water can descend by gravity from the surface of the fluid to fill the vacuity up. The efficient diameter of the screw is consequently greatly diminished, and a serious loss of power by slip is the necessary result. It is obvious that the velocity with which the water will rush into any empty space caused by the centrifugal or repellent action of the screw, depends upon the head of water above that empty space; or, in other words, upon the amount of the screw's immersion: and to prevent a vacant space from being formed, therefore, at the stern, the screw must be sunk in the water as deeply as possible. A deep screw is better than a large screw, as it presents less surface for friction, and will be equally efficient in preventing slip.

It will be seen from this recapitulation, that the centrifugal action of the screw operates detrimentally in two ways: first, in occasioning a dispersion of the water in a radial direction, whereby power is consumed without any compensating advantage; and, second, in so reducing the efficient diameter of the screw, that the necessary reaction cannot be obtained unless the screw moves with a very great velocity relatively with the velocity of the vessel. A wasteful amount of slip is thus produced, and the high velocity of the screw increases its centrifugal action and adds to the loss sustained from that cause. Under such conditions, I believe the effective part of the screw's disc to be reduced to a sort of half moon occupying the inferior portion of the circle. At the lower part of the disc the hydrostatic pressure compels the water to enter the circle described by the arms; but, in the other portions of the disc, I believe the water to be, to a considerable extent, shut out, or to be driven *outwards* instead of *backwards*, as ought to be the case. To recover some portion of the power thus dissipated, it has been proposed to surround the screw with a species of shrouding, which should receive an impulse from the moving water in the manner of a turbine; and the power thus recovered was to be rendered available in aiding the screw's rotation. But such an apparatus would be too complicated, and would cause too much friction to be usefully available in practice. It has also been proposed to inclose the screw in a tube; but screws working in this manner have been found to give less favorable results than screws working in open water. In Ericsson's propeller, a hoop encircles the propelling blades, which will prevent the radial dispersion of the water to some extent. Nevertheless, this expedient does not adequately meet the evil; but its efficacy would probably be somewhat increased if the hoop, instead of being made to encircle the blades, were set a little astern of them, so that it would more effectually encounter the conical column of water caused by the combined operation of the slip and the centrifugal force. In common screws, some benefit would probably be derived from bending or curving the blades sideways to a certain extent, so that the water, in flowing outwards, would impinge upon the curve, and aid the revolution of the screw. But the most effectual expedient of all is to sink the screw more deeply in the water; for, by this procedure, the centrifugal action and the inability of the water to obtain access to the heart of the screw will be simultaneously remedied. The deeper the screw is sunk in the water, the higher becomes the column which the centrifugal action must support, and an increased impediment to the radial dispersion of the water is thereby afforded. At the same time, the hydrostatic pressure of a high column compels the water to enter instantly into any vacuity caused by the action of the screw, or rather prevent such a vacuity being formed at all: and the screw will thus always have solid water to act upon. A vessel, of which the screw is sunk deeply in the water, will be able to contend with head winds as effectually as a paddle vessel; for the speed of the engines will be in all cases proportional to the speed of the ship, and the amount of slip will be nearly uniform whether the winds are favorable or adverse. No doubt, even with a deep screw, there will be some centrifugal action, caused partly by the impulse of the propelling blades and partly by the friction, which will cause some water to adhere to them, and acquire thereby a centrifugal motion. But when the slip is rendered uniform by the use of a deep screw, any centrifugal action which remains can for the most part be counteracted by giving a suitable form to the screw itself. With a uniform amount of slip there will be a uniform amount of centrifugal motion; and a uniform amount of centrifugal motion may be counteracted by imparting to the water such an amount of centripetal motion as will balance it precisely. This may be done by slightly bending backwards the arms of the screw, so that the centre of the arms shall be somewhat in advance of their extremities. Such a screw gives to the particles of water an impulse which would cause them to converge at a point if no counteracting force were applied; but, as they simultaneously receive a centrifugal impulse, they will follow a course intermediate between a convergent and a divergent one—or, in other words, they will be projected backwards from the screw in a cylindrical column of the same diameter as the screw itself.

THE CALORIC ENGINE OF ERICSSON.

THIS invention proposes to produce motive power by the application of heat to atmospheric air. The machinery by which this object is intended to be carried out may be thus described: Fig. 1, is a vertical section passing through V W, Fig. 2. Fig. 2, is a horizontal section through X Y, Fig. 1. (3) and (4) are two cylinders provided with pistons (2) and (5), fitted with air-tight metallic packing-

Fig. 192.

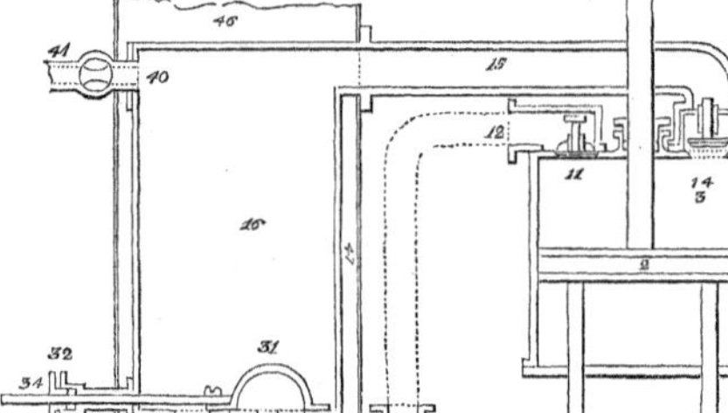

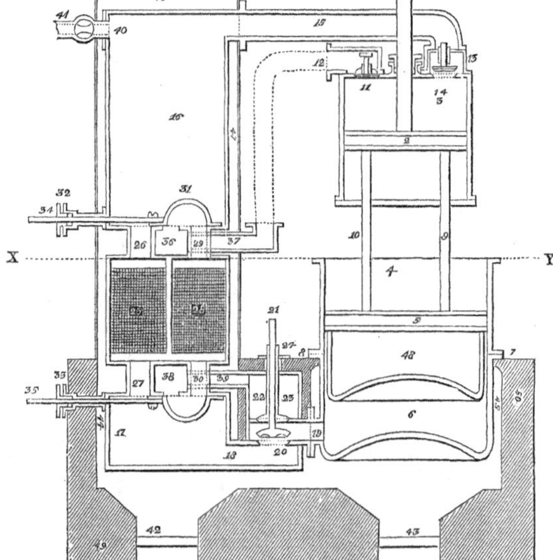

rings. (3) is called the supply cylinder, and (4) the working cylinder. (1) piston-rod, working in a stuffing-box, in the cover of the cylinder (3). (6) is a cylinder, the bottom of which is in the form of the segment of a sphere, and is attached to the working cylinder at (7) and (8). (9) and (10), four rods connecting together the pistons (2) and (5). (11) is a self-acting valve opening into the cylinder (3). (14) is a similar valve opening out of the cylinder and into the valve-box (13) (16) is a cylindrical vessel called the receiver, connected by the pipe (15) to the valve-box (13) (17) is another cylindrical vessel, called the heater the bottom of which is in the form of an inverted segment of a sphere like (6) and (48).

(20) is a conical valve, supported by the stem (21) working in the chamber (19), which forms a communication between (6), (17), and (18). (23) is another conical valve, supported by a hollow stem (24), and contained by the chamber (22).

(25) and (28) are squared vessels, like a cube, filled with disks of wire network, except small spaces at the top and bottom; these vessels are termed (for what reason I don't know) regenera

tors. (26), (27), (29), (30) pipes, forming a communication between (16) and (17), through (25) and (28). (31), (34), (35), two common slide-valves, worked so as to form alternate communications between the pipes (26), (27), (29), (30), and the exhaust-chambers (36) and (38). (34) and (35) valve-stems working in the stuffing-boxes (32), (33). (39) a pipe communicating between the valve-chamber (22), and the exhaust-channel (30). (37) a pipe leading from the exhaust-channel (36). (40) a pipe leading into the receiver (16), provided with a stopcock (41). (42) and (43) fireplaces, for heating the air in the vessels (17) and (6); (45), (44), (47), flues leading from the fireplaces and terminating at (46). (48) is a cylindrical vessel, attached to the piston (5), having

be driven through the valve (14) into the receiver (16). The stems (34), (35) of the slide-valves are so placed that, during this operation, the passages (26), (27) are open, the air from the receiver will pass through the wires in (25) into the heater (17), (18), and on to (6), as before observed; the temperature and volume of the air are increased as it passes through the heated wires (25) and over the fires (42) and (43). By this means, the smaller volume forced from (3), will fill the larger space in (6). Before (5) arrives at the top of the stroke, (20) will be closed, and (23) will be opened; the pressure from below is thus removed, the piston will descend, and the heated air in (6) will pass through (22), (39), (30), (38) into the regenerator (28), and in its passage through the wires it is

Fig. 193.

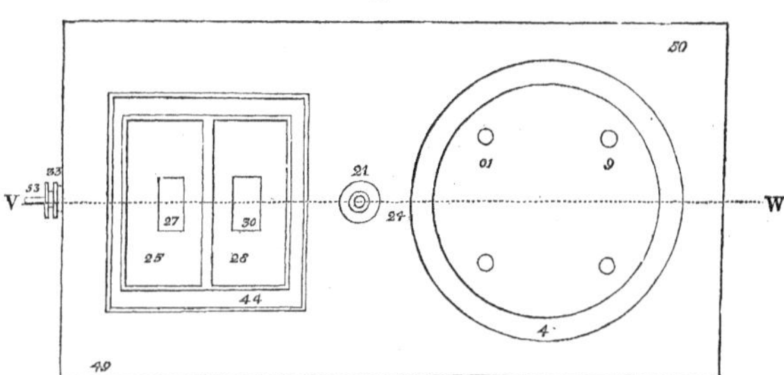

a bottom corresponding to (6); it is called the heat intercepting vessel, and filled with fire-clay at the bottom, and ashes, charcoal, or other non-conducting substances at the top, the object being to prevent the heat from reaching the piston (2), the bottom of which is open as well as the top of (4). (49), (50) is brickwork round the fireplaces and heaters. The valves (23) and (20) must be worked so that the valve (23) will open the instant the piston (5) arrives at the top of the stroke, and to be closed the moment the piston (5) arrives at the bottom of (6). Before the engine is started, the heaters and regenerators are brought to a temperature of more than 500° Fahr. by a slow combustion of the fuel in the fireplaces (42), (43). Before the fire is lighted, atmospheric air is forced into (16) by a pump, through (41), until there is a pressure of about 10 pounds on the square inch. The valve (20) is then to be opened, the air rushes from (16) through (26), (25), (27), (17), (18), (20), (19), and enters (6), which causes the piston (5) to move upwards, and the air contained in (3) will

supposed to part with most of its heat until it passes off at (37).

When any other fluid is used, the inventor proposes to connect the outlet pipe (37) and the valve-box (12), as indicated by the dotted lines, which represent such pipe. In this way the escaping air or other fluid through (37) will furnish the cylinder (3), independently of other external communication, and so the acting medium would perform a continuous circuit through the machine. When the piston (2) begins to descend, the valve (14) is closed, and the valve (11) is opened, by which a fresh supply of atmospheric air is taken into the cylinder (3). At the end of the down-stroke the valve (21, 23) is closed and the valve (24, 20) again opened, and in this way a continuous reciprocating motion is kept up. It is evident that after a short time the temperature of the wires in the regenerators will differ, that of (28) will be increased while that of (25) will be diminished; hence the positions of the slides (31), (35) have to be reversed at the end of every 50 or more strokes, by hand, or some connection to the engine. When the working is reversed, the heated air passing off from (6), will pass through the partially cooled wires in (25), while the air from the receiver (16) will pass through the heated wires in (28), and on entering (17, 18) will have attained a high temperature. In this manner it is supposed that the wires will take up and give out heat, and that the circulating medium will become heated independently of any combustion when the engine is put in motion. There are many fallacies involved in this arrangement; we have in another place alluded to some of them (page 88). It is clear that there is more friction about this arrangement than what belongs to that portion of the steam-engine for which it is substituted; the amount is at least doubled. There is but little doubt but that it *will go*, especially if every now and then air be pumped in on the sly through (41), so as to force it through the wires, and into (6). The heat required, before the machinery is put in motion, would generate steam of 40 lbs. pressure on the square inch. And the theory of the wires taking all the heat out of the used air and giving it back again to the fresh is very ridiculous, not to mention the impossibility of keeping for any length of time the vessels (16), (25), (28), (17), (18), (6), (48), (4) and (3) at different temperatures. A constant and steady difference in the *specific heat* of these vessels is required in order to secure a steady action to the engine. It puts us in mind of the inventor who dipped one-half a wooden wheel in water and the other half in air and expected it to turn on its axis perpetually. The non-conducting bottom of (48) is another thing that requires attention.

When we take into account that a bushel of coal will generate a room-full of steam, of almost any temperature or pressure, 200 feet long, 10 feet broad, and 10 feet high, the same amount of coal cannot, by this or any other machine, with which we are acquainted, develop the same amount of power.

It was shown at page 77, that whatever may be the pressure at which steam is formed, the weight of fuel necessary to evaporate a given volume of water is nearly always the same, and there the expression

$$V = \frac{20578}{P^{\frac{40}{43}}} + 13$$

was given, from which we readily find

$$P = \left(\frac{20578}{V - 13}\right)^{\frac{43}{40}},$$

in which V is the volume of a cubic foot of water, raised into steam, at a pressure of P pounds to the square inch. If the steam be 473 times the volume of the water from which it is produced, what is the pressure?

$$V = 473,$$

$$V - 13 = 460,$$

$$\frac{20578}{V - 13} = \frac{20578}{460} = 44.735,$$

$$\begin{aligned} Log.\ 44.735 &= 1.6506474 \\ & \times 43 \\ & 49519422 \\ & 66025896 \\ & 40)70.9778382 \\ Log.\ 59.4902 &= 1.7744459 \end{aligned}$$

$$\therefore P = 59\tfrac{1}{2} \text{ lbs. nearly.}$$

COMPARATIVE ADVANTAGES OF PADDLE AND SCREW VESSELS.

In smooth water, and with both vessels in their best trim, screw and paddle vessels are of about equal efficiency, or rather the advantage lies with the paddle, though the difference is so small as to be of no practical account. In deep immersions, screw vessels, however, have a very decided advantage; but paddle vessels again have a very decided advantage in the case of head winds. Screw vessels, when set to encounter head winds, are most wasteful of power; a means of remedying this defect, proposed by some engineers, consists in sinking the screw deeper in the water, and placing it further forward in the dead-wood; and with these modifications, screw vessels may not be so wasteful as paddle vessels when contending with strong head winds. Up to the present time, however, paddle vessels have a decided advantage over screw vessels in all cases in which a strong head wind has to be encountered; and if the comparison be made between the feathering-wheel and the screw, instead of between the radial-wheel and the screw—which last species of wheel the foregoing comparison supposes to have been employed—the advantage on the side of the paddles, so far as regards efficiency, will be still more decisive. The whole question turns upon the power of constructing screw vessels which shall be as efficient as paddle vessels, or more efficient, when set to encounter a head wind.

Nature and Laws of Slip.—Slip is of two kinds, positive and negative; but as the latter is only an accidental phenomenon, it is the first alone to which it is necessary here to attend. Positive slip is made up of two parts, of which the one is lateral slip, and the other retrogressive slip. Lateral slip is the lateral penetration of the screw-blades; retrogressive slip is the backward motion of the water, owing to its deficiency of inertia to resist the force which the screw applies. If the column of water upon which the screw acts were frozen, there would still be backward slip, as the inertia of the water would be just the same as before, but there would be no lateral penetration of the screw-blades, and, therefore, no lateral slip, except in so far as the column of water was put into revolution. The lateral slip will, in all cases, be reduced by increasing the length of the screw, but the friction of the screw will be increased in the same, or in a greater proportion. The retrogressive slip can only be reduced by increasing the quantity of water acted upon, and this may be accomplished by increasing the diameter of the screw or the speed of the vessel. In any given vessel the percentage of slip is about the same at all speeds; for though at high speeds the thrust of the screw is greater, yet the quantity of water with which the screw comes into contact is greater also. If, however, the thrust of the screw be increased without an increase of the speed of the vessel, there will be a large increase in the slip. The slip will also be increased by reducing the length of the screw and by increasing its pitch. If the pitch be increased in geometrical progression, the slip will increase in arithmetical progression, and this result will equally follow, whatever length of screw is employed. Screws with many blades have somewhat less slip than screws with few blades; but they have also more friction, and, to give satisfactory results, the pitch should be larger in the proportion of the number of blades, and a large diameter of screw should also be employed.

Thrust of the Screw.—The thrust of the screw will depend conjointly upon the pitch and the force exerted upon the screw-shaft to put it into revolution. The limit of the screw's thrust, computed on the supposition that it is not subject to friction, may be easily determined on the principle of virtual velocities, as in the case of a screw working in a solid nut; but as part of the rotative force is intercepted by friction, the actual thrust will never be so great as the theoretical thrust, but will be about one-fourth less. This diminution of the power is generally imputed to the operation of friction alone, but, in truth, a part of it is imputable, in the case of most screw vessels, to the existence of lateral slip; but as the lateral slip may be almost extinguished by increasing the length of the screw, and as the same loss would then be caused by the increased friction as is at present caused by the lateral slip, it is clear that the two elements are, in fact, convertible, and, in the case of screws with many blades, the difference between the theoretical and actual thrust is due almost wholly to friction.

Principle of Virtual Velocities.—These velocities are denominated *virtual,* because the system is really at rest; and they are only such as would happen if the equilibrium were disturbed. If a system of forces applied to the different parts of a machine be in equilibrium, and the points of application of these forces be made to undergo a very small displacement, dependent on their mutual connection with each other; the indefinitely small space described by the point of application of any force is called the *virtual velocity* of that point. Thus, if the force AP, applied at the point A, be moved into the position ap, the indefinitely small space Aa is called the virtual velocity of the point A. If from a, the new point of application of this force, a line am be projected or drawn perpendicular upon AP, the line Am is the *virtual velocity* of the point A, *estimated in the direction of the force.* The velocity is to be considered positive when it is measured from A, in the direction of the force, and negative when it is measured in the contrary direction. The forces themselves are always considered positive. If any number of forces P, Q, R, &c., act upon a machine, and keep it in equilibrium; and if p, q, r, &c., be the virtual velocities of their points of application, estimated in the directions of these forces respectively, then will

$$Pp + Qq + Rr +, \&c. = 0.$$

This important proposition is termed the *principle of virtual velocities.*

THE NEW THEORY OF THE STRENGTH OF MATERIALS, BY OLIVER BYRNE, THE AUTHOR OF THIS WORK.

The beams, or bars, the nature of the cross-sections of which we are investigating, are supposed to be supported at the ends and loaded in the middle. In small beams, the change in the particles that we are about to describe is not perceptible; yet it will be found very considerable in large girders, or in small girdles of a flexible nature.

Fig. 194.

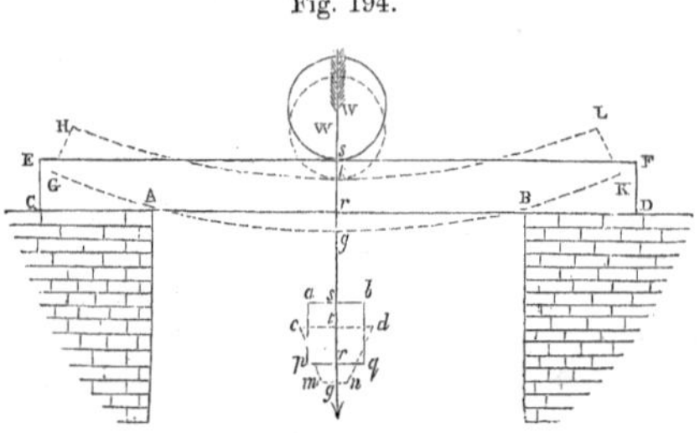

A very simple mode of illustrating what we shall describe relative to the molecular action of the particles in a cross-section, near the centre of the beam, may be obtained by taking a rectangular piece of caoutchouc India-rubber, whose cross-section would be represented by *abqp;* but it is to be understood that in point of structure we do not compare caoutchouc or India-rubber with iron, brass, or wood, but merely to show the manner in which the particles in the cross-sections of bodies, under the circumstances we have just described, endeavor to exert themselves. Let *ECDF* be the position of a beam before the weight W is applied, *HGABKL* its position after the application; the cross-sections in the two positions will be represented by the figures *abqp* and *cdnm.* The action of the weight or force *W* compels the point *s* to move to *t,* and the point *r* to move to *g,* and has a tendency to lengthen the whole beam; while at the same time, the filaments in the upper part of the beam, near the middle, become compressed in the direction of the length *AB,* and extended in the direction of the breadth *ab;* that is, the breadth *ab,* in one position, is represented by *cd* in the other. But the fibres in the lower part near *r,* in changing from *r* to *g,* become expanded in the direction of the length *AB,* and contracted in the direction of the breadth *pq,* so that *pq* in the cross-section becomes *mn.* From the rigidity of materials, this change may not have place, or may not be perceptible; but, in all cases, a force acting in the direction of the arrow, will have the tendency to change the cross-section *abqp* into one like *cdmn,* which if it be not able ultimately to effect, fracture must ensue.

Let *E s F* be the upper or lower surface of the beam, Fig. 195, before the weight *W* is applied. *Ht L,* Fig. 196, will represent the upper, and *Gg K,* Fig. 197, the lower, after its application. If the particles at *asb* in the bending process were such that they would merely become more dense, then the breadth at *asb* would not be changed; but it is not the case, for the harder parts of the material merely obtrude themselves into the softer, and partly become compressed and partly swell the breadth of the beam near these parts, as at *ctd* in the upper section *Ht L.* But in the lower surface *G g K,* or near it, the particles at *mgn* become separated, and the breadth becomes contracted from *ab,* which is equal to *pq,* Fig. 194, to *mn.*

Figs. 195, 196, 197.

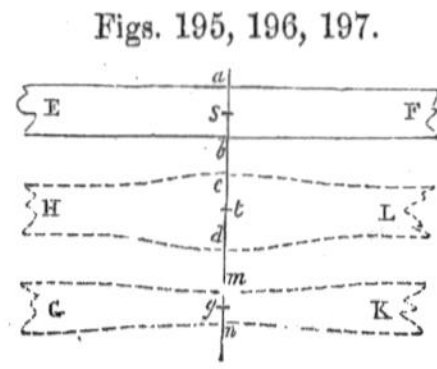

Let *x YZ,* Fig. 198, be a portion of a beam in the locality of fracture, caused by the forces *FF* acting in the directions of the arrows. The same process of reasoning which points out a neutral axis in the whole *AHDC,* will point out a neutral axis in any portion of the body *gabxtq,* no matter where it be situated; in fact, every fibre may be said to be compressed on one side and extended at the other, while the whole or each is bent round a common centre, as *S,* entirely outside the body. Then *SY* is the radius of curvature of the arc *C p D* at the point *p.*

Fig. 198.

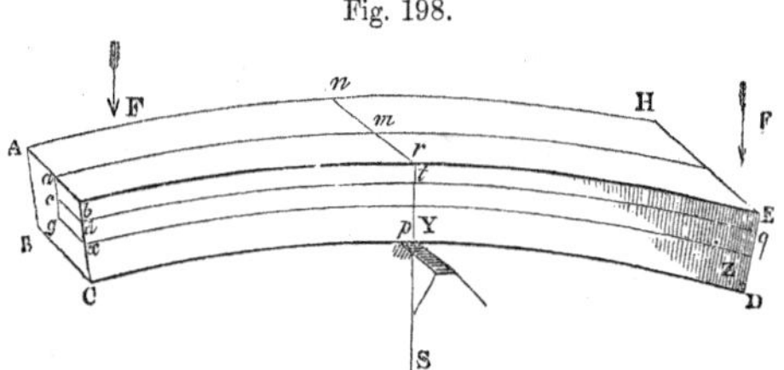

Now let us take *gcdxtYqZ,* any portion of the beam, it is evident that the filaments in the upper part near to *dtq* are expanded, and those near to *xYZ* are compressed; according to this reasoning there is a set of fibres between *dtq* and *xYZ* which are neither compressed nor expanded; hence, each portion of the beam is entitled to a neutral axis, which is relatively correct, but each neutral axis is itself bent round a centre in *rS.*

THE END.

www.ingramcontent.com/pod-product-compliance
Lightning Source LLC
LaVergne TN
LVHW021416110826
845150LV00007B/1947
* 9 7 8 1 4 2 5 5 0 9 9 5 8 *